Christopher Marlowe
and the Renaissance
of Tragedy

CHRISTOPHER MARLOWE AND THE RENAISSANCE OF TRAGEDY

DOUGLAS COLE

PRAEGER

Westport, Connecticut
London

The Library of Congress has cataloged the hardcover edition as follows:

Cole, Douglas.
  Christopher Marlowe and the renaissance of tragedy / Douglas Cole.
      p.   cm.—(Contributions in drama and theatre studies, ISSN 0163–3821 ;
      no. 63) (Lives of the theatre)
  Includes bibliographical references and index.
  ISBN 0–313–27516–5 (hardcover : alk. paper)
  1. Marlowe, Christopher, 1564–1593—Criticism and interpretation.
  2. Marlowe, Christopher, 1564–1593—Stage history—England.
  3. Theater—England—History—16th century.   4. Tragedy.   I. Title.
  PR2674.C59   1995
  822'.3—dc20   95–23019

British Library Cataloguing in Publication Data is available.

A hardcover edition of *Christopher Marlowe and the Renaissance of
Tragedy* is available from Greenwood Press, an imprint of Greenwood
Publishing Group, Inc. (Contributions in Drama and Theatre Studies,
Number 63, Lives of the Theatre; ISBN 0–313–27516–5).

Library of Congress Catalog Card Number: 95–23019
ISBN: 0–275–93673–2 (pbk.)

First published in 1995

Praeger Publishers, 88 Post Road West, Westport, CT 06881
An imprint of Greenwood Publishing Group, Inc.

Printed in the United States of America

The paper used in this book complies with the
Permanent Paper Standard issued by the National
Information Standards Organization (Z39.48–1984).

10 9 8 7 6 5 4 3 2 1

Copyright acknowledgments

The editors and publisher gratefully acknowledge permission to reprint the following copyrighted
material:

Excerpts from A. D. Wraight, *In Search of Christopher Marlowe: A Pictorial Biography*. Photography by Virginia F. Stern. London: Macdonald, 1965. Re-issued in paperbound edition, 1993,
London, Adam Hart.

Contents

	Illustrations	vii
	Foreword	ix
	by Josh Beer, Christopher Innes, and Simon Williams	
	Prologue	xi
	Chronology	xiii
1.	Matters of Life and Death	1
2.	The World of the Theatre in the Reign of Elizabeth	23
3.	*Dido Queen of Carthage*: Tragedy in the Classical Tradition	43
4.	*Tamburlaine the Great*: Tragical Discourse and Spectacle	59
5.	Machiavellian Tragedy: *The Massacre at Paris* and *The Jew of Malta*	79
6.	*Edward II*: Tragedy in the *De Casibus* Tradition	99
7.	*Doctor Faustus*: Tragedy in the Allegorical Tradition	121
8.	Marlowe's Legacy to Tragedy	149
	Appendix A: Thomas Kyd's Accusations of Marlowe	155
	Appendix B: Richard Baines' Note	157
	Notes	159

Works Cited   165
Index   171

Illustrations

1. Supposed portrait of Christopher Marlowe 18
2. Impression of a booth or platform stage set up in an inn-yard 25
3. Impression of a performance in an unmodified domestic hall 26
4. Sketch of the Swan Theatre 28
5. Panorama of London and its theatres 29
6. Portrait of Edward Alleyn 35
7. Woodcut from the title page of the 1631 edition of *Doctor Faustus* 40
8. 1951 Old Vic production of *Tamburlaine* 61
9. 1965 Royal Shakespeare Company production of *The Jew of Malta* 95
10. 1969 Prospect Theatre Company production of *Edward II* 110
11. 1968 Royal Shakespeare Company production of *Doctor Faustus* 134

Foreword

This book stems from the Greenwood Press series *Lives of the Theatre*. To facilitate use in college and university courses, some volumes have been selected to appear in paperback. This is such a volume. *Lives of the Theatre* is designed to provide scholarly introductions to important periods and movements in the history of world theatre from the earliest instances of recorded performance through to the twentieth century, viewing the theatre consistently through the lives of representative theatrical practitioners. Although many of the volumes will be centred upon playwrights, other important theatre people, such as actors and directors, will also be prominent in the series. The subjects have been chosen not simply for their individual importance, but because their lives in the theatre can well serve to provide a major perspective on the theatrical trends of their eras. They are therefore either representative of their time, figures whom their contemporaries recognised as vital presences in the theatre, or they are people whose work was to have a fundamental influence on the development of theatre, not only in their lifetimes but after their deaths as well. While the discussion of verbal and written scripts will inevitably be a central concern in any volume that is about an artist who wrote for the theatre, these scripts will always be considered in their function as a basis for performance.

The rubric "Lives of the Theatre" is therefore intended to suggest both biographies of people who created theatre as an institution and as a medium of performance and of the life of the theatre itself. This dual focus will be illustrated through the titles of the individual volumes, such as *Christopher Marlowe and the Renaissance of Tragedy*, *George Bernard*

Shaw and the Socialist Theatre, and *Richard Wagner and Festival Theatre*, to name just a few. At the same time, although the focus of each volume will be different, depending on the particular subject, appropriate emphasis will be given to the cultural and political context within which the theatre of any given time is set. Theatre itself can be seen to have a palpable effect upon the social world around it, as it both reflects the life of its time and helps to form that life by feeding it images, epitomes, and alternative versions of itself. Hence, we hope that this series will also contribute to an understanding of the broader social life of the period of which the theatre that is the subject of each volume was a part.

Lives of the Theatre grew out of an idea that Josh Beer put to Christopher Innes and Peter Arnott. Sadly, Peter Arnott did not live to see the inauguration of the series. Simon Williams kindly agreed to replace him as one of the series editors and has played a full part in its preparation. In commemoration, the editors wish to acknowledge Peter's own rich contribution to the life of the theatre.

Josh Beer
Christopher Innes
Simon Williams

Prologue

As is the case with most Elizabethan playwrights, including William Shakespeare, history has left us far fewer recorded facts about Christopher Marlowe's life in the theatre world than we would desire. The record does offer several intriguing details, however, of his life outside the theatre: a combination of facts, allusions, and allegations that has been used over the centuries to conjure up the image of a precocious poet, sometime spy, and swaggering blasphemer who died a violent death in a tavern brawl at the age of twenty-nine, the victim of either his own rash pugnacity, an avenging God, or an assassination plot devised by aristocrats in whose lives his own had become too dangerously entangled. It is not easy to separate Marlowe the man from the various myths that have been made of him, and it is not my intention in this study to unravel the mystery of who and what "he really was." I must rest content with showing briefly what sort of facts we have, how little they actually tell us, and how much more than that his biographers have wanted to make of them. The main purpose of this book is to assess the consequences of Marlowe's life in the theatre, to see how his plays transformed the varied dramatic and literary traditions of his time, and, above all, to suggest how they helped to recast and redefine the themes and modes of tragedy. I do not presume to find the man in the works, to interpret his works as products of a particular neurosis, as a cry of the heart, or as a concerted effort to challenge oppressive cultural institutions. They may be any or all of those things. Nevertheless, to see them in such perspectives, however revealing about the Marlowe we might like to imagine, blurs the central story of how his art was first crafted from earlier materials and traditions, and how it was then perceived, imitated, or echoed in those very competitive and energetic theatrical times.

Chronology

1564 Christopher Marlowe born at Canterbury.

William Shakespeare born at Stratford.

Birth of Galileo Galilei; deaths of John Calvin and Michelangelo Buonarroti.

1566 Birth of Edward Alleyn, future leading actor in Marlowe's plays.

1567 Birth of Richard Burbage, future leading actor in Shakespeare's plays.

1568 Founding of English College at Douai (France) to train Jesuits for the English mission.

1570 Publication of Abraham Ortelius, "Theatrum orbis terrarum": first modern atlas and a geographical source for *Tamburlaine*.

1572 Bartholomew's Day Massacre in Paris and French provinces.

Births of Ben Jonson and John Donne.

1575 Dramatic productions by the Children of Paul's.

1576 The Theatre, London's first permanent playhouse, opened by James Burbage.

Children of the Chapel Royal begin playing at the first Blackfriars Theatre.

1577 The Curtain Theatre built in Finsbury.

Publication of Raphael Holinshed's *Chronicles of England, Scotland, and Ireland*.

Francis Drake begins his voyage around the world (completed 1580).

1578   Douai College is moved to Rheims.

Marlowe enters the King's School in Canterbury on scholarship.

1579   Stephen Gosson's *School of Abuse*: anti-theatrical tract.

1580   Last recorded miracle play performed (in Coventry).

Publication of Michel de Montaigne's *Essays* and John Stow's *Annals of England* (source for *Edward II*).

Births of John Middleton and John Webster.

Marlowe enters Corpus Christi College, Cambridge, in December and is soon elected to a Matthew Parker Scholarship.

1581   English translations of *Seneca: His Ten Tragedies*.

1583   Formation of the Queen's Company of players.

1584   Marlowe receives the B.A. degree.

Publication of John Lyly's *Campaspe*.

Reginald Scot, *The Discovery of Witchcraft*, attacks superstition.

Sir Walter Raleigh arrives in Virginia.

1586   Sir Francis Walsingham uncovers the Babington plot to assassinate Elizabeth and enthrone Mary, Queen of Scots, in England.

Death of Sir Philip Sidney (b. 1551).

1587   The Rose Theatre is built by Philip Henslowe.

Execution of Mary, Queen of Scots.

Publication of *Historia von D. Iohan Fausten* (the "Faust-book") in Frankfurt.

5th edition of *A Mirror for Magistrates* published (orig. 1559).

Marlowe granted his M.A. degree after intervention by the Queen's Privy Council.

Probable first production of *Tamburlaine*.

1588   Defeat of the Spanish Armada.

Duke of Guise is assassinated in France.

Birth of Thomas Hobbes.

Robert Greene's *Perimedes the Blacksmith* refers to "that Atheist Tamburlaine" daring God out of heaven.

1589   King Henry III of France is assassinated.

Marlowe is arrested briefly for participation in a street duel in which his poet-friend Thomas Watson killed William Bradley.

1590   *Tamburlaine* published (without an author's name).

Publication of Edmund Spenser's *Faerie Queene I-III*, Philip
Sidney's *Arcadia*, and Mary Sidney (Countess of Pembroke)'s
Antonius: A Tragedy.

1591   Marlowe shares writing chambers with Thomas Kyd.

Probable first production of Shakespeare's *Henry VI*.

1592   *The Jew of Malta* is played at the Rose.

Marlowe is taken into custody for alleged counterfeiting at Flushing (in Dutch Isle of Walcheren), on the accusation of Richard
Baines (January 1591/92).

Death of Robert Greene (b. 1558), who provided the first allusion
to the theatrical activities of Shakespeare in London.

Death of Watson, and posthumous publication of his *Amyntae
Gaudia*, with Latin dedication by "C. M." (presumably
Marlowe) to the Countess of Pembroke.

Plague in London shuts down playhouses from July on.

Marlowe charged temporarily with assault upon William Corkine,
a tailor and musician, in Canterbury (September).

Publication of *The Spanish Tragedy* and of English translation of
the German Faust-book.

1593   *The Massacre at Paris* and *The Jew of Malta* are played at the
Rose in January; theatres are closed thereafter because of plague.

Pembroke's Men (who played *Edward II*) return from unsuccessful tour of the provinces.

May 12: a security search of Kyd's chambers reveals a heretical
manuscript alleged to have been owned earlier by Marlowe.

Baines prepares a list of Marlowe's "atheistical opinions."

May 20: Marlowe is sought at the estate of his patron Thomas
Walsingham in Kent and summoned to appear before the Privy
Council.

May 30: Marlowe, free on recognizance, is slain by Ingram Frizer
at Deptford.

July: *Edward II* is entered in the Stationers' Register.

September: Marlowe's translation of Lucan and his narrative
poem *Hero and Leander* are entered in the Stationers' Register.

Publication of Shakespeare's *Venus and Adonis*.

1594   *The Jew of Malta* is entered in the Stationers' Register.

Productions of *The Jew of Malta* continue at the Rose, together
with *Doctor Faustus*, *The Massacre at Paris*, and revivals of
Tamburlaine.

	Publication of *Edward II* and *Dido Queen of Carthage*.
	Admiral's Men and Chamberlain's Men (including Shakespeare) emerge as London's leading acting companies.
1595	Publication of Greene's *Friar Bacon and Friar Bungay*.
1597	Publication of Shakespeare's *Richard II* and *Richard III*.
	Jonson begins theatrical activity.
1598	Shakespeare's *The Merchant of Venice* is entered in the Stationers' Register.
	Publication of Marlowe's *Hero and Leander*.
1599	Chamberlain's Men open the first Globe Theatre on Bankside.
(?)	Shakespeare alludes to Marlowe, quoting *Hero and Leander* in *As You Like It;* in *2 Henry IV*, Pistol echoes lines from *Tamburlaine*.
1601	Henslowe revives *The Jew of Malta*.
	Dr. Faustus is entered in the Stationers' Register.
1602	Henslowe revives *Dr. Faustus*, paying William Birde and Samuel Rowley for "additions" to the script.
1603	Death of Queen Elizabeth, accession of King James I.
1604	Publication of *Dr. Faustus* (the so-called "A-text").
1606	Probable first production of Shakespeare's *Macbeth*.
	Jonson's *Volpone* is performed at the Globe.
1616	Publication of *Dr. Faustus* in an expanded version (the "B-text").
	Jonson publishes his *Works* in a folio edition.
	Death of Shakespeare.
1623	Publication of Shakespeare's plays in folio edition by members of his theatre company (the "First Folio").
1633	Publication of *The Jew of Malta*, with a title page citing revivals at court and at the Cockpit Theatre.
1642	Civil war forces the closing of the theatres.

Christopher Marlowe
and the Renaissance
of Tragedy

Chapter 1

Matters of Life and Death

Christopher Marlowe's life in the theatre was cut short violently at the age of twenty-nine; but the life of his plays in the world of the theatre goes on. In the age of Elizabeth I, he shone as the theatre's brightest star before the ascendancy of William Shakespeare, whose work owes a considerable debt to Marlowe's. In our own age, after a virtual absence from the stage for more than two and a half centuries, his plays are once again being produced and appreciated for their radically theatrical dimensions; as literary or poetic texts, they have enjoyed even more sustained attention. Doomed in a sense never to escape the shadow of Shakespeare, Marlowe nonetheless stands as a figure whose achievements and sensibility have come to be perceived as centrally important, not only to the development of dramatic art in one of its greatest eras but also to the expression of the Renaissance spirit in all its various and contradictory dimensions. His poetic drama helped to give symbolic shape to some of the more potent themes and myths of the Renaissance world—the drive for material empire and conquest, the subtle and often shadowy ironies of Machiavellian perceptions of how power is won and lost, the Faustian paradox of infinite aspiration and self-destruction. Along with Shakespeare, who enjoyed a much longer career and life, Marlowe pushed the poetic and psychological dimensions of drama far beyond the norms and ideals of Renaissance humanism, with its self-conscious emphasis on rhetorical style and classical learning. A genuinely new and passionate vitality energizes Marlowe's work, in conception, design, and expression; it borrows freely from both popular and learned sources, from both medieval and classical conventions, while creating from the mix not a derivative muddle but a new synthesis that, at its best, achieves mythic resonance.

Marlowe's touch on the pulse of the Renaissance was all too brief—he had only half a dozen years to live and write after earning his M.A. at Cambridge, and his dramatic legacy is limited to half a dozen plays. What teasing facts we know about those last six years suggest a life of intensity, audacity, and sensationalism that match such qualities in his drama; these have given rise in turn to conjectures and speculations that often outstrip their subject in their own extremes. Sixteenth-century documents attest that, just before the completion of his Cambridge studies, Marlowe was engaged in special (probably secret) service for the Queen; that he was involved some years later in two street duels and considered a threat to certain London constables; that he was arrested in the English-administered Low Lands (Netherlands) and sent back to England on charges of counterfeiting and possible treason; and that he was under investigation for atheism when he was stabbed to death in 1593 by Ingram Frizer, a personal servant of his current literary patron, Thomas Walsingham of Kent. The fatal stabbing, officially termed an act of self-defense against an attack initiated by Marlowe in a quarrel over the bill for food and drink consumed that day in the house of Eleanor Bull of Deptford, provoked grief and poetic tributes from his literary admirers. It also drew righteous diatribes from Puritan opponents of the stage and its wicked adherents; to the latter, Marlowe's death (reported with relish in a variety of inaccurate scenarios) represented an instance of divine retribution. Modern imaginations have spun even more complicated stories of intrigue around the violent circumstances of Marlowe's death. One of the earliest, S. A. Tannenbaum's *The Assassination of Christopher Marlowe* (1928), pointed the blame at Sir Walter Raleigh; the latest, Charles Nicholl's *The Reckoning* (1992), has contended that the Essex faction conspired to blacken Raleigh's name through association with Marlowe's alleged atheism and also to eliminate Marlowe as a witness. Others have even claimed that the murder was actually feigned to shield Marlowe from the imminent danger of being tried for heretical opinions and to allow him to continue writing plays under the name of William Shakespeare![1]

The hints of mystery and subterfuge surrounding Marlowe's short career are open invitations to fashion melodramatic myths about him. In the face of that temptation, however, it is good to remind ourselves of the facts that have been discovered, and of how much or little they demonstrate. The records we possess are of four main kinds: church records noting baptismal and burial dates; school and university documents noting attendance, scholarship stipends, and degrees; allusions in contemporary writings to his works and character, including authorship attribution on title pages of published works; and legal records documenting arrests, admonitions to keep the peace, and allegations prepared by informers. The names of the individuals mentioned in association with Marlowe have led to other recoverable data about them, which can add significant color to the scene. The category of allusions can be tricky, for, in instances when Marlowe's name is not mentioned directly, there can be doubt about whether he is indeed their subject; in other instances, contemporaries may have been responding to rumors or hearsay rather than to directly observed behavior. Similarly, in the case of allegations prepared by informers but never entered into trial records, there is little evidence about the extent to which such reports were given credence. For that matter, even when legal documentation does take the form of evidence accepted as true—as in the account of the events at Deptford—skeptics are always able to suspect a cover-up.

There is little in the church and school records before 1587 to suggest that Marlowe would have led anything other than a normal ecclesiastical life. Born in 1564, the son of a Canterbury shoemaker, he attended the King's School there and then went up to Cambridge in 1581 as an Archbishop Parker Scholar in Corpus Christi College, where, as all such scholars did, he read Divinity. Between the time of his B.A. degree and the M.A., the records of his stipend and buttery accounts show some absences from the university.[2] Then, in 1587, just at the time when Marlowe was scheduled to receive the M.A degree, a document appeared from the Privy Council, bidding the Cambridge authorities to grant Marlowe's degree and to cease their suspicions that he had defected to the English College at Rheims in France; this school had been established (originally at Douai) as the educational center for Catholic exiles and had become the training site for priests intending missionary work in Protestant England (an activity tantamount to treason in the reign of Elizabeth):

Whereas it was reported that Christopher Morley[3] was determined to have gone beyond the seas to Rheims and there to remain Their Lordships thought good to certify that he had no such intent but that in all his actions he had behaved himself orderly and discreetly whereby he had done her majesty good service, and deserved to be rewarded for his faithful dealing: Their Lordships' request was that the rumor thereof should be allayed by all possible means, and that he should be furthered in the degree he was to take this next commencement: Because it was not her majesty's pleasure that anyone employed as he had been in matters touching the benefit of his

country should be defamed by those that are ignorant in the affairs
he went about. (*Acts of the Privy Council*, cited in Bakeless [1942]
1970, 1: 77)[4]

In the context of the conspiratorial times, when England was threatened
with invasions by Catholic European powers sanctioned by the Pope and
when Jesuit priests were perceived as agents of sedition and treason, the
probable implication of this intervention is clear enough: Marlowe, the
Cambridge divinity student, had been enlisted as a secret agent and sent
to Rheims either to gather intelligence or to deliver messages to other
agents there. The university authorities, relieved of their suspicions about
his conversion or treason, duly granted his degree. But the new Master of
Arts did not go on to ordination and a career in either the church or the
academy.

We do not know the precise nature of Marlowe's "good service" at this
time, nor is there any other evidence of his having engaged in later
intelligence work. Nevertheless, later records show that he came into
fateful contact with figures who were involved in espionage and inform-
ing. In the meantime, the next set of records and allusions points clearly
to Marlowe's active life in London, where he quickly found himself among
poets and playwrights—many of them, like himself, university-educated
(and hence earning the nickname "University Wits")—who were turning
their skills to literary and theatrical enterprises. A 1588 allusion to Part II
of *Tamburlaine* establishes that Marlowe lost little time in making his mark
in his new profession. His two-part drama was published in 1590, though
without his name as author. This was a common practice in a time when
popular plays were considered neither the cultural equivalent of poetry nor
the property of their authors, who sold them (along with their rights) to
theatre managers or acting companies.

As an aspiring playwright, Marlowe had found himself in the right
place at the right time. Along with a handful of other recent university
graduates, such as John Lyly, Robert Greene, George Peele, and Thomas
Nashe (the last of whom Marlowe might well have met at Cambridge),
he saw new opportunities in the rapidly expanding needs of the commercial London stage. Within the preceding dozen years, London had seen
the construction of its first buildings expressly designed for the production of plays. Several groups of repertory players under the official
patronage of the aristocracy now had permanent places to perform, and,
even more importantly, places to draw large paying crowds from all
sectors of the city population. These groups of players competed not only
with each other but also with the "children's companies"—groups of boy

actors (originally, highly trained choristers subsidized to perform for cathedral and court functions), who put on plays in rented indoor halls; Marlowe's own play about Dido and Aeneas was performed by one such company, although we do not know when. All the companies hoped for the lucrative and celebrated invitation to play at court. Theatre records for these years suggest that the acting company to which Marlowe apparently sold his *Tamburlaine* script and which included the first great serious actor of the day, Edward Alleyn, also emerged as the court favorite by 1591–92. After that company's consolidation as the Lord Admiral's Men following the plague-induced ban on London theatrical production in 1592–93, its repertory also included Marlowe's *Jew of Malta, Doctor Faustus,* and *The Massacre at Paris.*[5]

The allusion that helps us to date *Tamburlaine* comes from Robert Greene (1558–92), a university man whose early attempts to carve out a literary career were prose romances (which included many lyric poems within their narrative). Before turning to playwriting himself, he had considered popular drama too vulgar a form. His preface to *Perimedes the Blacksmith* (1588) includes a long diatribe against the excesses of plays like *Tamburlaine* and of their authors as well:

> I keep my old course, to palter up something in prose, using mine old poesy still . . . although lately two gentlemen poets . . . had it in derision for that I could not make my verses jet upon the stage in tragical buskins, every word filling the mouth like the faburden of Bow Bell, daring God out of heaven with that atheist Tamburlaine, or blaspheming with the mad priest of the sun; but let me rather openly pocket up the ass at Diogenes' hand, than wantonly set out such impious instances of intolerable poetry, such mad and scoffing poets, that have prophetical spirits, as bred of Merlin's race, if there be any in England that set the end of scholarism in an English blank verse, I think either it is rather the humour of a novice that tickles them with self-love or too much frequenting the hot-house . . . hath sweat out all the greatest part of their wits. . . . If I speak darkly, gentlemen, and offend with this digression, I crave pardon, in that I but answer in print what they have offered on the stage. (Greene 1881–86, 7: 7–8)

The pun on Marlowe's name in "Merlin's race" attached to the use of blank verse makes it fairly obvious that he is one of the "mad and scoffing poets" intended, although it is impossible to decipher the other. Greene was clearly attacking both the attitude of his antagonists and the overblown style of their verse. It is noteworthy that his own first play, *Alphonsus, King of Aragon*, was, among other things, a kind of romantic travesty of Part I of *Tamburlaine*.

The first unambiguous record of Marlowe's physical presence in London—in September 1589—derives from his participation in a street duel that ended in the death of one William Bradley by the hand of Thomas Watson, an Oxford-educated poet and translator. The details of the incident were unknown until 1934, when Mark Eccles' archival discoveries were published in *Christopher Marlowe in London*. Bradley, a London man of twenty-six about whom very little is known, had recently been involved in some sort of feud with Watson and had gone before a justice of the Queen's Bench that very summer to complain that Watson and two others had threatened his life and safety. Such filings for "sureties of the peace," which required that the adversaries appear in court and offer bond that they would not injure the plaintiff, were a fairly common practice, and both sides in disputes often filed. In 1596, William Shakespeare and three others were so charged in an otherwise obscure incident. In May 1592, Marlowe had two neighbors offer bond for him that he would keep the peace with two local constables who had filed such complaints. In the 1589 incident, however, according to the report of the coroner's inquest, Marlowe himself was fighting with Bradley in Hog Lane near Cripplegate when Watson came upon them and Bradley turned his attack toward him. Marlowe, now out of the fight, watched while the other two fought with sword and dagger until Watson, hard beset, thrust Bradley through with his sword, killing him instantly. Watson and Marlowe were both arrested on charges of homicide and imprisoned in Newgate, but the inquest found Marlowe innocent and judged that Watson had acted in self-defense. Marlowe was released within two weeks, but Watson languished in jail for several months until freed by the Queen's pardon. The records of the fray also reveal that Marlowe and Watson were residing at this time at Norton Folgate, a suburban district close to the Shoreditch playhouses, The Theatre and The Curtain.

Watson (1557–92) was a learned writer who had studied abroad in Italy and France. He published Latin translations of Sophocles' Greek tragedy *Antigone* (1581), Tasso's *Aminta* (1585), and Coluthus' *Rape of Helen* (1586) but is remembered chiefly for his English love poetry, drawn from French and Italian models. His Latin pastoral, *Amyntae Gaudia*, was not published until just after his death in 1592, and it appears that Marlowe saw it through the press: its extravagant Latin dedication to the Countess of Pembroke, then at the height of her fame as a patron of the literary arts, was signed "C. M."

Perhaps even more important in the association of these two men, however, was their common link with their patron, Thomas Walsingham of Kent, second cousin to the head of Elizabeth's intelligence service, Sir Francis Walsingham. Eccles has noted that Watson's *Meliboeus* (1590) was dedicated to Thomas Walsingham; the work included an elegiac dialogue between Watson and his patron bemoaning the death of the late Sir Francis and referring to the start of their friendship during Watson's stay in Paris several years before (p. 8). We do not know the details or the chronology, nor whether Marlowe became Thomas Walsingham's friend before or after meeting Watson, but there is no doubt that Marlowe and Walsingham were on close terms in 1593, when the Privy Council sought Marlowe out at Walsingham's Scadbury estate. It is conceivable that the intelligence service of Marlowe's Cambridge days may then have brought him into contact with Thomas Walsingham, who had also carried messages to Europe for his cousin (Bakeless 1970, 1: 161). When, five years after Marlowe's death at the hand of Thomas Walsingham's servant, the printer Edward Blount published Marlowe's unfinished poem *Hero and Leander*, he dedicated it to Walsingham in tribute to their friendship. Walsingham also became patron to George Chapman (c. 1560–1634), another learned translator, playwright, and poet, who completed Marlowe's narrative poem on Hero and Leander in 1598.

Another literary associate of Marlowe's during this period was Thomas Kyd, with whom Marlowe shared writing chambers (it is unclear whether this implied shared living quarters) in 1591. Kyd's blank-verse revenge play, *The Spanish Tragedy*, was one of the most successful and influential Elizabethan plays. We do not know when it was first composed and performed (some conjectures put it as early as 1582), but it was still a strong item in the repertory at the Rose Theatre in the mid-1590s. All we know about the relationship between these two men comes from the testimony of Kyd himself, given two years later when his former link with Marlowe had borne bitter fruit: Kyd had been arrested, imprisoned, and tortured because authorities suspected that he had something to do with a libelous public threat against immigrants in London and because they had found among his papers a manuscript fragment that appeared to be heretical. Kyd claimed that the manuscript belonged to Marlowe, and, in letters written just after Marlowe's death, he attempted to disassociate himself from his earlier companion, virulently decrying Marlowe's character and beliefs (Appendix A).[6] The manuscript fragment was in fact a section of a sober theological argument disputing the divinity of Christ on scriptural grounds, originally written by a Unitarian heretic examined by Archbishop Cranmer in 1549. A book called *The Fall of the Late Arian*, published in the same year by John Proctor, had reproduced the argument in order to refute it step by step (Bakeless 1970, 1: 115–16). That a Unitarian perspective (or a Roman Catholic one, for that matter) could be called "atheism" is a useful reminder of how loosely the term was applied to any deviation from the officially accepted theology of the realm. But, as Kyd and others would make clear, Marlowe's own alleged atheism was of another strain entirely.

Before looking more closely at those charges and their consequences with respect to Marlowe's last days, we need to note one very dramatic but nontheatrical incident in 1592, which has come to light only recently. In 1976, R. B. Wernham published a newly discovered official letter dated January 26, 1591/2, from Sir Robert Sidney, governor of Flushing in the Dutch Isle of Walcheren, to Lord Burghley, reporting that the scholar Christopher Marly was being sent back to England as a prisoner along with a goldsmith, Gifford Gilbert. Both men had been accused of coining by their chamber-fellow, Richard Baines. Baines and Marly, according to the report, had in fact accused each other of drawing in the goldsmith with the intent to practice counterfeiting later on; only one coin had been struck so far. Moreover, each man had accused the other of intending to go over "to the enemy" or to Rome. Marly had also claimed to be well known to the Earl of Northumberland and to Lord Strange.

That the scholar-prisoner was indeed the dramatist Marlowe is evident from the connection with Lord Strange, the patron of the professional acting company that amalgamated with the Admiral's Men at the time that their repertory included Marlowe's plays, and with Baines, the informant who later drew up the charges of atheism leveled at Marlowe at the time of his arrest in the days before his death (Appendix B). The Northumberland connection also fits; the earl was a patron both of Thomas Watson, who had dedicated *The Rape of Helen* to him in 1586, and of Thomas Harriot, the noted mathematician, who had become a member of Northumberland's household at Syon by 1591, along with two other mathematicians, Walter Warner and Robert Hues (the earl called them his "three magi"). Both Harriot and Warner were named by Thomas Kyd as Marlowe's associates. Furthermore, one of Baines' later charges against Marlowe involved a reference made by Marlowe to Harriot.

Perhaps by reason of Marlowe's friends in high places, nothing further seems to have come of these charges of counterfeiting and treason. That Marlowe named these nobles in his defense, rather than any official in the intelligence service, suggests also that his presence abroad was not prompted by new or continued service of that kind. Moreover, the counterfeiting adventure, wild as it may seem, fits in with two other facts. Baines included among his later list of Marlowe's blasphemies the digressive charge that Marlowe had boasted "That he had as good right to coin as the Queen of England, and that he was acquainted with one Poole, a prisoner in Newgate, who hath great skill in mixture of metals, and having learned some things of him he meant, through help of a cunning stamp maker, to coin French crowns, pistolets, and English shillings." Eccles' researches into the circumstances of Marlowe's stay in Newgate at the time of the Bradley homicide disclosed that a counterfeiter named John Poole had been imprisoned there since 1587 (Eccles [1934] 1967, 37). Thus, it now seems quite probable that Marlowe was indeed attempting an experiment in counterfeiting with knowledge gleaned from his earlier Newgate internment. Ironically enough, at the very time that Marlowe was being shipped back to England as an accused counterfeiter, the players at Philip Henslowe's Rose Theatre were rehearsing, among other things, *The Jew of Malta*, a play that includes Barabas' gloating vision of "infinite riches in a little room."

It is easier to reconstruct a plausible, if unflattering, scenario for Marlowe in this incident than it is to piece together Baines' role. Sidney's letter does not explain why Baines was not sent back with the others, nor why his word seems to have won against Marlowe's in their mutual recriminations. The answer may lie in Baines' own background in the network of Elizabethan espionage. The most illuminating facts in that regard were discovered only in the late 1940s (Boas 1949), when historians of the English seminary at Rheims documented the imprisonment there of one Richard Baynes, a recently ordained priest who had conspired in 1582 to sell secrets of the Catholic seminary's leaders to Queen Elizabeth's intelligence secretary; Baynes had even confessed to a plot to poison the well of the entire religious community. His imprisonment lasted at least ten months, but the records do not reveal what became of him afterward. If, as seems likely, he escaped to take up service for Sir Francis Walsingham, he might first have been put in contact with Marlowe at the time that the Cambridge scholar was recruited for service involving Rheims. Whatever their relationship, it must have soured severely after their desperate cross-accusations of treachery in the Flushing affair. If Baines had been a confidant of Marlowe's for whatever reasons, this relationship would have provided him with some basis for the charges he later drew up in May 1593. At the same time, his earlier history suggests that he might do anything and everything if the rewards were great enough.

The year 1592 was not a good one for Marlowe, in or out of the theatre. His arrest in Flushing was a bad beginning, even though no penalties seem to have come of it. In May, two constables of Shoreditch filed complaints against him for threatening their safety. In June, bubonic plague took such hold of London that the theatres were ordered closed. In September, during a visit to his native Canterbury, he fell to fighting a local tailor, William Corkine, "with staff and dagger" in the public streets. Corkine sued for assault; Marlowe counter-sued and had his cause denied, but he managed to escape damage again when the charges were dropped (Urry 1988, 65–68). His friend Thomas Watson died that year, as did his enemy, Robert Greene, but not before he left behind another allusive diatribe aimed, presumably, at Marlowe:

> Wonder not, for with thee I will first begin, thou famous gracer of tragedians, that Greene, who hath said with thee (like the fool in his heart) there is no God, should now give glory unto His greatness, for penetrating is His power. . . . Why should thy excellent wit, His gift, be so blinded, that thou shouldst give no glory to the Giver? Is it pestilent Machiavellian policy that thou hast studied? O peevish folly! What are his rules but mere confused mockeries, able to extirpate in small time the generation of mankind. For if *Sic volo, sic iubeo* ["As I will, so I command"] hold in those that are able to command: and if it be lawful *Fas et nefas* ["Right and wrong"] to do anything that is beneficial, only tyrants should possess the earth. . . . Defer not (with me) till this last point of extremity: for little knowest thou how in the end thou shalt be visited. (Greene 1881–86, 12: 141–42)

Little did Greene know how prophetic his warning would be. By the end of the following May, Christopher Marlowe would meet a sudden and violent death.

Thomas Kyd was arrested on May 12, 1593. Six days later, the Privy Council issued an order to seek out Marlowe at "the house of Mr. Thomas Walsingham in Kent, or . . . any other place where he shall understand [him] to be remaining," to apprehend him and to bring him to court (Wraight 1965, 284). The presumption is that the order was provoked by Kyd's claim that the heretical document found among his papers was Marlowe's, although it is also remotely possible that the Privy Council may have wished to question Marlowe about the anti-immigrant libel. On May 20, Marlowe appeared before the court, which was presided over that day by the Archbishop of Canterbury. He was released immediately after entering his indemnity, with the understanding that he would provide his daily attendance upon the authorities until further notice. We do not know whether the Baines charges of atheism had been drawn up by this date.[7] It seems unlikely that Marlowe would have been treated so leniently if they had.[8] In any event, free on bond but obliged to stay on daily call, Marlowe had to stay close to London. His case was never resolved in court, however, for ten days later he lay dead in Deptford.

The details of that death, as officially documented in archival records, were discovered and lucidly put forth by J. Leslie Hotson in 1925. For the intervening centuries, however, the image of what happened on that fateful day derives from the hearsay reports of contemporary Puritan zealots, whose hostility toward the stage and anyone connected with it knew no bounds. The first of those reports, in 1597, appeared in Thomas Beard's often reprinted compendium of examples of divine retribution for sin, collected "out of sacred, ecclesiastical, and profane authors" and entitled *The Theatre of God's Judgments*. The entry on Marlowe falls among several accounts of wicked poets:

Not inferior to any of the former in atheism and impiety, and equal to all in manner of punishment was one of our own nation, of fresh and late memory, called Marlin, by profession a scholar, brought up from his youth in the University of Cambridge, but by practice a play-maker, and a poet of scurrility, who by giving too large a swing to his own wit, and suffering his lust to have the full reins, fell (not without just desert) to that outrage and extremity, that he denied God and His son Christ, and not only in word blasphemed the Trinity, but also (as it is credibly reported) wrote books against it, affirming our Savior to be but a deceiver, and Moses to be but a conjuror and seducer of the people, and the holy Bible to be but vain and idle stories, and all religion but a device of policy. But see what a hook the Lord put in the nostrils of this barking dog: It so fell out, that in London streets as he purposed to stab one whom he owed a grudge unto with his dagger, the other party perceiving so avoided the stroke, that withal catching hold of his wrist, he stabbed his own dagger into his own head, in such sort, that notwithstanding all the means of surgery that could be wrought, he shortly after died thereof. The manner of his death being so terrible (for he even cursed and blasphemed to his last gasp, and together with his breath an oath flew out of his mouth) that it was not only a manifest sign of God's judgment, but also an horrible and fearful terror to all that beheld him. (cited in Bakeless 1970, 1: 144–45)

Beard's anecdote was repeated in many other such works, including Edmund Rudierd's *Thunderbolt of God's Wrath* (1618), which aimed it more sharply at the writing profession: "But hearken, ye brain-sick and profane poets and players, that bewitch idle ears with foolish vanities," Rudierd admonished, to what befell this wretch, "who was a poet and a filthy play-maker" (Bakeless 1: 145). Francis Meres' commonplace book, *Palladis Tamia* (1598), which is often quoted for its commendation of Shakespeare's early works, did not share the Puritan animosity toward Marlowe's poetry, but he added to his citation of Beard's account a new note that others developed later: The poet was stabbed "by a bawdy serving-man, a rival of his in his lewd love" (Hotson, 14). Thus, by 1691, we find Anthony à Wood's embellishment in *Athenae Oxonienses*: "For so it fell out, that he being deeply in love with a certain woman, had for his rival a bawdy serving-man, one rather fit to be a pimp, than an ingenious *Amoretto* as Marlo conceived himself to be. Whereupon Marlo taking it to be an high affront, rushed in upon, to stab him, with his dagger" (Hotson 1925, 14).

How well does the legend fit the facts? Hotson's recovery of the records of the jury inquest following the homicide provides these basic details: Marlowe had spent most of the day with three associates—Ingram Frizer, Nicholas Skeres, and Robert Poley—dining at the house of one Eleanor Bull in Deptford, just east of Greenwich. Whether this house was a "public house" (or tavern) or only a lodging house serving meals is not at all certain; recent research has shown that the Bull family was very respectable and enjoyed some aristocratic connections (Urry 1988, 83–86). At any rate, Marlowe is said to have quarreled late in the day with Frizer about settling the bill for their food and drink. In a sudden outburst, he came up behind Frizer where he was seated at a table between Poley and Skeres, seized Frizer's own dagger from its sheath, and began striking him on the head. In the ensuing scuffle, Frizer received two scalp wounds before wresting the dagger from Marlowe and turning it against him to inflict a fatal head wound. Frizer was judged to have acted in self-defense and received the Queen's pardon.

Frizer, it turns out, was a serving-man, but not Marlowe's and not in the sense of a menial servant. He was in the employ of Thomas Walsingham, for whose family he continued to work as a successful business agent long after the homicide. Later records attest that he became a respectable landowner and church warden. Nevertheless, other records reveal that he and Skeres were shortly to be engaged in some unscrupulous business dealings. Boas (1940, 268–69) has acknowledged that it is difficult to trace his earlier history, because the name is so common, but there are two tempting pieces of data. One links a Nicholas "Skyers" with Matthew Royden in 1582 (Royden, a minor poet admired by Chapman and Nashe, was named by Kyd as an associate of Marlowe's); the other identifies a Skeres among those who had helped to uncover the Babington conspiracy to assassinate Queen Elizabeth in 1586. That Skeres, presumably, was also the man who was paid by the government in 1589 for delivering important messages from the Court to the Earl of Essex. The government connection links him in turn with the fourth member of the Deptford party, Robert Poley. Poley had a long and checkered history in secret intelligence. He had been instrumental in securing evidence leading to the disclosure of the Babington plot, and he later appeared frequently as a carrier of secret dispatches between the Court and Scotland, Denmark, and the Low Countries. Indeed, at the time of the Deptford incident he held a commission to deliver secret correspondence between the Court and Holland.

Thus, considering the past links of Marlowe, Skeres, and Poley with the intelligence network, as well as Frizer's position in the Walsingham household, the meeting at Eleanor Bull's takes on the character of a special sort of fraternity party among spies past and present. Inevitably, the discovery of the identity of Marlowe's companions on the day of his death has become an open invitation for conspiracy theorists to weave any number of melodramatic assassination plots. They have wanted to find something more insidious than a reunion gone awry or an accidental disaster. In an era of hypersensitivity to institutional cover-ups and to the victimization of the individual by oppressive elites, it becomes even more tempting to read another story between the lines. Such interpreters do not want to accept the coroner's inquest report as fact or to believe that Marlowe's own aggressive impulses could have been the real trigger of his death. They, together with more sentimental sorts who prefer their poets noble and pure, do not want to accept Kyd's characterization of Marlowe as one "intemperate and of a cruel heart," moved by "rashness in attempting sudden privy injuries to men." But Kyd did not need to make those particular claims in order to defend himself against charges of atheism. Furthermore, there is nothing in the revealed network of relationships that would rule out the possibility that the record tells the real story. It does not tell the whole story, however, and it is thus likely that the future will produce still further imaginative supplements to the unsatisfying and lean sketch of Marlowe's last days.

Although the official report of Marlowe's death has laid to rest the legendary accretions about pimps and lewd loves, it offers no help about the charges of atheism that were also part of the lurid image invoked in

Beard's "memorial." Beard cited what he called credible reports about Marlowe's having written books against the Trinity, debunking the Bible, and maintaining that Moses and Christ were frauds. The particularity of those charges, which is not found in the allusions by Greene, does find a parallel in the combination of charges made by Kyd and Baines. Thus, the fragment of the anti-Trinitarian argument found in Kyd's possession may have been the basis for Beard's alleged "books," while the other scoffing gibes about Moses, Christ, and religion, listed by both Kyd and Baines, fit the tone of the other blasphemies mentioned by Beard. Still, neither the Kyd letters nor the Baines note were public documents; if somehow their contents had been made known, it is highly unlikely that the moralists would have neglected to exploit Marlowe's alleged claim that "all they that love not tobacco and boys were fools."[9] We are left in the dark about the source (credible or otherwise) of the Puritan allegations.

With respect to Kyd and Baines themselves, there are certainly grounds to suspect their motivations and veracity: Kyd was desperately struggling to clear his own reputation at a time when Marlowe was no longer alive to contradict him; Baines the informer not only wore the badge of a questionable profession[10] but might also have borne Marlowe a grudge stemming from the Flushing incident. Nevertheless, their specific charges did overlap, and both men were quite confident that other witnesses could be found to corroborate them. Furthermore, Kyd's claim that it was Marlowe's custom in table talk to jest at scriptures and to argue against religion matched Baines' assertion that Marlowe introduced his atheistic opinions "almost into every company he cometh" and appears to have been supported by references to two of Marlowe's "converts." One was Richard Cholmeley, mentioned by Baines and later arrested and alleged to have maintained that "one Marlowe is able to show more sound reasons for atheism than any divine in England is able to give to prove divinity" (Wraight 1965, 354). The other, Thomas Fineux of Kent, began studies at Corpus Christi College, Cambridge, in Marlowe's final year there, and was reported, albeit in a very circuitous manner, to have been made an atheist by Marlowe.[11]

Although any single piece of such evidence may be tainted to some degree, there is still a sense of an underlying thread running through it all that is by no means at odds with the general characterization supplied by Robert Greene. The portrait is also consistent with the rather nasty lines set down by the poet and satirist Gabriel Harvey in 1593 in response to the news of Marlowe's death (which must have reached him only in the vaguest form, for Harvey assumed that Marlowe died of the plague):

Weep, Paul's, thy Tamburlaine vouchsafes to die.
Is it a dream? Or is the highest mind
That ever haunted Paul's or hunted wind
Bereft of that same sky-surmounting breath,
That breath that taught the tempany to swell.

He and the plague contended for the game. . . .
The grand disease disdained his toad conceit
And smiling at his Tamburlaine contempt,
Sternly struck home the peremptory stroke;
He that nor feared God, nor dreaded Devil,
Nor ought admired but his wondrous self . . .
Alas! but Babel Pride must kiss the pit. (in Boas 1940, 279)

In the same year, Harvey also called Marlowe "a Lucian"—referring to the Greek satirist who in his own time was noted for savage wit and blasphemy (Brooke 1922, 353).

Thomas Nashe, who had collaborated in some way with Marlowe in writing *Dido Queen of Carthage*, criticized Harvey for his denigration of both Marlowe and Greene after their deaths. Other poets, such as George Peele and Henry Petowe, penned tributes to Marlowe's artistry, and both Edward Blount and Chapman lauded him and his friendship with his patron Thomas Walsingham in their edition of *Hero and Leander*. Thus the paradox remains: Some of his contemporaries considered Marlowe a notoriously proud and mocking atheist, while others saw him as a person of rare gifts, whose works might be proudly dedicated in public to aristocratic patrons (hardly a risk worth taking if the poet's scandalous notoriety were uppermost in the public mind). As with the account of Marlowe's death, so here the record of facts leaves us wondering what the whole truth was. Peele's tribute, with its ambivalent allusion to the underworld, stands as a teasing epitome of the problem:

> . . . unhappy in thine end,
> Marley, the Muses' darling for thy verse;
> Fit to write passions for the souls below,
> If any wretched souls in passion speak? (Horne 1952, 246)

Yet one further factual problem with respect to Marlowe's life continues to tease: Was he, as so many biographies presume, an intimate of Sir Walter Raleigh's, who was also a figure of controversy connected to charges of atheism in his time? The facts remain inconclusive, and the sole documentary evidence linking their names rests on a very disreputable source—

the alleged atheist convert of Marlowe's, Richard Cholmeley. Baines mentioned that Cholmeley "hath confessed" that he was persuaded to atheism by Marlowe's reasons, but when Cholmeley's confession was made and under what circumstances is highly puzzling. The copy of the Baines note prepared for the Queen included a marginal addition next to the comment about Cholmeley that "He is laid for," indicating that efforts to arrest him were under way. Indeed, a warrant had gone out for his arrest on March 19, with a warning that he would be among many dangerous confederates.[12] He was not captured, however, until June 29, six weeks after Kyd and Marlowe were in trouble (Boas 1940, 253–55).

An undated and unsigned list of charges against Cholmeley indicates that he had once been in the service of the Crown, "employed by some of her Majesty's Privy Council for the apprehension of Papists," some of whom, he was said to have admitted, he set free for bribes. Among other items attributed to him were "that he speaketh in general all evil of the Council, saying that they were all atheists and Machiavellians, especially my Lord Admiral"; "that he made certain libelous verses in commendation of papists and seminary priests"; that he hated the Lord Chamberlain; that he wished he had slain the Lord Treasurer with his own hands during a recent mutiny; and that he could cozen the Council as he pleased. Tucked among these charges, we also find the claim about Marlowe's persuasive abilities in the cause of atheism and "that Marlowe told him that he hath read the atheist lecture to Sir Walter Raleigh and others." The relationship between Marlowe and Raleigh, then, rests on the hearsay evidence of an apparently scurrilous and remarkably brazen detractor of men in high places, who was himself accused, simultaneously and not untypically, of atheism and favoritism toward Catholics (Wraight 1965, 354–55).

We do not know the ultimate fate of Cholmeley, although there is a record of a request to the authorities by the Earl of Essex in November that his case be continued to allow time for establishing his innocence (Boas 1940, 255). As for the "atheist lecture," we do not know what that may have been either. It may be related to Baines' final claim that Marlowe "saith likewise that he hath quoted a number of contrarieties out of the Scripture which he hath given to some great men who in convenient time shall be named." "Contrarieties" in this context suggests a list of scriptural self-contradictions, which in turn can be linked with one of the other charges casting doubt upon the authenticity of Biblical chronology. Thomas Harriot's voluminous papers reveal his own calculations about that chronology. Hence, with the help of Kyd's information that Harriot was Marlowe's associate, there is another possible link to Raleigh and the kind of questions his circle was interested in investigating.

Yet we still have no hard evidence that Marlowe was in direct contact with Raleigh. It is certainly possible, since he claimed both Harriot and Northumberland as acquaintances. Nonetheless, in the later history of the inquiries and trials of Raleigh himself, including the Cerne Abbas inquiry (which related directly to heterodox theological arguments), no reference was ever made to Marlowe or to atheist opinions alleged to have been Marlowe's.

Although the questionable context of such evidence as Cholmeley's does not prove the evidence false, it leaves considerable room for doubt. Similarly, E. A. Strathmann has cast doubt on another repeated assertion related to Raleigh and Marlowe: that they were involved in a coterie of scientists and free thinkers. This claim seems to have originated in a diatribe by the Jesuit Robert Parsons against Queen Elizabeth's anti-Catholic edict of 1591. Parsons labeled the group a "school of atheism." Some modern literary scholars have speculated that Shakespeare's phrase "the School of Night" in *Love's Labour's Lost* may also allude to the coterie. If Parsons' charge is seen in the context of the bitter polemics between the Jesuits and those in charge of religious policy in England, then its value as objective evidence is considerably diminished (Strathmann 1951, 25–40).

Christopher Marlowe's life as we can piece it together is finally a bundle of "contrarieties": a divinity student turned spy, or "intelligencer," in the terminology of his time; a playwright with a quick wit, a quick temper, and a quick dagger; an adventurer and a schemer, consorting with underworld informers as well as with aristocratic patrons; an irreverent scoffer and mocker of religion; and a revered poet.

Ironically, Marlowe did not live long enough to see the peak of his celebrity as poet and playwright, which followed fast upon his death. In 1594, with the plague gone and the theatres in full revival, Henslowe's repertory included *The Jew of Malta*, *The Massacre at Paris*, *Doctor Faustus*, and revivals of *Tamburlaine*. *Edward II* and *Dido Queen of Cathage* were published. In a few more years, his poetry would also be published: *Hero and Leander* and his translations of Ovid's *Amores* and of the first book of Lucan's *Pharsalia*. Most of the later tributes to his art would be directed at *Hero and Leander*, for playwriting had not yet earned for itself the elevated status of poetry. That would all change in the coming generation, as Shakespeare, Ben Jonson, and others established their irresistible authority as literary giants in the theatre. But Marlowe had been there before them, supplying a new kind of passion and poetry to the life of the theatre.

Illustration 1. Supposed portrait of Christopher Marlowe. This 1585 portrait, discovered during the 1953 renovation of the Master's Lodge at Corpus Christi College, Cambridge, has been adopted by popular imagination to be that of Marlowe. The inscription supplies the sitter's age (twenty-one), which matches Marlowe's at the time, but no name. The paradoxical motto, "*Quod me Nutrit me Destruit*" (What nourishes me destroys me), has provoked irresistible applications to Marlowe's later career. Still, it is difficult to imagine a plausible social and financial context that would have provided Marlowe, the son of a cobbler and a scholarship student taking his bachelor's degree that year, with the opportunity to sit for such a portrait (or to afford the apparently rich garb of black velvet with touches of gold). It is even more difficult to comprehend the motivations for college authorities of the time to exhibit or store among their possessions the portrait of an uncelebrated student. (Photo courtesy of The Master and Fellows of Corpus Christi College, Cambridge. The College does not vouch for the identity of the portrait.)

And yet Marlowe's celebrity proved mutable, too. Even before the outbreak of civil war closed the theatres in 1642, new theatrical tastes had let most sixteenth-century plays drop out of repertory. The revival of *The Jew of Malta* in the 1630s seems to have been a notable exception. Publication records suggest that the reading public's interest in Marlowe's drama also waned; besides the single late appearance of *The Jew*, only *Doctor Faustus* continued to be reprinted after 1622. With the Restoration and the revival of the theatre in 1660, only *Faustus* reemerged, and then only briefly and fitfully, in much-revised form, before it disappeared entirely beneath a superstructure of spectacular farce. With one exception, Marlowe's plays would not be seen in the theatre again until the last decade of the nineteenth century, when William Poel revived *Doctor Faustus* as part of his experimental attempt to reconstruct the staging conditions of the Elizabethan theatre. The exception was again *The Jew of Malta*, which was performed by Edmund Kean in a much-altered version in 1818. In the life of the theatre, then, after his moment of fame at the end of the sixteenth century, Marlowe was pretty much dead and buried for the space of 250 years.

Offstage, however, another story was to unfold, a story with nearly miraculous dimensions. It started with the double image of Marlowe in the years just after his death, when he was praised by his peers for his poetic skills and blasted by the Puritans as an example of punished atheism and debauchery. A nearly total eclipse of interest in or appreciation of his work followed during the latter seventeenth century and throughout most of the eighteenth century. Then, in the wake of Goethe and of romanticism, a stunning metamorphosis occurred. Lifting passages from Marlowe's work as examples of inspired poetry and finding in those passages the themes and textures of their own ideals of sensuous excitement and dedication to beauty, romantic critics constructed a foundation for a new, enthusiastic assessment of Marlowe as poet. That enthusiasm mounted to a rapturous climax in the 1870s, when literary historians like Edward Dowden and Hippolyte Taine and poets like Algernon Charles Swinburne found in him the avatar of a divinely pagan spirit. The apotheosis was complete in these lines from Swinburne's sonnet on Marlowe, in which images of Apollo and Lucifer interfuse:

Crowned, girdled, garbed and shod with light and fire,
Son first-born of the morning, sovereign star![13]

It is worthwhile to note some of the steps along the way in this process of transvaluation, which Thomas Dabbs has detailed extensively in his recent book, *Reforming Marlowe*. Charles Lamb's *Specimens of English*

Dramatic Poets (1808) established the method of selecting passages out of context for comment and appreciation. William Hazlitt, in *Lectures on the Age of Elizabeth* (1820), illustrated how the imagery of a dramatic character like Faustus could be transposed into a description of Marlowe's own art and personality:

> There is a lust of power in his writings, a hunger and thirst after unrighteousness, a glow of the imagination, unhallowed by anything but its own energies. His thoughts burn within him like a furnace with bickering flames; or throwing out black smoke and mist that hide the dawn of genius, or like a poisonous mineral, corrode the heart. (Hazlitt 1931, 6: 202)

Half a century later, Dowden's characterization of early Renaissance drama as a pre-romantic capturing of "extremes of rapture and of pain" included a special claim for Marlowe's "taking art as the object of his devotion" (Dabbs 1991, 98–99). Swinburne, taking that cue, moved to a level of hyperbole worthy of Marlowe himself:

> In Marlowe the passion of ideal love for the ultimate idea of beauty in art or nature found its perfect and supreme expression, faultless and unforced. The radiance of his desire, the light and flame of his aspiration, diffused and shed through all the forms of his thought and all the colors of his verse, gave them such shapeliness and strength of life as is given to the spirits of the greatest poets alone. (Swinburne 1875, 164)

It should be noted that Swinburne's most ebullient praise was lavished on the sensuous surfaces of Marlowe's poem *Hero and Leander*, but he clearly let his overwhelming admiration for it color his judgments of all of Marlowe's work. Although hardly any other writer has matched Swinburne's virtual adoration of Marlowe's art, it is clear that the emerging critical consensus, fired by romanticism and estheticism, had elevated his work to a new and remarkably high status. Beard's justly damned sinner had finally been canonized in more ways than one.

And yet, the transformation had been made on the basis of "pieces" of Marlowe's art, in an age that offered no theatrical productions of them. Whether the force of the romantic ideology that imposed such glowing terms upon certain verse passages would have been resisted significantly by any experience of witnessing a whole play, with its contextual ironies intact, is impossible to say. One can well understand, however, how a play like *The Jew of Malta* might prove a mighty obstacle to under-standing, much less appreciation, if one came to it expecting a radiant passion for beauty in art or nature! It would take nearly another century to bring the totality of Marlowe back into view, including theatrical view. By the time that happened, in our own generation, the complex and often sardonic ironies of Marlowe's work would be revealed once again. In so much of that flaming aspiration admired by the nineteenth-century readers, viewers would also sense the encroaching "darkness visible" of a tragic perspective.

Chapter 2

The World of the Theatre in the Reign of Elizabeth

What was theatre like in the days of Marlowe? Where were plays to be seen? What sorts of acting companies performed them, and under what circumstances? What was the nature of their material, and who provided it? How did plays find their way into print? And what sort of esteem did playwrights enjoy, especially in comparison to poets? To appreciate fully Marlowe's interaction with the developing English theatre, we need to bear in mind the circumstances and conditions that governed the production and publication of plays in the last decades of the sixteenth century. This was precisely the critical time when the theatre in England was becoming professional. The economic and social conditions in London in particular made possible the phenomenon of a commercial theatre, consisting of several repertory companies competing for the allegiance of a broadly based popular audience, as well as for the special notice and prestige of performances at Elizabeth's Court.

Indeed, the favor of the Queen meant far more than the occasional rewards for command performance. Without royal support for theatrical production in general, plus the system of aristocratic patronage that gave legal standing to the acting companies, it is not likely that the actors could have prevailed against the pressures of hostile civic authorities that were continually anxious, for reasons of public safety, economy, and morality, to restrict and prohibit theatrical activity. Theatre gained its legal life-line as a sanctioned mode of royal entertainment through edicts of the 1570s. Actors were protected from the harsh measures affecting "rogues and vagabonds" and other men without official connection with a craft guild or an aristocratic household because they enjoyed the nominal patronage of the nobility (it rarely, if ever, extended to sustaining financial support). Hence, the names of the adult companies of the era: the Earl of Leicester's Men, the Earl of Worcester's Men, the Lord Admiral's Men, the Lord Chamberlain's Men, the Queen's Men, and so on.

As for most playwrights, they depended in turn on the commercial theatre, to whose companies they sold their scripts and, in several cases (including, most notably, that of Shakespeare), contracted themselves as company writers. But the commercial theatre itself was a relatively new thing. Although traveling groups of players had been known to wander throughout the land, performing in inn-yards, market places, or the private halls of individual nobles or city magnates (see Illustrations 2 and 3), it was not until 1576 that a permanent building expressly constructed for the production of plays sprang up in the north of London: it was called, simply, "The Theatre." Another, "The Curtain," opened nearby in the following year. Both were presumably built as roughly circular open-air arenas surrounded by roofed galleries, similar to the kind used for bull-baiting and bear-baiting. Within them, a platform stage projected from a section of the peripheral structure called a "tiring house" (what we now call "backstage") into the arena. At about the same time, Richard Farrant, master of the boy choristers known as the Children of Windsor Chapel, converted part of a London building called the Blackfriars (harking back to the time when it had been a monastery, before Henry VIII dissolved it) into an indoor theatre. There, until 1584, plays were staged for the more affluent public by various boy companies, including the Children of the Chapel Royal and the Children of Paul's (another choristers' school), bringing to a wider audience what had been their long-standing tradition of performing plays at Elizabeth's Court. While modern imaginations may find it difficult to take seriously the notion of children's acting as an accomplished art, we need to recall that the choristers in the schools that provided such actors were carefully selected and trained for their musical tasks; the discipline and skills of memorization, vocal projection, color, and dynamics all served them well in performing theatrical scripts as well as musical scores.

Thus were established the two venues for commercial theatre in Elizabethan London: the open-air stages where the men's companies performed, and the indoor stages where the boys held forth until 1590. Contemporary documents refer to the former as "public" and the latter as "private" playhouses. Further evidence suggests several contrasts between them. The public amphitheatres were apparently built to hold as many as 2,000 to 3,000 spectators, with the cheapest standing room in the yard

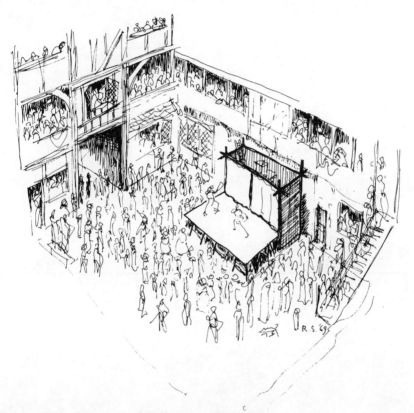

Illustration 2. Impression of a booth or platform stage set up in an inn-yard. (Sketch by Richard Southern. Copyright © Richard Hosley.)

Illustration 3. Impression of a performance in an unmodified domestic hall. (Sketch by Richard Southern. Copyright © Richard Hosley.)

priced at one penny; the more expensive seats in the galleries cost two or three times as much, and among these were sometimes "lords' rooms," partitioned off and priced at sixpence. In the much smaller private halls, with capacities estimated between 200 and 600, the lowest admission charge seems to have been sixpence. It seems clear that the higher admission prices of the indoor theatres (as well as some of the stylistically sophisticated material written for the boy actors) helped to establish a more elite clientele there. The distinction seems to have been maintained in the early years of the seventeenth century, when a second Blackfriars Theatre once again became the site of performances: first, by new boy companies, whose managers led them into legal trouble and ultimate extinction by staging dangerously topical and personal satires, and, later, by Shakespeare's company, the King's Men, who used it alternately with the Globe.

In the decade before 1584, records of theatrical performances at Court reveal a major transformation in royal preferences: The boy companies gradually gave way to the adult companies. In 1583, a group of twelve adult actors from various companies were chosen to comprise the Queen's Men, who monopolized the Court performances for the next seven years. During that time, a third London public playhouse, the Rose, appeared on Bankside; there, the Admiral's Men performed many of Marlowe's plays in the 1590s. By the turn of the century, the Swan and the first Globe Theatre had opened, and Elizabethan London was enjoying its Golden Age of theatre (see Illustrations 4 and 5). Estimates suggest that 15,000 of the population of roughly 250,000 frequented the theatres each week.

"Theatre," however, was by no means limited to the economically burgeoning success of London's acting companies. Long before these professional developments, acting and playwriting by amateurs had become a tradition in the educational system. Long before that, drama had been a vehicle for religious celebration and instruction. Both forms still lingered in the sixteenth century.

Religious drama was the form in which most Englishmen experienced theatre in the fourteenth and fifteenth centuries. Each year at the springtime feast of Corpus Christi, guildsmen in towns throughout England shared in the production of the mystery plays, which represented segments of the Biblical narrative from Creation to Doomsday. Whether played on pageant wagons or in a single outdoor locale, the staging of the mysteries was a major civic event. Supposedly forbidden after the Protestant Reformation, the tradition still held on in certain areas, as is attested by records of performances and edicts attempting to abolish them for good in the 1580s. Many Londoners hearing Hamlet's phrase about ranting players out-Heroding Herod could probably recall having heard and seen that actual

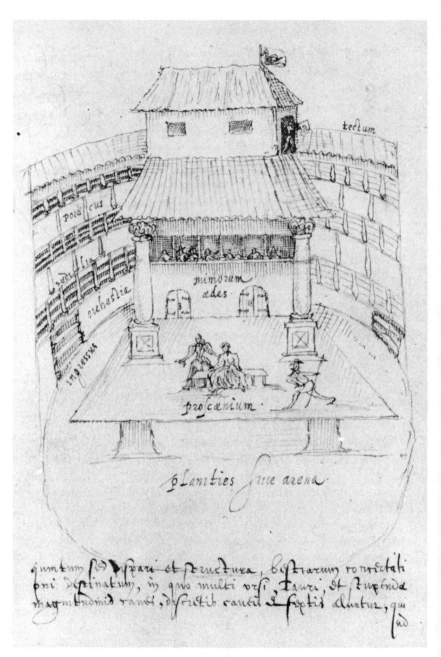

Illustration 4. Sketch of the Swan Theatre, constructed on Bankside in 1595, as copied by Arend van Buchell from a sketch by Johannes de Witt. This is the only extant contemporary rendering of the interior of an outdoor Elizabethan theatre. (Photo courtesy of University Library, Utrecht, MS 842,f.132r.)

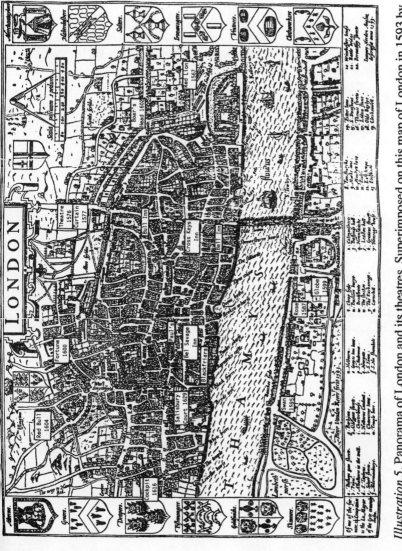

Illustration 5. Panorama of London and its theatres. Superimposed on this map of London in 1593 by John Norden are the approximate locations of inns known to have been used for Elizabethan performances and of playhouses built between 1567 (the date of a temporary theatre structure put up at a place called "The Red Lion") and 1629. The Rose Theatre, on the south bank of the Thames, was the site where most of Marlowe's plays were staged. (Adapted from the Norden map reprinted in Sugden 1925, 312.)

role (noted for its violent bombast) enacted in earlier times as part of the mystery cycles.

Still another mode of drama originally religious in nature was the morality play. *Everyman* is probably the most familiar example, but it is perhaps not the most typical in structure. The most repeated pattern was a story of temptation, fall, and repentance, represented by allegorical personifications of Mankind seduced by deceitful Vices (henchmen of the Devil and normally comic in their behavior) until some Virtue came to Mankind's rescue and taught him (and the audience) the needful lessons of Salvation. These patently moralistic plays were written for performance by small groups, either amateurs or traveling professionals, and could be staged either outdoors or indoors. Various kinds of morality drama developed from the theological origins: political lessons about the peculiar virtues and vices relevant to rulers; pedagogical lessons about the consequences of good and evil study habits; or—right into Marlowe's own time—civic lessons about vices that threatened to demoralize life in London. Several of the late moralities, or "interludes" as they were sometimes called, found their way into print in the sixteenth century, and the form did not finally disappear until the seventeenth. Moreover, elements of morality dramaturgy, including allegorical representation, the schematic rendering of temptation and conflict, and the comically guileful qualities of the various vices, found their way into the scripting of many Tudor plays dealing with quite secular characters, plots, and issues. The techniques associated with morality drama were still quite visible into the seventeenth century.

In the academy, meanwhile, other modes of theatre had established their own traditions. Comic plays by the Roman writers Terence and Plautus were part of the Latin curriculum in grammar schools, where pupils might be asked to recite and perform them; schoolmasters might also prepare new Latin or English scripts modeled on the Romans for their students' performances. A famous example of the latter is *Ralph Roister Doister*, an English comedy written by Nicholas Udall, headmaster in turn of the schools at Eton and Westminster in the early sixteenth century. At higher levels, it was also traditional in universities to write and perform plays for festival celebrations or as part of the entertainment of royal and/or diplomatic visitors. Thomas Legge, a noted Cambridge scholar (and the university's vice-chancellor in 1587–88), wrote a Latin play about Richard III that was produced at St. John's College in 1579. William Gager's Latin play about Dido and Aeneas was performed with great acclaim before the Queen on her visit to Oxford in 1592. So, too, in London's Inns of Court, the four training schools for young lawyers and other gentlemen, plays were written and performed at festival times. The earliest English tragedy in blank verse, *Gorboduc*, was written and produced there in 1561; two other tragedies, *Jocasta* and *Gismond of Salerne*, both, like *Gorboduc*, strongly imitative of the form and rhetoric of the Roman tragedian Seneca, followed shortly afterward. Later in the century, the Inns of Court hired professional acting troupes to perform during their festivities—both Shakespeare's *Comedy of Errors* and *Twelfth Night* are known to have been played there.

Drama under such academic auspices tended in the main to model itself upon classical Latin plays, although the use of spectacle and allegorical dumb-shows reveals a flexible, eclectic flair for incorporating other, more native traditions of theatrical performance, particularly emblematic pageantry and morality play conventions. Such dramatic enterprises lent a measure of value and esteem to the writing and production of plays, an aura of respectability not usually attached to the more popular arena of commercial theatre. Thus, Sir Philip Sidney in his *Apology for Poetry* could praise *Gorboduc* while decrying the implausibilities of much popular drama. Likewise, his sister Mary, Countess of Pembroke, the most celebrated patroness of literature in her time, could translate the French neo-Senecan tragedy of Robert Garnier into English and inspire a number of English authors to compose similar "poetic" tragedies never meant for the stage. The educational practices of the humanist tradition thus provided a sanctioned experience of theatre in the schools and also indirectly produced a line of amateur drama that was high in literary pretension and aloof from the marketplace of professional performance.

If it is true that the professional marketplace brought forth the more notable and enduring achievements in drama, it is also true that humanist education, with its stress upon the broad scope of learning, the skills of rhetoric and style derived from the study of classical literature, the appropriation of classical mythology's rich panoply of symbol and metaphor (all of which had become increasingly accessible through the proliferation of printed books), provided a remarkably fertile ground for gifted writers who were tempted to provide scripts for the newly flourishing English theatre. Whether or not one reached the university, the impact of that tradition was inescapable.

An interesting feature of the latter decades of the sixteenth century, however, was the notable attempt by several Oxford and Cambridge graduates to make their mark in a "literary world" that was expansive enough to include commercial plays as well as poetry, translations, prose romances, and topical pamphlets. A group of such men some six to eight years older than Marlowe were already busy at such tasks in the 1580s and

1590s: John Lyly, with a special eye on the Court, wrote stylishly man-
nered prose treatises and allegorical comedies for the boy companies to
produce before the Queen; George Peele tried his hand at both Court drama
and scripts for the public theatres; Robert Greene and Thomas Lodge
experimented with romance themes in prose and in dramatic comedy. And
they all, along with the younger Marlowe and Thomas Nashe from
Cambridge, seemed to read each other's work as well as that of their
non-university rivals. Marlowe, however, differed from the rest in limiting
himself to poetry, classical translation, and drama; in that, he prefigured
the pattern developed by such slightly later authors as Ben Jonson and
George Chapman.

   Despite the interest in drama among educated writers, there was a
marked cultural bias among the *literati* of the sixteenth century against
plays associated with the popular or commercial theatre. Indeed, when
Jonson brought out an expensive folio edition of his plays, masques, and
poems in 1616, he was much derided by his contemporaries for having
included his stage plays under the collection's title, *Works*, a term
conventionally associated only with poetry and "serious" literature.
Shakespeare's career had run its course by then, but, even so, the status
of commercial plays as literature was still controversial. Indeed, the
conventions of play publication, judging from the evidence of title pages,
more often linked a play with the performers who acted it than with the
person who wrote it—a clear sign of a very important pattern in the
professional world of Elizabethan theatre: Performance came first, publication afterward (if at all).

   The life-line of the burgeoning theatre was in its performing companies,
playing in London's inn-yards and new theatre buildings, or touring the
provinces. During Marlowe's brief career, there are records of at least half
a dozen active adult companies, several of which underwent considerable
fluctuation and exchange among their memberships. Before the Privy
Council's 1598 decree limiting the number of officially licensed London
companies to two—the Admiral's Men and the Chamberlain's Men—had
come a decade of competition, mergings, and winnowings. Of special
interest to anyone trying to trace Marlowe's involvement with the theatre
is the somewhat complicated amalgamation of the Lord Strange's Men
with the Admiral's Men at The Theatre in the late 1580s. Actors who
would eventually turn up as members of the two great rival companies
a decade later were then coworkers. Edward Alleyn, who would soon
become the leading actor of the Admiral's Men, apparently joined them
in 1589, when he was twenty-three, after half a dozen years with
Worcester's Men. He was celebrated in his lifetime and afterward for his

roles as Tamburlaine, Faustus, and Barabas the Jew of Malta, but it is not certain that he originated the role of Tamburlaine, which Greene's 1588 allusion implies had been performed a year or so before Alleyn joined the Admiral's Men. The company is named on the 1590 title page of *Tamburlaine*; in fact, this is the first of extant play editions that specifies an adult company as performers. It is clear from later records that *The Jew of Malta*, *The Massacre at Paris*, and *Doctor Faustus* were all in the Admiral's repertory from 1592 through 1594, and a major reason for that company's financial success. Hence, the simplest conjecture is that Marlowe may have begun his professional playwriting career by selling Part One of *Tamburlaine* to the Admiral's Men at The Theatre, quickly writing Part Two in the wake of its success, and then supplying the other scripts as he completed them.

Dido, according to its 1594 title page, was acted by a children's company and is thus one exception to the pattern. If the play is an early work, as many have argued, it could well represent the effort of a young writer to prepare a marketable script for the other major venue in professional theatre.

Edward II, performed by Pembroke's Men, as we learn from its 1594 title page, seems to be another exception to the general pattern but in fact may be only a slight variant. We have no records of the company's activities before 1592, when they were on tour, but there is some evidence to suggest that among their number were some members of the amalgamated Strange's/Admiral's group of two years earlier, which was in the process of splitting up in the wake of a financial argument between Alleyn and the owner of The Theatre, James Burbage (Gurr 1992, 40). When Pembroke's Men fell upon hard times in their 1593 tour, they were forced to sell some of their costumes and playbooks, among them *Edward II*, which then found its way into print. Although Marlowe may have sold his play to Pembroke's Men in the first place, it is also possible that it became a part of their repertory by way of members earlier affiliated with the amalgamated company at The Theatre. Seventeenth-century company records indicate that one practice among companies in the process of breaking up was to parcel out the properties, including plays, among the sharers.

In any case, the evidence is very clear that in the Elizabethan commercial theatre, the usual pattern was for a playwright to sell a play outright to an acting company or a company's agent. The company then "owned" the play and, in most cases, guarded it from publication (and thus from appropriation by competing companies) so long as it continued to be a profitable part of their repertory. Indeed, in the case of those companies that, besides purchasing plays from several authors, contracted with an individual writer to supply a given number of plays per year for a stipulated time, it was normal for the writer never to publish the plays for the duration of the contract. At the same time, seventeenth-century practice shows that individual playwrights who were neither under contract nor shareholders of the company (as Shakespeare was) were free to publish their plays independently of any company that might have bought their works for production. Such was the case, for example, with Ben Jonson and George Chapman.

There were still other ways in which a play might find its way into print, apart from authors, acting companies, or their agents. Contemporary references point to the fairly common practice of pirating scripts, often through stenographic means and/or memorial reconstructions by unscrupulous actors or former members of a company. Several early editions of Shakespeare's plays, including *Romeo and Juliet* and *Hamlet*, are notorious examples. In Marlowe's case, the prime example is the only extant edition of *The Massacre at Paris*.

Elizabethan plays belonged to the performers in more ways than one. Once a script was paid for, the company could alter it at will, making cuts or additions as the actors saw fit. In many cases, playwrights other than the original author would be contracted to supply additions to a play that was about to be revived in the company repertory. We know from theatre records that *Doctor Faustus* went through such a process of revision, after Marlowe's death and before its first publication. A company could, if it so wished, sell a script to publishers without any consultation with the original author.

Because of the extremely fragmentary nature of documentary evidence regarding theatrical repertories in the 1580s, it is very difficult to tell what sorts of plays acting companies were then most eager to secure. Some Court records exist of payments made for performances by boy and adult companies in that decade, but they tell us next to nothing about the commercial repertory at large. Our best glimpse of that repertory system is provided by some accounts for the period 1592 through 1602 preserved from the career of theatre manager Philip Henslowe. Henslowe held a major financial interest in the Rose Theatre when it was built in 1587, and he refurbished and expanded it at considerable expense in 1592 when the Admiral's Men moved there. (His association with Edward Alleyn became even closer when Alleyn married his step-daughter in October 1592 and eventually became his heir; see Illustration 6).

Henslowe's *Diary* records a variety of financial transactions, including receipts from performances of titled plays during seven scattered periods

Illustration 6. Portrait of Edward Alleyn (1566–1626), leading actor of the Admiral's Men. Noted for his roles in Marlowe's plays, Alleyn also became a theatre manager and owner. His financial and family alliances with the theatre manager Philip Henslowe helped him become the wealthiest of the famous London players by the end of the sixteenth century. By his benefactions in 1619, he founded Dulwich College, where this portrait by an anonymous painter is to be found. His second marriage was to the daughter of the Dean of St. Paul's, John Donne. His increasing wealth and social status marked an exceptional career in the often demeaned theatrical profession of his time. (Photo courtesy of The Trustees of Dulwich Picture Gallery, London.)

between 1592 and 1597. G. E. Bentley has summed up some figures emerging from the forty-odd recorded months:

> The total number of different plays mentioned in these . . . incomplete records of the activities of this single manager is about 280. Of these 280 named plays, only about 40 are still extant, and at least 170 would now be totally unknown—even by title—had Henslowe's accounts been destroyed as were the vast majority of all other theatre records of the period 1590–1642. (Bentley 1971, 15)

With surviving plays representing such a small fraction of the greater list, and allowing for the several companies competing with those logged by Henslowe, it is clear that nowadays we can see only a sliver of the theatrical output of the time.

But even that fragment discloses significant aspects of the commercial theatre, not least among them the sheer number of different scripts performed by a repertory company. From this we can infer how intense the demand for new material must have been. Andrew Gurr has provided a helpful summary:

> The Admiral's in their 1594–5 season, performing six days a week, offered their audiences a total of thirty-eight plays, of which twenty-one were new to the repertory, added at more or less fortnightly intervals. Two of the new plays were performed only once, and only eight survived through to the following season. Even the most popular plays the Admiral's performed, those of Marlowe, would be put on stage not more often than once every month or so. The first part of *Tamburlaine* appears in Henslowe's records for this season fourteen times, its second part six, *Faustus* twelve, *The Massacre at Paris* ten and *The Jew of Malta* nine. The repertory in the next season, 1595–6, was again large—thirty-seven plays, of which nineteen were new—and in 1596–7 thirty-four plays were performed of which fourteen were new. (Gurr 1992, 103–4)

Performing a different play each afternoon, six days a week, put enormous demands upon the actors, even when allowing for type-casting, given the size of an adult company. Most plays required casts of twenty or more. London companies in the late sixteenth century apparently consisted of a central group of eight to twelve contractual "sharers"—principal actors who bought into a company, sharing both profits and costs (scripts, costumes, properties, rent, and so on)—and an equal or usually greater number of "hired men" (including three or four boys to play female parts, musicians, and other stage attendants). Companies traveling in the provinces were considerably smaller, usually six to eight men; they would obviously have had to get by with fewer props and costumes, and to use (or abridge) scripts that permitted individual actors to "double" in multiple roles.

It is also from Henslowe that we derive our clearest sense of the sequence in which an Elizabethan play would find its way to commercial production. His record of payments as financial agent for Worcester's Men and the Admiral's Men suggests the following sequence of events. After a dramatist had brought his script to the attention of a playing company and the company had shown an interest, the players or their agent (Henslowe) paid the author, who supplied a fair copy, either complete or with an agreement to supply any incomplete sections by a certain date. The company then submitted the completed script to the Master of the Revels, who was the official censor for the realm and screened all plays prior to production.[14]

Henslowe's process involved his lending the purchase money for a play to the company; when the play was performed, the loan was repaid with part of the house receipts. The going rate for a new play in the period averaged £6, a sum that needs to be measured in relation to other contemporary market values. Bentley has suggested as a point of comparison the annual salaries for curates, schoolmasters, and lecturers, which ranged between £10 and £20 (Bentley 1971, 96); a dramatist who sold two or three plays a year would do as well. Smaller payments for providing additional scenes or otherwise reworking old scripts were also possible, and there was the variable remuneration that came with "benefit performances" on the second or third presentation of a play, when an author would receive a portion of the receipts from the acting company (Bentley 1971, 99). After the benefit, however, there was no additional financial reward for an author of any play that continued successfully in active repertory or was revised at some later time.

As recorded by Henslowe, the Admiral's repertory in the mid-1590s indicates a wide variety of genres, although, once again, our estimates can be only approximate, given the high proportion of plays known only by title. Comedy, tragedy, history, and all the hybrid combinations summed up by Shakespeare's Polonius in his introduction of the traveling players at Elsinore seem to be represented: "The best actors in the world, either for tragedy, comedy, history, pastoral, pastoral-comical, historical-pastoral, tragical-historical, tragical-comical-historical-pastoral, scene individable, or poem unlimited; Seneca cannot be too heavy, nor Plautus too light" (*Hamlet*, 2.2.396–401). Polonius, who also says that he acted the role of Julius Caesar once in the university, cites Roman authors and, to that extent, invokes the tradition of humanist drama. Still, his menu of combined genres clearly reflects the more eclectic practices of Elizabethan playwrights, who blithely mixed tragic and comic modes, as well as several others derived from their sources in history, romantic fiction, legend, or whatever. Henslowe listed play titles bearing names from Roman history, from English and European history both recent and remote, and from romantic legend; revivals of *The Spanish Tragedy* appeared in repertory with "The Spanish Comedy." Henslowe noted performances of the old *King Leir* play (whose romantic happy ending Shakespeare would later reverse), but there were no titles from the works of Seneca, Plautus, or Terence—the academically "hallowed" classics. The theatrical market-place at the Rose Theatre was marked by novelty, variety, and—if it is safe to extrapolate from the evidence of extant plays—a taste for the exotic, adventurous, and sensational.

Another index of that taste is the list of roles associated with Edward Alleyn (see Illustration 6), who so quickly established himself as the leading actor of the 1590s. Earlier, only famous clowns were more celebrated and noticed, but Alleyn became noted for his playing of the extravagant warlord Tamburlaine (and a presumably similar "Tamar Cam"), the tragically mad Hieronimo of *The Spanish Tragedy* and the comically mad Orlando Furioso, and the grotesque comic villain Barabas in *The Jew of Malta*. The Elizabethan appreciation of the exotic and the extravagant may well suggest that popular "entertainment values" do not seem to have changed all that much between then and now. One dimension that was clearly different, however, was the Elizabethan interest in the artfully spoken word and an appreciation for stylized and extended speeches amplified with the sundry techniques of rhetoric, derived originally from the study of classical literature. Indeed, the contemporary phrase most often used to describe theatre-going was "to *hear* a play." Alleyn obviously possessed the physical stature, charisma, and voice that would capture "listening" spectators, and, in the scripts provided him by Marlowe in particular, he found excellent vehicles for the display of those gifts.

The circumstances of commercial theatre, then as now, are bound to play some part in shaping the kind of dramatic art that writers create. The average size of Elizabethan acting companies would have had a direct impact on the size of a play's cast; the companies' exclusively male composition also meant that most roles would be masculine. And, in the sixteenth century, when most adult acting companies were not guaranteed an individual theatre or playing space of their own, a "practical" script would be one that could be performed in a variety of spaces, including inn-yards and private halls as well as the new outdoor theatre buildings. Scenery and props would be minimal; action would flow from one place or time to the next without interruption, with verbal cues providing the necessary recognition of such shifts. An upper playing space at one of the gallery levels would provide for action "above"—simulating an upper window, balcony, or even a city wall, and a trapdoor in the main platform would allow for such special effects as the appearance of devils from hell (see Illustration 7). Many scripts called for a "discovery space" in which a character or characters would be revealed upstage by the removal of a curtain, after which they would usually move downstage to continue the action. When props were used, dramatists could exploit their emblematic or symbolic possibilities—as Marlowe did with Tamburlaine's chariot and bridle, Edward's throne and crown, or Barabas' cauldron (the bridle and cauldron appeared in an inventory of Henslowe's properties at the Rose, along with Tamburlaine's cage and a dragon for *Faustus*). Costumes were apparently lavish and often spectacular; Henslowe's accounts indicate that greater sums were spent in furnishing them than for plays or props. But, for all the peculiar features of Elizabethan staging details, the most important items continued to be the talents of individual writers and performers.

Christopher Marlowe's dramatic success in his own time, like Shakespeare's soon after, was thus bound up with the particular traditions and developments of a commercial theatre world in an especially active period. The happy coincidence of gifted authors, gifted performers, and a broad and eager audience that ranged from the Queen to the workman's apprentice made possible what we now see as triumphs of dramatic art. Nevertheless, we need to remember how important and special the "gifts" were and to recall that, while the Elizabethan theatre world stood ready and eager for all sorts of new material to produce, not many of the hundreds of plays performed there have survived, much less prevailed. Writers like Marlowe, Jonson, and Shakespeare—for all their dependence on the context of commercial theatre—did have peculiar and unique literary power, which has made a difference in how we still think of drama, long after the reigns of Elizabeth and James. In Marlowe's case, it was not just a matter of transforming the spoken word on stage and bringing a poet's skill to bear on sensational plots in ways that would please a popular audience. It was also a matter of spirit and of vision, a gift for orchestrating the sights and sounds of lively drama. In his works, a new sense of tragedy emerged, an ironic sense of human will and self-destruction that moved,

Illustration 7. Woodcut from the title page of the 1631 edition of *Doctor Faustus*. This illustration of the initial conjuring scene appeared in the 1616 edition and in five reprints of that edition through 1631. The emergence of Mephistopheles from below strongly suggests the theatrical use of a trapdoor. (Photo courtesy of The Newberry Library.)

in its best configurations, far beyond the formulaic and often banal Renaissance concept of tragedy as any disaster overtaking the high, mighty, or prosperous. Marlowe's contributions to the Elizabethan theatre may well have enhanced the wealth of a Henslowe or an Alleyn, but, more significantly, they enriched, sharpened, and deepened our experience of what might be called the psychology of tragedy: an exploration of the motives and consequences of destructive and self-destructive action. The variety of modes in which Marlowe explored those patterns and their relation to conventional traditions of literary and dramatic tragedy now deserve our closer attention.

Chapter 3

Dido Queen of Carthage:
Tragedy in the Classical Tradition

Renaissance playwrights with an eye for tragic subjects in the Latin literary tradition found their most obvious models in the Roman plays of Seneca; these were themselves adaptations of ancient Greek tragedies concerning the myths of Oedipus, Medea, Hercules, the fall of Troy, and the house of Atreus. Virgil's *Aeneid*, the Roman epic that had become a fixture in humanist education at nearly every level, provided in its episode of Aeneas' relationship with Dido another ready-made tragic story. Various sixteenth-century playwrights in Italy, France, and England adapted the story for the stage, and among them was the young Christopher Marlowe. Unlike Marlowe's other plays, which, according to Elizabethan records, enjoyed a considerable popular and literary impact, *The Tragedy of Dido Queen of Carthage* seems to have gone relatively unnoticed.[15] Nonetheless, it stands as a revealing instance of how Marlowe's dramatic imagination worked in relation to a powerful classical model and to the larger Renaissance conventions of tragedy based on such models.

First published in 1594, the title page informs us that the play had been written by Christopher Marlowe and Thomas Nashe and had been played by the Children of Her Majesty's Chapel, one of the children's acting companies that performed in London's "private" or indoor theatres.[16] We have no firm evidence of when *Dido* was written, nor of the extent of Nashe's collaboration in its composition. The play shows clear signs of having been tailored to the peculiar features of boy acting companies and indoor theatre production (for which Nashe wrote at least one play of his own). To this degree, *Dido* contrasts with Marlowe's other plays, which were played by adult companies in the "public" or outdoor theatres. The scant records of the Chapel Children's performance history do not offer any help in fixing a date; only a few provincial appearances are on record for the years 1586–91 (M. Shapiro 1977, 16–17). Analyses of the play's verse technique, while agreeing on the preponderance of end-stopped lines as a mark of relative "immaturity" in the practice of blank verse, also note several instances of close parallels with *Dr. Faustus*, in which Marlowe's skills were often at their highest level. Most scholars have concluded, mainly on the rather soft evidence of the text's vaguely "academic" closeness to Virgil, that the play was an early work; but if so, it also shows a canny sense of how theatrical dimensions of gesture, physical interaction, and the use of props and costume can animate and amplify a script based on a classical poem. *Dido*, in this regard, is far more theatrical than most of the learned literary attempts of the time to imitate Senecan tragedy. Moreover, its several departures from Virgil's narrative, especially those that give more scope to the presentation of character and feeling in Dido herself, suggest patterns of configuring the human response to affliction that recur in Marlowe's major plays.

Few of the surviving Renaissance plays that treat the story of Dido and Aeneas are content merely to translate Virgil into dramatic form, nor do they attempt seriously to provide a framework of interpretation that coincides with the epic's thematic stress on the importance of founding what would become the Roman empire. Two Italian plays of the 1540s, one by Giraldi Cinthio and the other by Lodovico Dolce, reshape the story in a formal structure derived from Seneca. Scenes comprised of very long monologues or of moral debates between masters and servants alternate with choral passages; sententious generalizations (termed *sententiae* by rhetoricians) occur throughout; and the climactic violence of Dido's suicide is reported in a messenger's speech. Cinthio's version presents the story as an allegory of prudence (Aeneas) eventually triumphing over sensuality (Dido); his choral passages offer explicitly Christian admonitions that seem hardly pertinent to the setting and characters. These included a final appeal to avoid seeking the unstable goals of Fortune and Love and to prefer the true good, which is the love of God and the hope of His grace. Dolce's explicitly Christian moralizing rests uneasily with the pagan mythology of his fable, which stresses the cruelty of love and the fatalistic power of the gods over humankind. His play opens with a long soliloquy by Cupid, disguised as Ascanes, proclaiming himself the cruelest of the gods; it ends with the additional reports of Anna's suicide (prompted by grief for Dido) and of Iarbas' invasion of Carthage. A mid-century French version by Estienne Jodelle echoes the harsh themes:

Love is a minister of blind evil, and destiny is inevitably hopeless.[17] It is doubtful whether any of these plays were known to Elizabethans, but the more literate among them would have been familiar with the Senecan paradigm that influenced these and most other efforts to create what we now refer to as "humanist tragedy"—plays that adapted Senecan style and form to the poetic treatment (whether in Latin or in the vernacular) of historical and Biblical subjects.[18]

In Marlowe's time, this sort of playwriting went on in schools and universities, including the law schools of the Inns of Court, as well as in the circles of aristocratic literary culture. In 1590, Mary Herbert Sidney, Countess of Pembroke, translated Robert Garnier's *The Tragedy of Antony* from the French, leading several members of her courtly circle to write Roman-style tragedies in the following decade. Samuel Daniel's *The Tragedy of Cleopatra*, dedicated to the Countess, was an exceptionally popular work of this kind among the reading public, going through eight reprintings (and several revisions) in the seventeen years after its initial publication in 1594. Had Marlowe seen himself primarily as a poetic dramatist of this sort, rather than one with a sharp sense of theatrical opportunities, his *Dido* would probably have taken on a more predictable and conventional literary shape—five acts separated by choral interludes, plus a maximum of moral commentary provided not only by the chorus but also by debates and even by the solitary confessions of self-accusing protagonists. The thematic possibilities of destructive passions in the courts of the great were obvious in the stories of both Cleopatra and Dido, and one characteristic of humanist tragedy was to insist on such themes explicitly and repetitively. Thus, Daniel filled his first act with one long monologue by Cleopatra, elaborating her resolution to die, beginning with her reflection on the death of Antony:

Who now thrown down, disgraced, confounded lies
Crushed with the weight of Shame and Infamy,
Following th'unlucky party of mine eyes,
The trains of lust and imbecility,
Whereby my dissolution is become
The grave of Egypt, and the wrack of all;
My unforeseeing weakness must entomb
My country's fame and glory with my fall.
(Daniel [1599] 1966, 1.17–24)

Berating her own sins of lust and pride, she hopes to restore some sense of dignity by a courageous suicide, thereby making an example of herself to posterity, so that future princes will not fall into the same trap of self-indulgent pleasures. Daniel followed the scene with an Egyptian chorus lamenting the sufferings that had resulted from "her disordered lust," these "momentary pleasures, fugitive delights" (1.256). The confessional stance of Cleopatra, her attempt to make amends for her past evils in the act of suicide, and, above all, her self-conscious sense of her exemplary status all reveal the play's insistence on her moral significance: This is tragedy with a message. The Senecan rhetoric of emotional amplification has been infused with moral categorization. And it is relentless, above all in the choral passages.

The circumstances of Dido's situation, especially the role of the gods in inflicting love upon her, make her more the victim of others than is the case with Daniel's Cleopatra. More revealing is the difference in how Daniel and Marlowe treated their heroines, measured by the kind of psychological focus permitted these women in their distress. The emotive, confessional, and reflective mode derived from the Senecan monologue is not found in Marlowe's script. Dido has her monologues, to be sure, but they are never focused on herself, much less on herself as moral *exemplum*, nor are they ever retrospective. Instead, they are always focused on the crisis of the moment. Similarly, Marlowe provided no chorus or subsidiary character to render judgments about Dido. Here the action must work upon the audience directly, as indeed is the case in most Elizabethan popular theatre. In rejecting the conventions of humanist tragedy, even for a subject that comes out of the humanist literary tradition, Marlowe opted for a theatrical mode of communication, a mode that accents action and emblem as its chief signals.

The variety of action and of tone that marks the play also sets it apart from its principal source, Virgil's *Aeneid*. Virgil's gods and goddesses sometimes behave with the arbitrary cruelty and jealousy that characterizes their behavior in the myths and writings of the ancient Greeks. There is no precedent in the Roman epic, however, for the comic dimensions of such scenes as the opening one of Jupiter "dandling Ganymede upon his knee," or those in which the touch of the disguised Cupid impels Dido into a see-saw mix of polite decorum and rude disdain with Iarbas (3.1.1–54) or turns the aged Nurse to thoughts of lusty love (4.5). Of quite another color is the melodramatic amplification of the thwarted-love motif in the roles of Iarbas and Anna, whose suicides mimic Dido's own at the final conflagration. Dido's role, too, is more complex, not only in scenes that show her as the victim of conflicting impulses but also in other non-Virgilian passages where the more love-lorn and forgiving aspects of her character, derived probably from Ovid's image of her in *Heroides*, overcome the outraged vindictiveness of Virgil's characterization. In still another innovation—namely, the doubling of Aeneas' attempts to depart—Marlowe managed to complicate his character as well, while developing with more irony the perspectives on tragic love. Notable for variety, too, are the uses of scenic devices, props, and spectacle, including the statue of Priam, the portrait gallery of Dido's suitors, the storm, the ceremonial bestowal of crown and scepter upon Aeneas, the confiscated ships' tackle that becomes the target of Dido's complaint, and the ritual pyre.

Comic scenes had no part in humanist tragedy, but, in the less formal and self-consciously literary drama of the Tudor popular stage, they were often present. One popular play from the 1560s could proclaim itself unabashedly *A Lamentable Tragedy, mixed full of pleasant mirth, containing the life of Cambises, King of Persia.* "Mixing" mirth or comedy into otherwise serious plays often took the form of a comic subplot or a group of "underling" characters, whose actions might or might not intersect with those of the major figures. As we know from Shakespeare's later work, such characters can be put to excellent use within those limits; what matters most is how they are made to function in relation to the whole. Comic scenes appear in all of Marlowe's plays, with the exception of *Edward II*. In mixing comedy into his tragedies, Marlowe was thus following a common tradition.

In the case of *Dido*, moreover, several of the comic scenes depend for part of their effectiveness on the casting of very small boys in the roles of Ganymede, Ascanius, and Cupid, who can sit easily in the lap or be carried in the arms of the older boys who play Jupiter, Dido, and the Nurse. Moreover, the small boys' roles are rendered with very childlike detail: Jupiter woos Ganymede with the promise of delights that his unbounded power can provide—Vulcan (the lame) will dance for him, Juno's peacocks will be plucked for feathers to make his fan, or even Hermes' wingfeathers will be plucked if Ganymede should fancy them; meanwhile, Jupiter gives the lad Juno's wedding jewels. Ganymede, much too ingenuous to appreciate the irony of any of these "godlike" gifts, simply responds:

> I would have a jewel for mine ear,
> And a fine brooch to put in my hat,
> And then I'll hug with you an hundred times. (1.1.46–48)

Similarly, the Nurse coaxes Cupid/"Ascanius" (who asks to be carried in her arms) with sweet things to eat and the sight of pretty flowers, colorful fish, and waterfowl in a garden stream; Venus had attracted Ascanius earlier with the promised gifts of a bow and arrow, and she had taken him in her arms where she put spangled feathers in his hat, gave him sweets to eat, and sang him to sleep with a lullaby (2.1.310–16). One may well wonder if this emphasis on the extreme childlike qualities in the small boy roles was an effort to increase the illusion that the other roles (also played by boys) were supposedly adults, or whether the effect was intended to call attention to the paradox that all of these actors were but boys. In any event, such moments seem far removed from the graver matters of tragedy, unless and until one discovers the way their motifs echo not just one another but also some of the more serious encounters in the play's main line of action.

That love can make fools of us all is a virtual proverb in all ages, and the ancient myths also implied that "even the gods" were not immune. That may not have been Marlowe's point precisely, but one can detect something close to it in the way he positioned and repeated the scenes that involve these smallest boys. Most obvious is the implication that Cupid's mischief knows no bounds. Although his touching Dido is part of a greater plan set up by Venus, his afflicting the Nurse is pure improvisation; he delights in her absurd flush of lustiness and invites us to enjoy it, too. What is only ridiculous in this instance sets forth by contrast the more pitiable consequences of his wounding Dido. Far more interesting, however, is the way that Marlowe paralleled the "wooing" rhetoric of Jupiter, Venus, and the Nurse in their interactions with the small boy in their arms by providing an analogous scene between Dido and Aeneas. Jupiter, Venus, and the Nurse are all intent on enticing the child before them with pleasant prospects, "comfits," and gifts, in a way that suggests a child's version of Marlowe's famed love lyric, "Come live with me and be my love." (Jupiter's appeal, in fact, ends with the phrase, "if thou wilt be my love.") In the case of Venus and the Nurse, those gifts are innocent enough and do not reflect negatively on the givers. But those suggested by the great god Jupiter are tinged with many ironies: As marks of his power, they seem absurdly trivial, but they also imply some harm or loss to others. That he should lavish upon Ganymede the wedding jewels stolen from his wife is of course the most blatantly ironic, and this action tends to reduce Jupiter to a different sort of absurdity from the one later to be seen in the love-struck Nurse. But in between these comic scenes is still another emblematic bestowing of gifts—by Dido upon Aeneas. It concludes their "cave" scene on the day of the hunt, marking their mutual profession of love:

Stout love, in mine arms make thy Italy,
Whose crown and kingdom rests at thy command;
Sichaeus, not Aeneas, be thou call'd; . . .
Hold, take these jewels at thy lover's hand,
These golden bracelets, and this wedding-ring,
Wherewith my husband woo'd me yet a maid,
And be thou King of Libya, be my gift. (3.4.56–63)

Dido's former spouse, Sichaeus, unlike Juno, is long dead, and Dido's action is not so much an act of betrayal as it is one of new dedication to a new husband. The parallel with Jupiter's giving of jewels accentuates the moral differences between the doting god and the more dignified woman. Jupiter makes a fool of himself, as later the Nurse is made foolish by Cupid. Dido, however, even though under the spell of Cupid, impresses us by contrast as having more of a sincere stake in her expression of love. She will become its tragic victim, but not its absurd example. Marlowe's scenario accentuates the tragic by framing it with comic contrasts.

Marlowe stayed fairly close to those sections of Virgil's poem that he used in his play, but did not attempt to reshape them according to Senecan conventions. He provided no chorus, no *sententiae*, no lurid rhetoric involving the mythological underworld to express the chief moments of grief or rage. His closest approach to the Senecan mode is in Aeneas' tale of the fall of Troy, where certain divergences from Virgil, such as Pyrrhus' hacking off of old Priam's beseeching hands, reflect the Senecan penchant for grotesque detail. Similarly, Marlowe did not use the gods' command that Aeneas depart for Italy as an opportunity to stage a moral debate about the decision, as Dolce had done, for example. Marlowe's Aeneas (in 4.3), commanding his followers immediately to prepare to sail, does imagine for a moment what Dido's reaction is likely to be, reflects to himself that leaving without bidding farewell "were to transgress against all laws of love" (line 48), yet abruptly concludes:

I may not dure this female drudgery:
To sea, Aeneas, find out Italy! (4.3.55–56)

But Aeneas is not in the event so brusquely dismissive as his phrasing suggests, for Marlowe invented an episode in which Dido does succeed, albeit temporarily, in persuading Aeneas to stay. The elaboration of this unprecedented interval is of the greatest significance in highlighting what Marlowe wished to emphasize about the love of Dido and Aeneas. In it one senses more intrinsically the seductive power of love, which had been staged in more extrinsic and comic terms in the earlier scenes depicting Dido's wounding by Cupid and her wooing of Aeneas at the cave. Then, Marlowe had focused the audience on Dido's self-embarrassing revelations of the new desires that Cupid had secretly instilled in her; Dido's struggle to hide those desires becomes a comically impossible task, and the comedy is exaggerated by the role reversal involved in her initiation of the courtship. Now, Marlowe was still working at the portrayal of vulnerability in love, but with the emphasis no longer on comic victimization. Puckish Cupid is no longer a figure in the scene; human passions play themselves.

We begin to see the direction in which those passions move, as well as the kind of character they reveal, as Aeneas returns from his ships with Anna to confront Dido (4.4). To the Queen's forthright challenge, "Is this thy love to me?" Aeneas lamely lies that he had only gone to the shore to bid farewell to Achates. Dido is notably quick to forgive, confessing:

> Love made me jealous, but to make amends,
> Wear the imperial crown of Libya,
> Sway thou the Punic sceptre in my stead
> And punish me, Aeneas, for this crime. (4.4.33–36)

Aeneas returns a kiss for his "fair Dido's punishment" and, newly vested in the symbols of Carthaginian royalty, stands for a moment uneasily, saying "a sword and not a sceptre fits Aeneas." At that point, Marlowe again reminded his audience of the surprising opening scene of the play by having Dido liken Aeneas to Jupiter:

> O keep them still, and let me gaze my fill.
> Now looks Aeneas like immortal Jove:
> O where is Ganymede, to hold his cup,
> And Mercury to fly for what he calls?
> Ten thousand Cupids hover in the air
> And fan it in Aeneas' lovely face! (4.4.44–49)

What Dido expresses as an admiring compliment, the audience must take ironically, recalling the tone of the play's irreverent opening tableau. Aeneas' worthiness, like Jupiter's, is called into question. Dido's addition of angelic Cupids to attend Aeneas evokes still another irony, since the agency of Cupid in this story has been to victimize Dido. The lover Dido looks upon as divine at this moment (who is thus marked as less than what she perceives him to be) becomes a sad sign of her deluded devotion, again accenting her vulnerability while leaving the image of Aeneas at this moment awkwardly ambivalent.

Their next interchange reinforces the impression. Dido's tone turns from one of jubilant admiration to romantic intimacy:

> O that the clouds were here wherein thou fled'st,
> That thou and I unseen might sport ourselves!
> Heaven, envious of our joys, is waxen pale,
> And when we whisper, then the stars fall down,
> To be partakers of our honey talk. (4.4.50–54)

The allusion to the clouds presumably harks back to Virgil's description of how Venus hid Aeneas in a cloud to get him safely to Carthage. Now Dido yearns for such a miracle simply to be alone with Aeneas. Her lyricism then invokes other sorts of "miracles" in which the heavens emerge inferior to the joys of their intimacy. Marlowe's skill in modulating the tone of his lovers' imaginations is really quite remarkable. Compare these lines of Dido's with those that Aeneas, in the preceding scene, imagines her saying in response to the news of his departure:

> "Come back, come back!" I hear her cry afar,
> "And let me link thy body to my lips,
> That, tied together by the striving tongues,
> We may as one sail into Italy." (4.3.27–30)

The more blatant eroticism here, redolent of the Ovidian elegies that Marlowe translated, may possibly be an attempt to distinguish a masculine perception of sex from Dido's feminine one; it surely stresses by contrast the superior richness of what Dido experiences in love. Back in the reconciliation scene, Marlowe provided still another contrast to Dido's love rhetoric in Aeneas' decidedly unlyrical response to her lines above:

> O Dido, patroness of all our lives,
> When I leave thee, death be my punishment!
> Swell, raging seas, frown, wayward Destinies;
> Blow, winds; threaten, ye rocks and sandy shelves!
> This is the harbour that Aeneas seeks. (4.4.55–59)

Blow, winds, indeed. Aeneas may mean what he says, for the moment, but it is much harder to take his protestations seriously in the context of the vacillation and prevarication that Marlowe has invented for him. We know, of course, that he will go back on his word, just as we knew it when we heard his first grand vow of fidelity in the cave scene (3.4.42–50); that Marlowe should give him two such moments to swear undying loyalty is further indication of the sense of self-delusion he persistently stressed in lovers' behavior.

Marlowe bestowed on Dido a greater imaginative range than he did for Aeneas, with practical foresight at one end and hallucinatory wish-fulfill-ment at the other. Just after she yields the crown to Aeneas, and even as she glories in his kingly image, fears that he will try to leave again push to the surface (she obviously has not been totally convinced by his newly proclaimed vows). Her initial emotional response to that fear is a mixture of wish-fulfilling fantasy and erotic vision, but Marlowe made her catch herself in mid-fantasy and turn to more practical ways of keeping her man:

> O that I had a charm to keep the winds
> Within the closure of a golden ball,
> Or that the Tyrrhene sea were in mine arms,
> That he might suffer shipwrack on my breast
> As oft as he attempts to hoist up sail!
> I must prevent him; wishing will not serve. (4.4.99–104)

She orders her nurse to take his son Ascanius hostage to a country retreat, and she has her servants confiscate his ships' oars, tackling, and sails; still, she cannot go so far as to burn his ships—for fear of "Aeneas' frown." There are little ironies built into each of these measures as the extrapolated plot unfolds: The real Ascanius, of course, is in Venus' hands, and he will be returned by Hermes directly to Aeneas along with the direct behest to leave; when Aeneas finds his rigging gone, his rival Iarbas is more than ready to supply him with substitutes. But Marlowe invested another kind of irony in Dido's concluding lines from the speech above:

> If he forsake me not, I never die,
> For in his looks I see eternity,
> And he'll make me immortal with a kiss. (4.4.121–23)

Hyperbole, fantasy, and eroticism merge again in a moment of emo-tional intensity that is undercut absolutely by our prescient knowledge that she *will* die as a result of his abandoning her and that the only immortality he will grant her, indirectly, is the memorable legend that she will become in death. (Marlowe used that "immortal with a kiss" line in still another intensely rapturous and radically ironic speech in *Doctor Faustus*, when Faustus embraces the demonic form of Helen of Troy.)

Marlowe rounded out the scene with another major monologue for Dido, provoked by the confiscated rigging that her servants deliver to her. With somewhat artificial formality, the scene moves her through a triple apostrophe to the sails, the oars, and the tackling, in which she berates *them* for the disloyal departure attempt, rather than Aeneas ("O Dido, blame not him, but break his oars"). Marlowe's image of Dido is again closer to Ovid's here than to Virgil's, conveying her essential reluctance to censure him, or to direct her anger against him. Using the props as ways to deflect her anger and her hurt is a theatrically effective means to demonstrate simultaneously the strength of those feelings, her soft spot for Aeneas in spite of her sense of his readiness to leave, the ironic futility of her delusion that she can assume actual rather than imaginary control of her situation, and the tragic irony of her absolute dedication to the one thing that will ultimately destroy her.

Dido does, of course, vent her wrath directly at Aeneas in their last encounter, which stays very close to Virgil (even incorporating five lines of direct quotation from the Latin). But again, an exceptional alteration in the scene's conclusion signals Marlowe's insistence on Dido's more vulnerable and wish-fulfilling traits. Virgil's Dido, after accusing Aeneas and vowing revenge, walks out on him, leaving him deeply troubled about having to leave one whose passion has been expressed with such force. Marlowe's Dido also moves toward a wrathful climax but then offers an ultimatum suggesting that all may yet be redeemed:

> Why starest thou in my face? If thou wilt stay
> Leap in mine arms: mine arms are open wide.
> If not, turn from me, and I'll turn from thee;
> For though thou hast the heart to say farewell,
> I have not power to stay thee. (5.1.179–83)

The lines prescribe the actors' movements. She stands with arms extended to him; unable to say anything, he turns away from her. She then turns her back on him—at which point he must exit. She turns once more to discover his absence, as we see from the continuation of her speech:

> Is he gone?
> Ay, but he'll come again, he cannot go,
> He loves me too too well to serve me so. (5.1.184–85)

Her wrath is gone, too. In its place, the playwright introduced a rapid alternation of despair and hope; the hope drifts into a hallucinatory mode, making Dido imagine Aeneas at the shore, being greeted by his men:

> But he shrinks back, and now, rememb'ring me,
> Returns amain: welcome, welcome, my love! (5.1.190–91)

The line suggests that she rushes toward the door, expecting to see him come through it, but the next line brings her back to reality: "But where's Aeneas? Ah, he's gone, he's gone!" That Dido is raving and crying at this point is made explicit by Anna's remark on entering. That she is still fundamentally unwilling to blame Aeneas shows in her defensive response to Anna's calling him wicked: "Call him not wicked, sister, speak him fair" (5.1.200). Anna is sent again to ask Aeneas to return, this time for "a tide or two," so that Dido can gradually learn to bear the separation. With each detail, Marlowe stressed Dido's efforts—in imagination, in commands and petitions—to remake the painful events, to turn things around from the way they unhappily are. With each new attempt, the audience's sense of inevitable futility mounts.

Once more, before Dido moves to her resolution of suicide, Marlowe invented for her a further hallucinatory monologue. He did not push her in the direction of Virgil's picture of a maddened woman dreaming that she is hunted by Aeneas, a frenzied victim likened to Orestes fleeing the Furies or to mad Pentheus (*Aeneid* IV.469–73). Dido's dreams are not nightmares but romantic fantasies of recuperation; her mythological invocations stress reunion rather than persecution:

> I'll frame me wings of wax like Icarus,
> And o'er his ships will soar unto the sun
> That they may melt and I fall in his arms;
> Or else I'll make a prayer unto the waves
> That I may swim to him, like Triton's niece;
> O Anna, fetch Arion's harp,
> That I may tice a dolphin to the shore
> And ride upon his back unto my love!
> Look, sister, look, lovely Aeneas' ships!
> See, see, the billows heave him up to heaven,
> And now down falls the keels into the deep.
> O sister, sister, take away the rocks,
> They'll break his ships. O Proteus, Neptune, Jove,
> Save, save Aeneas, Dido's liefest love!

Now is he come on shore safe, without hurt; . . .
See where he comes; welcome, welcome, my love! (5.1.243–61)

Now it is Anna's turn to bring Dido out of her "idle fantasies." The
last of them echoes the hallucination that concluded the farewell scene
(5.1.189–91), reinforcing the urgency of Dido's obsessive wish, in the
face of reality, that Aeneas will return. Dido herself, after regaining her
composure, calls these imaginings "thoughts of lunacy" (5.1.273); still,
there is a basic truth expressed in her irrational ravings about the strength
and intensity of her devotion to Aeneas. It survives even the ritual of
"renunciation" that Dido stages as her last act. Although Marlowe altered
some of the details in the Virgilian account, the basic symbolism is
substantially the same, as Dido burns the relics of Aeneas and utters a
prophetic curse on the future relations of Rome and Carthage. Yet, one
telling exception intrudes just before Dido's final line (quoted in Latin
directly from Virgil). It is an antithesis that shows Dido's inability to
wish death upon her lover, even as she takes her own life: "Live, false
Aeneas! Truest Dido dies" (5.1.313). That attitude is to be found in
Ovid's Dido of the *Heroides*, and there is perhaps still another Ovidian
inspiration in the deeply ironic line in which Dido presages her suicide—
"I, I must be the murderer of myself" (5.1.270). Ovid had Dido end her
letter to Aeneas with her own epitaph:

From Aeneas came the cause of her death, and from him the blade,
From the hand of Dido herself came the stroke by which she fell.
(VII.195–96)

The irony of conscious self-destruction is blended in Dido's last actions
with a paradoxical quality of assuming control over her destiny. As in the
Aeneid, she tricks others into thinking that the ritual pyre is intended only
to destroy the mementos of Aeneas. This is a death she chooses and directs.
That Marlowe should change the immediate means of suicide from stabbing to burning indicates not only his instinct for spectacular stage effects
(the actor playing Dido presumably falls into a trapdoor behind the
flames), but, more significantly, his stress on the ironically emblematic
aspects of his protagonists' death scenes. Do we not still hear the echo of
Dido's uncontrollable plea of longing to Aeneas in the cave scene?

The man that I do eye where'er I am,
Whose amorous face, like Paean, sparkles fire, . . .
Prometheus hath put on Cupid's shape,

And I must perish in his burning arms.
Aeneas, O Aeneas, quench these flames! (3.4.17–22)

Dido's deepest desire and the way she dies reflect one another; indeed, her earlier cry of passion unknowingly prophesies her fate.

That the frustration of passionate desire can lead to self-destruction is a theme further amplified by Marlowe's invented love-suicides of Iarbas and Anna, although the surprising speed with which they dispatch themselves in the wake of Dido's last grand speech lends a mechanically contrived quality to the finale. Still, these other frustrated lovers, who have not been literally targeted by Cupid himself, do suggest that Marlowe was reaching for a way to universalize his theme without relying on the more conventional commentary of choral pronouncements. He preferred the emblematic action, although in this instance he may have forced it too awkwardly. It is a preference we will see again and again in the concluding scenes of his other plays.

Dido remains the only major female role that Marlowe developed in his short career. She is clearly the central figure in the play, dominating all others, including Aeneas, in terms of psychological and histrionic interest. Marlowe and Nashe may well have been drawn to the subject as theatrical material by its suitability for the particular talents of boy acting troupes; these companies seem to have developed a certain degree of specialization in what Michael Shapiro has called the "pathetic heroine play," which stands out among their other specialties—romantic comedy, satire, and parody—as the one serious or tragic category where they could compete with the adult companies (Shapiro 1977, 154ff.). Writing a script with a leading female role would be a risky venture indeed without a very talented boy actor to render it. As H. J. Oliver has noted after having seen a modern revival of the work by a boys' cast, he was struck by how much more "realistically" the women's parts appeared in contrast to the male roles (Oliver 1968, xxxiii). We should remember that the acting projects of the children's companies were ancillary to their original and continuing functions as choirboys for such prestigious precincts as the Chapel Royal and St. Paul's Cathedral; moreover, their membership lasted only until their voices "broke" at puberty. Records indicate that the subsidized, full-time training of choristers started at about age seven or eight. It may be difficult for us to envision plays like *Dido* acted by boys of grammar school age, especially since we have no modern counterpart for the level and extent of training that such Elizabethan boys underwent. One may still imagine, for all that, that singing might have been less of a demanding challenge than acting for the majority of them, that bold and simple roles (as all but those of Dido and Aeneas themselves are in this play) would be handled with less trouble, and that the few who could meet the demand of the major roles would do well with them if they could be handled in a style of "oratorical declamation"—such as we find, for example, in Aeneas' narrative of Troy's fall.[19] We have already noted how the play makes special use of the smaller boys in the troupe. And it is at least possible that one of the factors in Marlowe's transformation of Dido into a softer and more vulnerable figure than Virgil's character was his sense that such a role might be rendered more convincingly by a boy actor.

But *Dido* is more than an exercise in adaptation to particular theatrical circumstances. The tragic pattern in the relationship of Dido with Aeneas was already a given in the literary tradition, but its special treatment by Marlowe reveals tendencies in the playwright that are suggestive of his own pattern for tragedy—a pattern that elaborates with unusual subtlety the manifold and often ironic connections between desire and destruction. This pattern is not reducible to the moralistic cliché that giving in to lust leads to ruin. His play is not really about lust, or even lust glamorized by its adherents. Nor is it shaped to emphasize in some lugubrious way the cruel impact of fate and the gods upon innocent human victims. Although Virgil brought the agency of Venus and Cupid into the narrative (and Marlowe followed him, with comic variations), in neither the epic nor the play do we find ourselves "blaming" the gods for the love affair—Cupid dissolves all too readily into a walking symbol. Once Dido and Aeneas proclaim their love for one another, we do not discount Dido's passionate feelings as an artificial imposition. Aeneas may do so when Hermes tells him that Cupid started it all, but no audience is likely to side with him in that instant dismissal. Marlowe has been too busy showing us the intensity and sincerity of Dido's rapturous devotion, inventing new scenes to do so, making us sympathetic with her longing to keep the love intact even in the face of Aeneas' attempts to leave. And yet, even as he elaborated on her sense of longing, he impressed upon us its inevitable frustration. The one thing that Dido feels has fulfilled her (and it is Marlowe's new scenes of her poetic raptures that convey this feeling) is the one thing she must lose. The tragic paradox is *there*, in that mutual contradiction, rather than in the death of a mighty queen.

Marlowe's skill gets us far more interested in Dido's struggle than in Aeneas' decision to leave or stay. It is at first a comic struggle to maintain her poise and dignity when first beset by Cupid's touch. That quickly becomes a struggle to express herself freely in a situation where decorum argues otherwise, but, in the cave scene, it is no longer wholly comic, for even there the sense of her being Cupid's puppet is already evaporating.

When she does speak freely and achieve her desire, Marlowe has framed it ironically, by reminding us both of the flames we know lie in her future and of the doting gestures of Jupiter that began the play. Thereafter, the struggle is to hold on to the treasure she has briefly won—a doomed struggle that is now tragic rather than comic. Increasingly thwarted by an adverse reality, she takes refuge in fantastic visions of reconciliation and reunion that cannot be. The desire for the impossible, rather than outraged humiliation, defines her radical suffering. Again, Marlowe has merged sympathy with irony: His Aeneas is not quite worth such devotion, but Dido can see nothing of worth apart from him. The intensity of her love is unarguable, but it also blinds her. Indeed, it leads to the final irony of becoming her own murderer. Desire, delusion, and destruction plot the curve of her experience (as they do for Faustus and Edward II). In Marlowe's conception of tragedy, these are all bound together in one.

Equally important is the technique Marlowe employed to communicate that conception. He avoided the more conventional, generalizing captions typical of humanist tragedy, but he did manage, as some humanist tragedy has done, to establish a certain degree of tension in projecting a double perception of his protagonist. Daniel's *Cleopatra*, for example, for all its choral moralizing, manages to generate considerable sympathy for Cleopatra (a good bit of it by making her so self-conscious of her past excesses); there is a manifest tension between the judgment an audience is likely to make about her on the basis of her own speeches and the negative judgment continually supplied by the chorus. Marlowe's double perception of Dido is not so much one of conflicting judgments as it is of perspectives. One perspective emerges from the protagonist's speeches, together with the images and visions that inform the feelings in those speeches; the other is supplied by some framework of irony that reveals to the audience a contradictory aspect of the protagonist's feelings, a destructive double meaning in her imagery or gestures that she cannot see at the moment. The result is not moral ambivalence so much as it is tragic paradox: a complexity that resists disentanglement.

Chapter 4

Tamburlaine the Great:
Tragical Discourse and Spectacle

Marlowe's *Tamburlaine* is a curious phenomenon in theatrical history: a play that had such an immediate impact on the audience of its time that the name of its protagonist became a cultural byword, invoked more often than Hamlet, Falstaff, or Lear would be, although not always within a respectful context. Tamburlaine was one of the more notable roles for Edward Alleyn of the Admiral's Men, the Elizabethan theatre's first greatly celebrated tragic actor. Together with Thomas Kyd's *Spanish Tragedy*, Marlowe's play seems to have set the standard for blank verse as the poetic means best suited for the writing of tragedy for the popular stage. Its initial success inspired several attempts at imitation, and yet, within a dozen years or so, it had become identified with a theatrical style ridiculed by such discerning playwrights as Ben Jonson. Despite his nod to "Marlowe's mighty line," Jonson inveighed against styles of writing and acting that flew "from all humanity, with the Tamerlanes and Tamar-Chams of the late age, which had nothing in them but the scenical strutting, and furious vociferation, to warrant them to the ignorant gapers" (Jonson 1947, 8: 587). (*Tamar Cam*, now lost, was a popular play in Alleyn's repertory.) Shakespeare's Pistol in *2 Henry IV* expresses himself in just such a manner, garbling and parodying lines from Marlowe's play and others like it in his ludicrous attempt to be a Tamburlaine of the tavern-world:

> Shall pack-horses
> And hollow pamper'd jades of Asia,

Which cannot go but thirty miles a-day
Compare with Caesars, and with Cannibals,
And Trojan Greeks? nay, rather damn them with
King Cerberus; and let the welkin roar! (2.4.176–81)

Whether viewed as an attempt at the sublime or as a now outdated example of the ridiculous in playwriting, Marlowe's play was clearly a theatrical experience to remember. Its combination of rhetoric and spectacle struck its early audiences with unprecedented force, leaving them with indelible images of an Asian warlord not many of them were likely to have known primarily from the reading of history. Spectators from Marlowe's time recall Tamburlaine's treading upon the backs of conquered kings and using them as chariot-drawers (see Illustration 8); they cite his furious and "bedlam" behavior as a terrorizing tyrant and scourge of nations (Brooke 1922, 366–69; Gurr 1968, 98–100). Marlowe had clearly chosen a subject with impact, and, in Alleyn, he had the actor to represent that subject with stunning effect.

Indeed, one mark of the play's impact is to be seen in the structure of the drama itself. The original play, now called Part I, was apparently written as a complete story in itself; its production proved so successful, as we learn from the prologue to Part II, that Marlowe wrote an immediate sequel. Scholars who have examined the use Marlowe made of his historical sources concur that the first play was structured to conclude within its own terms and that the second shows many more signs of inventing or importing materials that are not directly related to the available accounts of Timur's reign.[20] Marlowe certainly built his second part on the basis of the first, but Part II moves in significant new directions, teasing out novel challenges for the apparently unconquerable hero that are not found in history and that underline, albeit ambiguously, some of the more trenchant ironies in Tamburlaine's self-mythologizing behavior. Each part deserves separate attention, especially in reference to the sometimes confusing boundaries of what the Elizabethans considered as tragedy.

Tamburlaine is the only play by Marlowe that we know was printed in his own lifetime; the earliest edition is 1590. None of the early editions (there were four reprintings through 1606), however, bore Marlowe's name as author—a fairly common practice for Elizabethan plays, which became the legal property of the acting company that bought them from writers. Its singular verse style marks it as Marlowe's work. Robert Greene's 1588 allusion to the "atheist Tamburlaine," "daring God out of heaven," presumably refers to the concluding act of Part II. Hence, we

Illustration 8. 1951 Old Vic production of *Tamburlaine*. Tamburlaine (Donald Wolfit) whips his "pampered jades" in the spectacular chariot scene as rendered by Tyrone Guthrie. (Photo courtesy of John Vickers Theatre Collection, London.)

surmise a probable date of composition in 1587, the year Marlowe left Cambridge.

We can gain some sense of what the Elizabethan audience may have been expected to find of interest by the way the title page is set, for title pages often served as advertisements. This read: *Tamburlaine the Great. Who, from a Scythian shepherd by his rare and wonderful conquests became a most puissant and mighty monarch, and (for his tyranny, and terror in war) was termed The Scourge of God. Divided into two tragical discourses, as they were sundry times showed upon stages in the City of London by the right honorable the Lord Admiral his servants.* In addition, Part II's highlights were later given the following billing: *The second part of the bloody conquests of mighty Tamburlaine. With his impassionate fury for the death of his lady and love, fair Zenocrate, his form of exhortation and discipline to his three sons, and the manner of his own death.* "Rare and wonderful" (if also "bloody") conquests by a shepherd-turned-monarch, notorious for his "tyranny and terror in war"—such is the stuff of tragedy as implied by this extended title. One of the later reprints added a heading that reads "The Tragical Conquests of Tamburlaine"—still another indication of how flexibly the adjective could be applied. Rather than referring primarily to a formal or structural pattern, or even to a disaster that befalls a protagonist, "tragical" yoked to "discourses" and "conquests" denoted a style or a quality. Marlowe's brief but characterizing prologue to Part I includes a similar usage:

> From jigging veins of rhyming mother wits,
> And such conceits as clownage keeps in pay,
> We'll lead you to the stately tent of war,
> Where you shall hear the Scythian Tamburlaine
> Threatening the world with high astounding terms
> And scourging kingdoms with his conquering sword.
> View but his picture in this tragic glass,
> And then applaud his fortunes as you please. (1–8)

The "tragic glass" of Part I involves no defeat for its hero, no suffering or disaster for him to endure; on the contrary, it is Tamburlaine's adversaries who suffer disaster. Marlowe was setting a tone here, establishing a claim for the elevation of his style above the puerile rhyming verse or low comedy of other plays. The rhetoric he offered to represent his martial subject would thus be in tune with its stateliness and with the astounding eloquence of its hero.

In line with this emphasis on a high or tragic *style* is the exceptional note provided by the printer of the first edition, Richard Jones, who apparently took upon himself the task of cutting from the acting text (which served as his printer's copy) certain scenes of low comedy that he judged inappropriate:

> I have (purposely) omitted and left out some fond and frivolous gestures, digressing (and in my poor opinion) far unmeet for the matter, which I thought, might seem more tedious unto the wise, than any way else to be regarded, though (haply) they have been of some vain conceited fondlings greatly gaped at, what times they were showed upon the stage in their graced deformities: nevertheless, now, to be mixtured in print with such matter of worth, it would prove a great disgrace to so honourable and stately a history.

Whether the sections Jones omitted were original with Marlowe or additions made to his text in the course of production we shall never know. Clearly, there are still comic touches that remain intact, such as the characterization and behavior of the foolish king Mycetes in Part I and of the battle-scorning son of Tamburlaine, Calyphas, in Part II, but these could hardly have been cut without serious damage to the main narrative. It is more likely that the offending scenes involved the actions of subordinate figures not directly engaged at the moment with the major characters. In any event, Jones' unusual action in cutting the text bespeaks a heightened sense of literary decorum, usually associated with the classical criteria espoused by such writers as Sir Philip Sidney, whose *Apology for Poetry* (c. 1583) expressed several reservations about the free-ranging conventions of the popular stage. From such a perspective, the tragic muse should not tolerate comic intrusion.

On the other hand, the tragic muse did tolerate bloody tyrants as appropriate subject matter. Renaissance definitions of tragedy often emphasized the downright evil of potentates whose careers were dramatized as tragic. Sidney's *Apology* defended the "right use" of "high and excellent tragedy, that openeth the greatest wounds, and showeth forth the ulcers that are covered with tissue; that maketh kings fear to be tyrants, and tyrants manifest their tyrannical humours" (Sidney [1595] 1904, I, 177). The anonymous *Art of English Poesy* (1589) offered a historical description of how and why tragedy came to be written:

> But after that some men . . . became mighty and famous in the world, sovereignty and dominion having learned them all manner of lusts

and licentiousness of life, by which occasion also their high estates and felicities fell many times into most low and lamentable fortunes: whereas before in their great prosperities they were both feared and reverenced in the highest degree, after their deaths, when the posterity stood no more in dread of them, their infamous life and tyrannies were laid open to all the world, their wickedness reproached, their follies and extreme insolencies derided, and their miserable ends painted out in plays and pageants, to show the mutability of fortune, and the just punishment of God in revenge of a vicious and evil life. (Anonymous 1904, 2: 35)

Such stress upon tragic protagonists as great "negative examples" is only part of a larger picture whose margins were continually being stretched by the experiments of practicing playwrights. Certainly, this tendency helps to explain why both the early Shakespeare and others could find the villainous career of King Richard III an appropriate subject for tragedy. In the case of Marlowe, and of *Tamburlaine* in particular, however, the paradigm of tragedy as a story of tyrannical vice and retribution is not so obviously followed. Indeed, if we focus again on the outline of Part I, we discover a career that not only defies both defeat and retribution but invites, through its constant waves of self-glorifying rhetoric, a response of admiration or wonder, in spite of the tyrannies enacted there. Tamburlaine's acts of insolence are derided only by his adversaries, who inevitably fall before him. Even Zenocrate, who is given sentiments that express moral discomfort with his ruthless ways, cannot find it in her heart to renounce him or her love for him; his charismatic *élan* sweeps all before it. In Part II, the figure of the tyrant becomes ever bloodier and more extreme; his "impassionate fury" spills over into fits of madness, and Marlowe's touches of irony explore more deeply the mutability that can be found even in the career of such an extraordinarily victorious conqueror. As Marlowe did so, he approached ever more closely some of the issues implicit in conventional Elizabethan notions of tragedy but never yielded completely to the pressures of those conventions.

In their search for tragic "tyrants," Tudor playwrights had turned regularly to the pages of both history and romance. In many cases, they tried to adapt the stories and situations they found there to the form and rhetorical style associated with Senecan tragedy. Two notable examples were produced at the Inns of Court in the latter part of the sixteenth century: *Gorboduc* (1561–62), famous also as the first tragedy composed in blank verse, and *The Misfortunes of Arthur* (1588). Both works stress the disastrous results of tyranny, rebellion, ambition, and revenge on political stability, drawing explicit morals in that regard. On the popular stage, one found much less deference to Senecan form or style; instead there prevailed a free-ranging mix—even in such a play as the somberly titled *Lamentable Tragedy of Locrine* (c. 1587)—of the serious and the comic, of verse and prose, of elaborate, static set speeches and rough–and–tumble action involving a variety of characters. Marlowe's treatment of Tamburlaine, however, while an experiment both in the creation of a high style and in the elaboration of spectacular and varied action, stands apart from these other tragedies in its unprecedented investment of imaginative energy in the portrayal of its tyrannical protagonist. To label Tamburlaine an ambitious tyrant is somehow both an understatement and a tautology. Even when such labeling takes place on stage, as it does in the frequent diatribes leveled against Tamburlaine by his numerous enemies, there is a paradoxical sense of futility in the censure, as the irresistible waves of superior rhetoric and force wash over the protesters.

It is not merely the military invincibility of the protagonist that deflects the judgments. It is the magic of his "working words"—the charismatic grandiloquence, charged with cosmic and mythological allusion, that transforms Tamburlaine's ambition from a dangerous political vice into something more akin to transcendent rapture, that expresses a vision that bundles into itself strains of elemental, human, and divine aspiration that become surprisingly concretized in "the sweet fruition of an earthly crown."

> The thirst of reign and sweetness of a crown,
> That caused the eldest son of heavenly Ops
> To thrust his doting father from his chair,
> And place himself in the empyreal heaven,
> Moved me to manage arms against thy state.
> What better precedent than mighty Jove?
> Nature that framed us of four elements,
> Warring within our breasts for regiment,
> Doth teach us all to have aspiring minds:
> Our souls, whose faculties can comprehend
> The wondrous architecture of the world:
> And measure every wandering planet's course,
> Still climbing after knowledge infinite,
> And always moving as the restless spheres,
> Wills us to wear ourselves and never rest,
> Until we reach the ripest fruit of all,
> That perfect bliss and sole felicity,
> The sweet fruition of an earthly crown. (2.7.12–29)

Marlowe, quite unlike his dramatic predecessors, did not try to dress his tyrant-protagonist in borrowed Senecan robes. Instead, he invented a style of speech that defines more particularly the motivation and the passion that drives Tamburlaine and mesmerizes his allies. For them, and, to a certain degree, for the audience as well, to listen to Tamburlaine is to undergo seduction. "Come live with me and be my love" is in Part I transformed into "Come war with me and be my tributary kings." The raw political bribe at the core of the invitation is enameled over with the more visionary delights of newfound power—riding "in triumph through Persepolis." Ordinary moral criteria are blurred in the ecstasy of antici-pated bliss. The temptation is irresistible—at least for Theridamas, Techelles, and Usumcasane, whose roles evolve from converts to allies to cheering (and jeering) squad to choral angels singing the praises of their demigod. This pattern also applies to Zenocrate, whose more orthodox sentiments and misgivings of conscience are always over-whelmed by her devotion to Tamburlaine. At the end of Part I, they are all wearing crowns.

The originality of Marlowe's transformation of the tyrant-protagonist is all the more remarkable when one considers the historical image of Tamburlaine available in sixteenth-century European accounts. Al-though these varied in some specific details, they shared a general estimate of this late fourteenth-century Tartar conqueror as a courageous, energetic, military and administrative genius with a reputation for his barbaric treatment of enemies and for both generosity and firm discipline in dealing with his armies. The measure of his success as a conqueror seemed to them nearly beyond parallel but akin to that of Alexander the Great. In documenting his long career (which culminated, by the way, with the defeat of the Turkish Emperor Bajazet when Tamburlaine was already in his late sixties), the sixteenth-century historians provided several details that Marlowe incorporated into his play: Tamburlaine's origins as a poor herder, his early plunders as a brigand, his conversion of a cavalry leader and his conspiracy with the Persian king's brother to usurp the crown, his own usurpation of the Persian throne, his practice during sieges of changing the colors of his ensignia to signify the mounting severity of his threatened reprisals, his humiliation of the conquered Bajazet by caging him and feeding him table scraps, and his wholesale slaughter of an unarmed civilian embassy sent by a besieged city to plead for mercy. And, although he did not use it in the context in which it appeared in the accounts, Marlowe found there also Tambur-laine's personal response to a charge of cruelty with respect to the slaughter of those innocent ambassadors:

he answered in most furious wrath, and ire, his face red and fiery, his eyes all flaming, with burning sparkles as it were blazing out on every side, "Thou supposest me to be a man, but thou too much abusest me, for none other am I but the wrath and vengeance of God, and ruin of the world." (Fortescue [1571] 1951, 296)

This seems to be the only report of Tamburlaine's own words. That they "worked" in this instance is attested by the additional comment that the protester was never seen in camp again. They provide an important key to Tamburlaine's self-concept, as well as a mark of his pride and passion, but they are a far cry from the more romantic self-glorification expressed in Marlowe's play. Indeed, the whole outline of the historical Tamburlaine's extraordinarily successful accomplishments in war and in building the sumptuous city of Samarkand includes no reference to any gift of eloquence or persuasion. Marlowe gave him that.

It was a gift central to Marlowe's dramatic strategy for conveying Tamburlaine's dominating power (a strategy Shakespeare later found valuable in portraying Henry V as a master of rhetoric). The martial prowess of Tamburlaine might have been demonstrated by staged battle scenes, but Marlowe seems to have taken pains to avoid that: Most of the battles are off-stage, and we are presented instead with pre-battle scenes of boasting or challenge and with post-battle scenes of victorious vaunting. Even Part I's climactic encounter between Tamburlaine and Bajazet rages off-stage while the audience watches Zenocrate and Zabina engage in a verbal barrage of mutual insults and threats. Words and the force of will behind them are the theatrical weapons of choice here. The opening of the play sets the tone, with the Prologue's invitation to listen to Tamburlaine "threatening the world with high astounding terms," contrasted at once with King Mycetes' confessed inability to express even his own grief because he lacks a "great and thundering speech."

The greatness, we discover, is not merely in the volume but also in the range and scope of the imagery through which Tamburlaine magnifies everything about himself and his dreams, in the piled-high hyperbole and swelling periods of the verse paragraphs of his oratory. It seems inconceivable that Marlowe would have orchestrated such a role without some confidence that it would find an actor with the requisite talent to bring it off successfully, and it is at least possible that, among other things, we have in *Tamburlaine* a script written with precisely such an actor as Edward Alleyn in mind. In any case, the choice to make Tamburlaine a word-warrior also provided a means of letting poetic craft rather than sensational martial action convey the image of greatness.

Marlowe certainly did not shrink from staging sensational things, but when such things do appear on stage, we discover that they are not feats of martial art but emblematic spectacles of domination; it is not the struggle but the satisfying taste of power that counts most. Marlowe, taking his cue from the historical anecdote of Bajazet's treatment, added the extra humiliation of using a human as a footstool and amplified the visual image in the spectacle of Tamburlaine's king-drawn chariot in Part II. The combination of these two theatrical choices in the representation of power—breath-taking magniloquence and humiliating spectacle—sums up in little the basic paradox of Tamburlaine, the superhuman achiever who relishes subhuman gestures.

Besides granting Tamburlaine an eloquence undocumented in history, Marlowe added several other significant gifts. He provided him with Zenocrate, who, as the kidnapped princess of a rival ruler, bears more relation to the world of chivalric romance than to the historical Tamburlaine's harem of wives, including a Tartar "head" wife whose counsel in government Tamburlaine habitually sought. Marlowe provided him with a glorious physique, celebrated in Menaphon's heroic description at the start of Act II—again, a notable "elevation" from the historical Tamburlaine, whose name in the sixteenth century was a corruption of "Timur the Lame," a title given to Timur Khan after a crippling accident. And, for a brief but significant moment near the end of Part I, Marlowe provided Tamburlaine with his only inner conflict: an uncharacteristically self-questioning moment when he wonders whether his desire for Zenocrate's beauty is fitting for a martial hero. The answer seems to be "of course"— beauty is the spur to valiant and transcending deeds. Marlowe drew this motif out of the treasury of chivalric romance as well.

In many ways, Part I almost becomes a chapter out of heroic romance, were it not for the occasionally disconcerting signs of a kind of violence and a delight in humiliation that seem to defy chivalry. The treatment of Bajazet and his wife, as well as the slaughter of the virgins of Damascus, are the chief examples here. Marlowe accentuated the melodramatic in both instances, amplifying the historical account in the case of Bajazet considerably by staging a double suicide and an interval of insane raving for Zabina. He then added a third corpse to the final tableau of Part I by bringing on the dying Arabia, the other lover of Zenocrate. "All sights of power to grace my victory," Tamburlaine comments on the three dead bodies beneath him. After all that seductive glory, the audience is presented with the problem of adjusting its response to the carnage that, in Tamburlaine's own gloss, holds up a mirror "wherein . . . may be seen / His honour, that consists in shedding blood." Is this a reminder of the "tragic glass" of the prologue? And if so, do we applaud Tamburlaine's fortunes or not? The pattern of romance (the hero triumphs; Zenocrate is crowned as she consents to wed Tamburlaine with the blessing of her father) and the force of rhetoric assert the affirmative. The pattern of tragedy (the corpses of the maltreated victims, the memorable images of sadistic humiliation, the disconcerting identification of honor with bloodshed) casts a dark shadow on that affirmation.

The shadow deepens in Part II, despite new triumphs by Tamburlaine over ever-escalating armies and nations in opposition. Marlowe's expanded inventions in this sequel, particularly those that relate to the hero's domestic realm as opposed to the battle campaigns—the death of his wife, the murder of his anti-warrior son, his own fatal disease—introduce new tragic ironies. The warrior who boasted he was master of Death in Part I is radically challenged by the adverse reality of death, weakness, and disease not under his control. In framing Tamburlaine's response to those challenges, Marlowe embodied new modes of expression in speech and in spectacle. The rhetoric of persuasion and self-glorification becomes the mad rant of the impotent; the effort to master reality takes on new verbal and visible shapes that increasingly stress the hallucinatory quality of Tamburlaine's myth-making will and imagination. In Part I, his words of glorious prophecy and his color-coded threats always came true; now his words and symbolic acts, although continually grand, striking, and even shocking, prove hollow and ineffective. Marlowe could hardly have rewritten history in such a radical way as to strip Tamburlaine of his imperial power—that pattern for tragedy would not fit. But he could suggest a new pattern, in which the downfall is not material so much as psychological, in which the sense of loss would not be measured in yielded crowns or defeat in battle but by the reaction of the self to a world once "his own" but now no longer swayed and shaped by the force of individual will, word, or act.

The supreme confidence of Tamburlaine in Part I gives way in Part II to "impassionate fury" as he meets the resistance of mortality itself. Marlowe gave an edge of madness to the conqueror's violent expressions of rage and frustration, which clearly form the basis for such later allusions by Thomas Dekker to "mad Tamburlaine" or by Michael Drayton to "bedlam Tamburlaine" (Brooke 1922, 368–69). When Zenocrate dies, Tamburlaine shifts from his tone of grand elegy into one of hallucinatory revenge:

> What, is she dead? Techelles, draw thy sword,
> And wound the earth, that it may cleave in twain,

> And we descend into th'infernal vaults,
> To hale the Fatal Sisters by the hair,
> And throw them in the triple moat of hell,
> For taking hence my fair Zenocrate.
> Casane and Theridamas, to arms!
> Raise cavalieros higher than the clouds,
> And with the cannon break the frame of heaven, . . .
> Behold me here, divine Zenocrate,
> Raving, impatient, desperate and mad,
> Breaking my steeled lance. (2.4.96–113)

His orders to mount a campaign against heaven and hell, accompanied by the wild gesture of wounding the earth, are, of course, quite in line with the way he has always asserted power, but here they are manifestly futile. His followers try to bring him back to reality, and urge patience: "She is dead, / And all this raging cannot make her live" (2.4.119–20).

Together with this new emphasis on Tamburlaine's impotent rage in the face of death and disease, we discover in Part II a shift in the imagery that Marlowe wove into the boasts and visions of Tamburlaine. The glories of his power, still often figured in celestial or divine metaphors, are associated more and more starkly with gore and violence. The persistent ironic juxtaposition of the grotesque with the glorious increasingly calls into question, if not into revulsion, the habit of mind that identifies one with the other.

Marlowe provided a sort of prelude to this theme in the first scene of Part II, where Tamburlaine is concerned that his three young sons may lack the martial vigor he considers so vital to carrying on the task of world conquest. "Revenge, war, death and cruelty" must reside in a fitting heir:

> For in a field whose superficies
> Is covered with a liquid purple veil,
> And sprinkled with the brains of slaughtered men,
> My royal chair of state shall be advanced:
> And he that means to place himself therein
> Must armed wade up to his chin in blood. (1.4.79–84)

Two of his sons are quick to respond in kind. One avers that he would sail to the throne over that sea of blood; the other, even closer to his father's imagery, proposes:

And I would strive to swim through pools of blood,
Or make a bridge of murdered carcasses,
Whose arches should be framed with bones of Turks,
Ere I would lose the title of a king. (1.4.92–95)

With approving paternal pride, Tamburlaine beams, "Well, lovely boys, you shall be emperors both" (96).

The metaphor of blood turns literal in father's next lesson, when Tamburlaine finishes his discourse on fortifications with an exhortation to fearlessness in the midst of carnage and stabs his own arm to help demonstrate that "Blood is the god of war's rich livery" (3.2.116). He bids his sons to bathe their hands in his blood, "While I sit smiling to behold the sight" (129). Two of them do so and even urge their father to cut their own arms, too. Calyphas, however, the black sheep of the family, protests that he finds it "a pitiful sight."

Calyphas never does accept Tamburlaine's teaching and prefers to sit out the next great battle, playing cards with a servant. In a comic scene with his brothers, he sends them off to fight with a slogan prophetic of Shakespeare's Falstaff: "Take you the honour, I will take my ease, / My wisdom shall excuse my cowardice" (4.1.49–50). But Tamburlaine does not excuse him. Learning of Calyphas' truancy, he kills him in a burst of self-glorifying rhetoric:

Here Jove, receive his fainting soul again,
A form not meet to give that subject essence,
Whose matter is the flesh of Tamburlaine,
Wherein an incorporeal spirit moves,
Made of the mould whereof thyself consists,
Which makes me valiant, proud, ambitious,
Ready to levy power against thy throne,
That I might move the turning spheres of heaven,
For earth and all this airy region
Cannot contain the state of Tamburlaine. (4.1.109–18)

This is the only instance in either part of the play where we see Tamburlaine himself kill someone directly. That the victim happens to be his own unarmed son is already a dreadful irony; that Tamburlaine should wrap that murder in the megalomaniacal vision of himself as Titan and god, turning the spheres of heaven, is an even more horrendous irony. Marlowe here did all he could to emphasize the gap between rhetoric and spectacle, with the result that Tamburlaine's "sublimity" is perceived as grotesque.

The incident also reinforces another contradiction that Marlowe infused into his chief character in Part II: his erratic stance vis-à-vis the gods. Tamburlaine's sense of himself as the divinely commissioned "scourge of God" (derived from the historical source material) now alternates with an increasing feeling of rivalry and hostility toward the gods. What provokes the animosity, of course, is the experience of affliction: first the loss of Zenocrate and now the humiliation of having a son who scorns violence. Here, at the murder of Calyphas, Tamburlaine goes on to claim that Jove has made Tamburlaine his enemy by sending him such inferior progeny, yet a moment or two later he reinvokes his role as the scourge of God to justify any action that might be called cruel and barbarous:

> Nor am I made arch-monarch of the world,
> Crowned and invested by the hand of Jove,
> For deeds of bounty or nobility;
> But since I exercise a greater name,
> The Scourge of God and terror of the world,
> I must apply myself to fit those terms,
> In war, in blood, in death, in cruelty. (4.1.148–54)

Terror is greater than nobility, and extraordinary power must display itself in extraordinary destruction. Whatever remnants of chivalric romance may have lingered about Tamburlaine in this play (and there are a few in his effulgent praises of the ailing Zenocrate), they are clearly gone by now. His extravagant measures in mourning her death by burning the city where she died, in killing his son, in treating his conquered enemies like beasts, in executing the Governor of Babylon and annihilating its population—*all of which are Marlowe's inventions*—accumulate a hideous countervailing force that ultimately belies the self-styled divinity of his mission and meaning. The infinite longings and high aspirations invoked in Part I have turned into nightmarish megalomania, with the extra irony that Tamburlaine himself goes on exulting in it all as a dream coming true. This is no tragedy of disillusionment, in which the protagonist suffers a crisis to learn the limits of his true identity. It is rather a tragedy of delusion, in which the seductive greatness to which he believes himself to have been called is defined ultimately in ever-increasing, gratuitous slaughter and cruelty.

Marlowe did employ motifs from chivalric romance in some of the by-plotting of Part II, chiefly in the relationship between Theridamas and the vanquished widow Olympia. Olympia, dedicated to her husband who was slain by Tamburlaine's forces, kills her own son to preserve him from the cruelties of their captors, presenting as she does so a compassionate and pitiful image of a loving parent forced to slay her child—an image obviously contrasted with the later killing of Calyphas by Tamburlaine. Her captor Theridamas, Tamburlaine's first convert, tries very hard to imitate the winning amorous ways of his lord, echoing in less expanded form the sorts of enticements Tamburlaine had offered in his courtship of Zenocrate:

> Thou shalt be stately queen of fair Argier,
> And clothed in costly cloth of massy gold,
> Upon the marble turrets of thy court
> Sit like to Venus in her chair of state,
> Commanding all thy princely eye desires. (4.2.39–43)

Theridamas' words do not "work," however, and his inferiority to Tamburlaine is further proved by his frustrated threat of rape. In a device of subterfuge borrowed by Marlowe from Ariosto's *Orlando Furioso*, Olympia tricks her captor into killing her. Thus, although the episode bears no relation to the movement of the main plot, its themes and contrasts work to the advantage of Olympia, whose death and whose son's death wear a badge of honor and courage, and to the disadvantage of both Tamburlaine and his would-be understudy Theridamas.

In Part I, Marlowe attempted to provide a sense of climax to his pattern of repeated Tamburlainean victories by escalating the magnitude of each successive campaign and by providing some shocking spectacle to portray the final triumphs. An identical strategy informs Part II, but the specific spectacular events we find there—the chariot drawn by conquered kings, the execution of Babylon's governor, and the burning of the Koran—were invented by Marlowe, rather than developed from hints in history. The chariot image offers an emblem of Tamburlaine's notion of material power; it is an amplified version of the sort of delight he took earlier in caging Bajazet and in using him as a footstool. The visual image may well have been derived from the opening dumb show of a 1566 play, *Jocasta*, which had been reprinted for the second time in 1587. There, the allegorical tableau of an emperor with scepter and orb being drawn in a chariot by four crowned kings represented Ambition; this image, in turn, was based on a report of a historical incident illustrating "unbridled ambitious desire" in the reign of the Egyptian king Sesostres (Cunliffe 1912, 69). Presented as fact rather than allegory in Marlowe's play, the image has added shock value, which is exaggerated even further by the sadistic mockery and torture inflicted on the defeated kings by Tamburlaine's whip and his associates' taunts. The mocking and humiliating tone adheres as well to the treatment of the Governor of Babylon, who is suspended from the "city walls" (or upper stage) and shot to death after having been tricked by Tamburlaine. The final image, however, in which Tamburlaine dares Mahomet to stop the burning of his holy books, moves in another direction, for it discloses Tamburlaine's mocking challenge to unseen powers rather than to material adversaries. Greene's familiar allusion attaches the "atheist" label to this scene, but the details of the scene and its context do not accommodate that judgment: The challenge is, after all, to Mahomet, and no Elizabethan audience was likely to expect him to work a miracle. Nevertheless, the spectacle still carries its force as an expansion of Tamburlaine's hubris, which is next indicated by his presumption that disease cannot touch him, for that would prove him but a man.

> Shall sickness prove me now to be a man,
> That have been termed the terror of the world?
> Techelles and the rest, come take your swords,
> And threaten him whose hand afflicts my soul,
> Come let us march against the powers of heaven,
> And set black streamers in the firmament,
> To signify the slaughter of the gods.
> Ah friends, what shall I do? I cannot stand. (5.3.44–51)

The Titan image resurfaces at the moment of Tamburlaine's greatest physical weakness. He will bring death to the gods for having brought disease to his presumably superhuman body. But just as he tries to rise to this greatest campaign of all, he literally cannot stand. Reality undercuts his rhetoric, but his bewildered acknowledgment of helplessness does not last long, for Marlowe has moved him into new levels of delusion and hallucination. Ever the mythologizer, Tamburlaine bids Theridamas go to the court of Jove to fetch Apollo to cure his wounds. He then imagines that he sees Death personified, appearing and disappearing—"Look where he goes, but see, he comes again" (75).[21] His hallucinations and ravings are calmed this time by a potion administered by an earthly physician, who can work no Apollonian miracles.

The accelerating spectacle of power is thus displaced at its peak of audacity by the spectacle of impotence. Even so, Marlowe did not manufacture any change of heart or lately won wisdom for his protagonist. Tamburlaine persists in the myth of himself, and he rationalizes his inevitable death as the desire of the gods to invest him in "a higher throne"; he now looks to sweeter fruitions than earthly crowns and grieves for his sons and fellow warriors who will have to live without him. He goes out, as he came in, blazing his own glory.

How that glory has been defined in the interval, however, remains as the signal irony of Marlowe's double play. He did not present the conventional story of a tyrant who meets with retribution but instead exposed the workings of an imagination that conceives of greatness painted in blood, finds delight in gratuitous humiliation, destruction, and terror, and invests it all with a divine, transcendent significance. The tragic implication is felt by the audience in the sense of the ironic gap between the godlike claims that Tamburlaine imposes on all his motives and deeds, on the one hand, and the grotesquely violent actuality of their consequences, on the other. Superhuman aspiration has become subhuman destruction and still calls itself divine.

The Elizabethan response to *Tamburlaine*, as documented in allusions to it, focuses, not surprisingly, on the bold and sensational surfaces of the play as performed, rather than on its implicit ironies. The play's ambivalent combination of heroic motifs from chivalric romance and grotesque violence indicating perverse cruelty seems to have been split in two for the Elizabethans and thus drained of its irony. Hence, two apparent attempts to capitalize on the play's popularity: *The Comical History of Alphonsus, King of Aragon* and *The Tragical Reign of Selimus. Alphonsus*, generally attributed to Greene, follows the pattern of Marlowe's Part I by tracing the successive victories of a superhuman conqueror who boasts that he controls Fortune herself, crowns his three associates, and moves to a climactic triumph against a Turkish potentate whose daughter he marries in triumph at the end. Still, this work lacks any imitation of Tamburlaine's peremptory or sardonic cruelty. *Selimus*, on the other hand, takes the opposite tack, as its full title promises: *The First Part of the Tragical Reign of Selimus, sometime Emperor of the Turks, and grandfather to him that now reigneth. Wherein is shown how he most unnaturally raised wars against his own father Bajazet, and prevailing therein, in the end caused him to be poisoned. Also with the murdering of his two brethren, Corcut and Acomat.* The play shows the rise to power of a totally evil and unscrupulous tyrant who meets with no retribution for his misdeeds. One of three sons to Bajazet (a descendant of the Bajazet of Tamburlaine's time), Selimus plots to overthrow his aged father and block his brothers from power. More interesting than this raw ambition, however, is his elaborate self-justification, set forth in a 150-line monologue in rhyme royal, expounding his contempt for the sanctions of religion, of political order, and of family, all of which he discounts as mere expedients to keep lesser men in check. The only authority he respects is that of individual power:

> But we, whose mind in heavenly thoughts is clad,
> Whose body doth a glorious spirit bear,
> That hath no bounds, but flieth everywhere,
> Why should we seek to make that soul a slave,
> To which dame Nature so large freedom gave? (349–53)

Selimus thus echoes Tamburlaine's invocation of Nature as the force that teaches us to have aspiring minds, and his "heavenly thoughts," like Tamburlaine's, are also directed to very material goals. Such thoughts are certainly not those of religion, or even of a classical mythological "beyond," for he goes on to assert that there is neither life, punishment, nor reward after death. Later in the play, he also invokes the Machiavellian icons of the lion and the fox to explain the strictly pragmatic "virtues" of his violence and treachery, calling the "lion's force" and "fox's skin" the "two wings wherewith I use to fly / And soar above the common sort" (1737–42). The playwright seemed to take considerable pains to align Selimus with all the bugbears of Elizabethan religious and political orthodoxy, and to pose him as an aspiring—and successful—example of the self-glorifying atheist, tyrant, and schemer.

His success, however, is not so swiftly and easily accomplished as was Tamburlaine's rise to power. He meets with special resistance from his brother Acomat, who proves a particularly vicious opponent, demonstrating a use of violence that goes far beyond pragmatism. Acomat's atrocities are further extensions of the symbolic and sardonic cruelties of Tamburlaine, a kind of grotesque theatrical game of "Can you top this?" After conquering his sister's son, the young prince of Natolia, Acomat has the boy thrown down from the castle wall upon upright spears, next has his young niece strangled, and then sends both bodies to his father Bajazet as tokens of his hostility. Shortly thereafter, as the climax to a heated debate with Bajazet's ambassador Aga, he gouges out Aga's eyes and hacks off his hands, stuffing them into Aga's blouse, from which they are gruesomely extracted in the following scene of Aga's return to court. Selimus' subsequent crimes, which include poisoning his father by means of a Jewish doctor and several on-stage stranglings, pale by comparison, but they do eventually get him the uncontested sovereignty he wants. What the author felt his audience wanted is evident in the epilogue's last lines:

If this first part, gentles, do like you well,
The second part shall greater murders tell.[22]

Closer to the ironic Marlovian formula of aspiring rhetoric and destructive action are two tragedies of George Chapman's, the translator of Homer who also continued Marlowe's narrative poem, *Hero and Leander*. Chapman's 1596 comedy, *The Blind Beggar of Alexandria*, performed with popular success by the same company that had enacted *Tamburlaine*, contains several parodic references to Marlowe's play, but his later tragedies, *Bussy D'Ambois* (c. 1604) and the two-part *Conspiracy and Tragedy of Charles Duke of Byron* (1608), represent a serious and peculiar development of the paradoxes displayed in Marlowe's protagonist. Neither Bussy nor Byron is a tyrant or a conqueror, but both their characters are given a heroic aura that supposedly sets them apart from ordinary men and tempts them to see themselves as laws unto themselves. Byron's opening speech includes a kind of motto worthy of Tamburlaine:

To fear a violent good abuseth goodness,
'Tis immortality to die aspiring,
As if a man were taken quick to heaven. (1.2.30–32)

The antithetical quality attached to each of Chapman's protagonists is an engagement in corrupt actions of betrayal, rather than in Tamburlaine-style violence. Nonetheless, Chapman seems to insist that they both configure some extraordinary greatness by his putting speeches that attest to such in the mouths of their adversaries. Byron's case is developed with a heavy stress upon his self-deception, but, for all his delusions, there is a persistent sense that his character cannot be explained adequately by any simple moral categorization. Chapman focuses instead on the paradox of a special strength that carries within itself the germs of its own destruction. One of his characters, Epernon, provides a sort of choral summation of the problem:

Oh, of what contraries consists a man!
Of what impossible mixtures! Vice and virtue,
Corruption, and eternness, at one time,
And in one subject, let together loose!
We have not any strength but weakens us,
No greatness but doth crush us into air.
Our knowledges do light us but to err,
Our ornaments are burthens, our delights

Are our tormentors, fiends that, rais'd in fears,
At parting shake our roofs about our ears. (5.3.189–98)

As a technique, this sort of meditative generalization is a far cry from
Marlowe's dramaturgy, but the substance of this tragic paradox is woven
into nearly all of his plays. Is it mere coincidence that Chapman should
dedicate this drama to the young son of Marlowe's patron, Thomas
Walsingham?

Chapter 5

Machiavellian Tragedy:
The Massacre at Paris and *The Jew of Malta*

Hyperbole and caricature are verbal and visual modes of artful exaggeration. In Elizabethan treatises on the art of rhetoric, hyperbole as a device was also labeled "the overreacher" or "the loud liar," indicating to some degree how careful a rhetorician must be in employing it to keep its effectiveness intact. An excess of superlative comparisons can easily become sheer bombast; fantastic claims in speeches of praise or self-praise can easily ring false. Whatever its self-defeating risks, however, hyperbole remains a device intended for elevation, magnification, or intensification; caricature, when intentional, uses exaggeration to demean rather than to elevate. It is thus more akin to satire in its style and purpose. One of the curious aspects of Marlowe's art is his tendency to combine both modes of exaggeration in his drama. The imagination that could provide such poetic and rhetorical speech for a Scythian warlord and also invent for him such an antithetical son as the wise-cracking Calyphas bespeaks a perspective that teases constantly with subversive mockery, as does the sensibility that could juxtapose with Dido's love-lorn desperation her old Nurse's comical rediscovery of sexual passion. Even more important is the degree to which that mockery is directed not just at conventional sentiments but also at the very unusual and at times daring aura that Marlowe created around his protagonists. In the case of Tamburlaine, one recalls, for example, the vaunt of the disease-struck warrior:

Come let us march against the powers of heaven,
And set black streamers in the firmament,
To signify the slaughter of the gods. (Pt. II: 5.3.48–50)

This is followed at once by the humiliating and unsuccessful struggle of
the speaker to stand up ("Ah friends, what shall I do? I cannot stand").
In a more self-conscious vein, there is Tamburlaine's own confidential
aside just after his initial grandiloquent proclamation of love to the
captured Zenocrate: "Techelles, women must be flattered" (Pt. I:
1.2.107)—a statement that humorously acknowledges the "loud lying"
implicit in the fantastic hyperbole of such preceding images as:

With milk-white harts upon an ivory sled,
Thou shalt be drawn amidst the frozen poles,
And scale the icy mountains' lofty tops:
Which with thy beauty will be soon resolved. (1.2.98–101)

At such a moment, Marlowe himself seems to be taking his audience into
special confidence, winking at the extremes of expression that he has
conjured up for his warrior lover, yet mindful of their efficacy at the same
time.

How much exaggeration can a poetic dramatist get away with, and in
how many different directions can the device be pushed? Questions like
these seem to lie at the heart of Marlowe's further experiments in playwriting, especially in two dramas that adapt, develop, and transform—
each in a very different way—the popular mythological figure of the
Machiavellian villain. In *The Massacre at Paris*, Marlowe turned to
contemporary French history for a tale of violence and intrigue centered
on the notorious slaughter of the Huguenots in 1572, finding his focus in
the character of the scheming Duke of Guise, who was himself assassinated in 1588. In *The Jew of Malta*, he invented a villain of consummate
treachery and a plot of cunningly executed slaughters to project in farcical
contours the image of a perverse world energized by greed and revenge.
The Massacre's Guise is an irreligious political Machiavellian at work in
a sectarian civil war that is depicted in a style that we today might call
tabloid sensationalism. The title role in *The Jew* is an emblematic "infidel"
whose underhanded machinations against Christians and Turks are caricatured extrapolations of tactics associated in the popular mind with
Machiavellian statecraft, but whose motives and style have little or nothing
to do with political ambition. For him, it is not a case of the end justifying
the means but rather of the means becoming an end in themselves—out-

rageous and destructive cunning enjoyed for its own sake in what we might call a comic-book world. In both plays, the tragic ironies evident in *Dido* and *Tamburlaine* give way to less deep-seated effects, where melodramatic oversimplification in the one case and satiric farce in the other dominate.

In late sixteenth-century England, the writings of Niccolò Machiavelli (1469–1527) had achieved a largely undeserved notoriety for wickedly advocating ruthless treachery, amoral force, manipulative cunning, and religious hypocrisy as the most effective means of achieving and maintaining political power. Although it is difficult to trace precisely the evolution of this reputation, it seems fairly clear that the writings of European opponents, such as Innocent Gentillet's *Contre-Machiavel* (1576), had a prevalent impact that seems to have preceded the widespread availability of Machiavelli's own works in English translation. Historians have also noted that Gentillet, a Protestant magistrate from Grenoble, clearly intended his work not just as an attack on what he thought were Machiavellian principles of statecraft, but as a primary warning that contemporary French politics had become dangerously contaminated by the practice of those principles. For him, the culminating example of that corruption was the Bartholomew's Day massacre of the Huguenots.[23]

The distorted and exaggerated image of Machiavelli, in other words, was the first to impress itself upon the popular imagination, and it did so in connection with the recent violent events in France. That image seems to have been in circulation before the dramatists of the 1580s and 1590s began to exploit it and to subject it to further transformations. (Recall how the author of *Selimus* provided his Turkish protagonist from an earlier century with a catalogue of Machiavellian attitudes; similarly, Shakespeare's Richard of Gloucester in *3 Henry VI*, once he has proclaimed his own regal ambition, takes confidence in his skill at deception, boasting—quite anachronistically—that he can "set the murderous Machiavel to school.") Marlowe's earlier place in the line of playwrights who set their own murderous Machiavels to work is anchored by his two arch-villains, the Duke of Guise and Barabas the Jew.

For an era that saw the stuff of tragedy in the outrageous acts of tyrants, it was only a short step to reconceive the character and motivation of tyrants—above all, those who used guile and deception to advance their power—in Machiavellian terms. It was a method more conducive to the creation of moral monsters rather than of heroes, but that did not faze the Elizabethans. What the Senecan classics had sanctioned in their own way now became possible in more "modern" formats, a mode of depicting villainy inspired by the controversial political writings of an Italian iconoclast, as well as by the duplicity and violence of political acts perpetrated under the mask of religious zeal in Italy and France. The new accent on deception and treachery as crucial components of such tyranny had two further consequences for the drama. On stage, the display of these traits in a character could take the form of that character's assuming various "roles" to meet the needs of the moment, thus lending a kind of theatrical bravura to the role at large. With respect to plot, the display of these traits would require a series of intrigues and manipulations. If history could provide much of the raw material for those intrigues, so much the better.

THE MASSACRE AT PARIS

Such seems to have been the case in *The Massacre at Paris*, a play that Marlowe must have written sometime after the summer of 1589, the date of the French King Henry III's death, with which the play ends. Its first recorded production, by Lord Strange's Men at the Rose, was in January 1593; Henslowe's diary of receipts and expenses also records revivals (now by the Admiral's Men) in the summer of 1594, in 1598, and in 1601. The undated printed version of the text that survives seems to be one of those garbled Elizabethan scripts whose highly irregular features have been attributed to the contemporary practice of pirating play texts by way of "memorial reconstruction"—piecing together speeches with the aid of collaborating actors' memories. It is only about half the length of Marlowe's other plays, includes only fifteen speeches longer than a dozen lines, and is marred by many textual confusions and repetitions. In addition, it includes a number of lines found also in other Elizabethan plays. Such a corrupted and patchwork text provides little basis for poetic or rhetorical analysis, but it does nevertheless offer a basic sketch of the scenario and general tone of the action presented. Moreover, the particular role of Guise, rendered with fuller detail than those of the other characters, suggests that an actor who played Guise is likely to have been one of those whose memories pieced the text together.

In any event, the outline of the play and the basic characterization of the Duke of Guise reveal a fairly crude effort on Marlowe's part to convert the already sensationalistic reports of French political and religious bloodshed into sensationalistic theatre. Scholars, especially Paul Kocher (1947) and Julia Briggs, who have examined the contemporary sources of the play (mainly by outraged Protestant pamphleteers and historians, but also some by Catholic reporters) have demonstrated how closely Marlowe adhered to the events and judgments provided in them.

The St. Bartholomew's Day Massacre of 1572, in which thousands of Protestants were slain in a brutal surprise attack that began in Paris and spread even more disastrously through the provinces, is one of European history's notorious atrocities. In Elizabeth's England, racked by religious controversy and fears of Catholic treason, the massacre became a lurid warning flare of the violence and deception that one might expect in the current unrest. Roughly the first half of Marlowe's play is given over to the depiction of this event, which is portrayed as the brain-child of Guise; all but one of the half-dozen scenes that stage the killing of individual innocent Protestants include him as the leader of the assailants. The remainder of the play telescopes several events of the next seventeen years, including the death of King Charles, the succession of Henry III, Guise's assassination of his wife's paramour, the growing division between the King and Guise, leading to the assassination of both Guise and his brother the Cardinal, and, finally, the double deaths of King Henry III and his friar assailant. A total of eighteen violent deaths on stage may not seem very great when measured against the casualty statistics of the actual massacre, but the theatrical impression produced by so many victims, dispatched by poison, stabbing, shooting, and strangling in the space of several short scenes, amounts to a kind of visual hyperbole that threatens at times to become farcical self-parody.

Beneath the panorama of intrigue and bloodshed, one can discern at least three patterns of unifying interpretation. The first, already patent in the historical sources, insists on the events as evidence of a Catholic conspiracy against Protestantism everywhere. The second derives from the familiar pattern of "tyrant-tragedy," in which the source of evil is the over-reaching will of a politically ambitious protagonist, who wreaks violence on his adversaries, only to meet with retributive destruction in the end. The third, more peculiar to Marlowe's dramaturgy, juxtaposes the expression of ambition in "high aspiring terms" with the crude display of raw violence. The wit of the protagonist is used to glorify the self and to mock his victims, revealing an ironic fascination with the inhuman effects of the self-defined Extraordinary Man.

The first pattern reads the story of Guise and his family as the saga of evil Catholics doing atrocious things to pious Protestants, with some of the Catholics ultimately suffering violent retribution for their crimes. The dimension of religious and political propaganda is typically high-lighted throughout the script. This occurs most blatantly in the last speeches of Henry III, who, for example, not yet apprised of the poisonous nature of his stab wounds by the friar, addresses the English emissary:

> Agent for England, send thy mistress word
> What this detested Jacobin hath done.
> Tell her, for all this, that I hope to live;
> Which if I do, the papal monarch goes
> To wrack, and antichristian kingdom falls.
> These bloody hands shall tear his triple crown,
> And fire accursed Rome about his ears;
> I'll fire his crazed buildings, and enforce
> The papal towers to kiss the lowly earth.
> Navarre, give me thy hand: I here do swear
> To ruinate that wicked Church of Rome,
> That hatcheth up such bloody practices;
> And here protest eternal love to thee,
> And to the Queen of England specially,
> Whom God hath bless'd for hating papistry. (Sc. 21.57–71)

The depiction of Henry of Navarre as the consistently God-fearing and pious Protestant leader is similar (an image that must have struck English audiences at revivals of this play after July 1593 with unintended irony, since Henry became a Catholic at that time). The inescapable link between the religious and political warfare of the day is further stressed in such moments as King Henry III's earlier triumphal gloss on his assassination of the Duke of Guise, which lists among Guise's crimes several items that issue implausibly from this Catholic monarch's mouth:

> Did he not draw a sort of English priests
> From Douay to the seminary at Rheims,
> To hatch forth treason 'gainst their natural queen?
> Did he not cause the king of Spain's huge fleet
> To threaten England . . . ? (Sc. 18.102–6)

With such strokes, the play depicts Guise as the avatar of international anti-Protestant treachery, including, interestingly enough, his protection of the seminary where Marlowe the Cambridge scholar had probably once been sent in the service of Queen Elizabeth and where Baines had even earlier attempted his ambitious conspiracy.

The second pattern of "tyrant-tragedy" emerges from Marlowe's decision to tie as much of his historical narrative as possible to the central figure of the Duke of Guise, to make him the cause of as much of the civil dissension and violence as possible, including events that follow his death, such as Henry III's assassination, depicted here as an act of revenge commissioned by Guise's brother. Marlowe, without basis in his sources, ascribed to Guise the responsibility for the first fatality in the play, the poisoning of the Queen of Navarre; he also transformed from suspicion to fact Guise's role in the initial assassination attempt upon the Lord Admiral.[24] Although the Queen Mother, Catherine de Medici, is shown in the play to be complicit with Guise in planning the massacre, Marlowe reversed the historical accounts by making him, rather than Catherine, the initiator of the plot. So, too, Guise is given a dominant role in the scenes depicting the murder of Protestant preachers, teachers, and even the philosopher Ramus. As a ghoulish climax to the day's bloody events, Marlowe staged a visit by Catherine, Guise, and the Cardinal to the place where the decapitated corpse of the Lord Admiral has been hung up (his head has been sent as a victory token to the Pope):

GUISE Now, Madam, how like you our lusty Admiral?

QUEEN CATHERINE Believe me, Guise, he becomes the place so well
    As I could long ere this have wish'd him there. But come, let's walk
    aside, th'air's not very sweet.

GUISE No, by my faith, Madam. Sirs, take him away, and throw him in
    some ditch. (Sc. 11.13–18)

From first to last, the Duke of Guise is portrayed as supremely contemptuous of his adversaries and victims. The sole modification in his attitude arises in his reaction to King Henry III's demand that he disband his army. Then, playing for time, he switches from unabashed insolence to feigned compliance, marking the shift with an explicit aside: "I must dissemble" (Sc. 19.61). This example of Machiavellian expediency is matched immediately by his royal opponent, who resolves secretly to do away with Guise. This is the point where the Duke is seen to have over-reached himself and where the King turns the tables on him. The assassination of Guise follows a short intervening scene that provides the Protestant Navarre with an opportunity to express his resolve to aid Henry in the godly cause of defeating the Duke. When Guise walks into the King's trap, the text captions the moment in a none-too-subtle aside by King Henry (which also happens to mirror the ironic climax of *The Jew of Malta*): "Come, Guise, and see thy traitorous guile outreach'd, / And perish in the pit thou madest for me" (Sc. 21.33–34).

Even though the pattern of retribution is here played out, Marlowe insisted that his protagonist maintain his sense of superiority, remorselessness, and disdain for his adversaries to the end. Like the Jew Barabas and like Mortimer in *Edward II*, Guise breathes his last with defiant pride for what he has done. Responding to the advice of one of his murderers to pray to God and ask the King's forgiveness, he retorts:

> Trouble me not, I ne'er offended him,
> Nor will I ask forgiveness of the King.
> O that I have not power to stay my life,
> Nor immortality to be reveng'd!
> To die by peasants, what a grief is this!
> Ah, Sixtus, be reveng'd upon the King;
> Philip and Parma, I am slain for you!
> Pope, excommunicate, Philip, depose
> The wicked branch of curs'd Valois his line!
> *Vive la messe!* Perish Huguenots!
> Thus Caesar did go forth, and thus he died. (Sc. 21.77–87)

That the Duke should invoke in his last words the hated enemies of the Protestant cause, Pope Sixtus V, King Philip II of Spain, and Philip's general, the Duke of Parma, is yet another index of the propagandistic quality of his characterization. So, too, is his Catholic slogan, "Long live the Mass!" This final glimpse of Guise the Catholic monster, while consistent with the judgment leveled at him in the Protestant sources Marlowe used, is curiously inconsistent with the more Machiavellian notion of Guise as a man who values religion only as a means to serve his personal goals of power. Such is the unequivocal impression Marlowe built up in the extraordinarily long monologue of Scene 2 in which Guise reveals his innermost thoughts and motivations. In one passage, he sums up the financial support he receives to mount his anti-Protestant seditions:

> For this, from Spain the stately Catholics
> Sends Indian gold to coin me French ecues;
> For this, have I a largess from the Pope,
> A pension and a dispensation too;
> And by that privilege to work upon,
> My policy hath fram'd religion.
> Religion: *O Diabole!*
> Fie, I am asham'd, however that I seem,
> To think a word of such a simple sound,
> Of so great matter should be made the ground. (Sc. 2.57–66)

Guise is forthright in displaying his contempt for religion, but he uses a hypocritical zeal to gain support that will advance his own aims. Like Tamburlaine, he is focused on the sweet fruition of an earthly crown; like Tamburlaine, too, his rhetoric surrounds that goal with the aura of a transcendent quest:

> Oft have I levell'd, and at last have learn'd
> That peril is the chiefest way to happiness,
> And resolution honor's fairest aim.
> What glory is there in a common good
> That hangs for every peasant to achieve?
> That like I best that flies beyond my reach.
> Set me to scale the high Pyramides,
> And thereon set the diadem of France,
> I'll either rend it with my nails to naught
> Or mount the top with my aspiring wings,
> Although my downfall be the deepest hell.
> For this, I wake, when others think I sleep;
> For this, my quenchless thirst whereon I build
> Hath often pleaded kindred to the King;
> For this, this head, this heart, this hand and sword,
> Contrives, imagines, and fully executes
> Matters of import, aim'd at by many,
> Yet understood by none;
> For this, hath heaven engender'd me of earth;
> For this, this earth sustains my body's weight,
> And with this weight I'll counterpoise a crown . . . (Sc. 2.34–55)

The hyperbolic image of what he would do if the crown were set atop the pyramids defines his sense of energetic purpose, but it is already shadowed by the destructive or self-destructive force of the alternatives: on the one hand, tearing away at one of the wonders of the world with his own hands to reduce it to naught; on the other, flying Lucifer-like to the heights even if it means being cast down to hell. This is one of the rare moments in the text in which Marlowe's metaphorical subtlety can be glimpsed, and it is noteworthy that this passage shows the playwright using motifs that he orchestrated in *Tamburlaine* and in *Doctor Faustus*, before he went on to add the more Machiavellian notes of religious hypocrisy and the cunning manipulation of a political power-base. Here, and here only in the received text, one senses the deep irony of the self-affirming ego

whose extraordinary energies harbor within them the explosive capacity
for both destruction and self destruction. By contrast, the curses and
vaunts of the dying Guise seem mere bluster. In between these moments,
Marlowe indulged in another kind of contrast: the macabre demonstration
of how the aspiring Guise executes his self-glorifying mission. Guise's
career in action is a caricature of mordant cruelty.

His initial victim, Queen Margaret of Navarre, is killed by the exotic
means of gloves scented with a poisonous fragrance—a detail supplied in
the sources but not associated with Guise. His role in the assassination of
the Lord Admiral, the leader of the Huguenot cause, is presented with
crude savagery. After Guise's posted sniper succeeds only in wounding
the Admiral, other henchmen stab him in his bed; the corpse is then thrown
down into the court where the waiting Guise tramples on the body. Other
victims of the massacre are presented as defenseless and unarmed; their
helpless situation at the moment of death is nearly always marked with
some derisive jest on the part of Guise or his companion slayers. There is
an odd effect in the handful of scenes that represent the massacre itself:
Guise's recurrent presence suggests that he personally is engaged in
directing the slaughter of as many individual victims as possible—here,
there, and everywhere. This is more a representation of brutal energy than
of Machiavellianism, where the art is to remain concealed and have others
execute one's destructive aims. By that standard, the figure of Catherine
de Medici in this play is more clearly the Machiavel, willing even to poison
her own sons secretly if they stand opposed to her will. Nonetheless, as a
dramatic tactic, giving Guise such ubiquity in the violent actions (multi-
plied beyond the historical accounts), following so swiftly upon his long
soliloquy, is Marlowe's way of ironically matching aspiring rhetoric with
degrading practice. It is the trademark for his brand of tragedy. In *The
Massacre at Paris*, this pattern is seen in its crudest form, and it is so
overlaid with the ideological vilification of Guise as Protestant Enemy
Number One that its psychological interest is barely visible. How much
of an impact Marlowe's play had on early seventeenth-century treatments
as Guise's career, such as John Webster's *The Guise* or Henry Shirley's
The Duke of Guise, we shall never know, for these later plays have not
survived.

THE JEW OF MALTA

The Duke of Guise and Machiavelli are explicitly linked in the unusual
prologue that introduces *The Jew of Malta*:[25]

Albeit the world think Machevill is dead,
Yet was his soul but flown beyond the Alps,
And now the Guise is dead, is come from France,
To view this land, and frolic with his friends. (1–4)

The speaker, we learn in the next few lines, is "Machevill" himself, and "this land" is not Malta, but England (the "Britanie" of line 29). Machiavelli has friends here, even though those who love him will not mention his disreputable name. He goes on to suggest that even those who hate him or denounce his books read his writings and attain power (even papal power, the image asserts) by putting his unscrupulous principles into practice, until they in turn are ousted by other disciples through treachery and bloody force.

The tone is set: knowing, satiric, inviting the audience to enjoy a display of hypocrisy and treachery that their orthodox moral standards condemn but that, the speaker cannily implies, they may secretly admire and even practice. Machiavelli is not only introducing Barabas the Jew and asking the audience to "grace him as he deserves." He is also introducing the audience to themselves, challenging them to acknowledge their own hidden complicity in the qualities that define the popular image of Machiavelli as the ultimate opportunist whose crafty and unscrupulous tactics work beneath a mask of righteousness. "Here I am, among you," Machiavelli says in effect, "a figure of evil with whom you have a love-hate relationship; and this fellow traveler of mine, Barabas, is not merely a Wicked Other (as you like to categorize me, too) but a distorted mirror of your own secret values."

This is a remarkable introduction, most unusual in the way it compromises the presumed moral standards of the audience, as well as in the way it establishes an emblematic perspective for the unfolding drama. This "tragedy of a Jew" is to be seen as an image of our hypocrisy. Our response to it, the author implies, may prove as deeply ambivalent—and self-exposing—as our response to Machiavelli's challenging ideas. If, as the subsequent action quickly shows, Barabas becomes a caricature of evil, it is not, as in the case of the Duke of Guise, a caricature that can be comfortably identified with the enemy. Marlowe's strategy here includes the manipulation of thematic context and satiric tone to trap his audience into a kind of unheeded comic alliance with his monstrous protagonist. It is a strategy that tries to catch us comically admiring what we presumably hold as morally hateful.

Such a strategy and such a tone do not fit as well with sixteenth-century conventions of tragedy as they do with certain conventions of Tudor morality drama, above all the character of the Vice. Sixteenth-century developments of the late medieval allegorical moral play had turned the originally theological basis of such drama toward a variety of didactic aims, some political, some pedagogical. But more important than the wider range of moral lessons to be demonstrated in the late morality play or interlude was the theatrical concentration of interest in the character of the Vice, who more often than not became not only the driving force in the plot, but also a satirical master of ceremonies.[26] The typical pattern of action would begin with the Vice's self-defining introduction of himself to the audience, in which the particular evil or sin he personified would be spelled out and illustrated. Next he would proclaim his immediate project: to bring about the downfall of the human protagonist of the play by luring him into that sin, using a disguise or false identity as some apparent or specious good. While executing the project, the Vice would characteristically engage the audience in a series of asides, mocking the gullibility of his human target. When the everyman figure has fallen—often by action that indulges in farcical dimensions—the Vice, again in direct intimacy with the audience, gloats over the triumph, taking every opportunity to underline his morally destructive power. Even if the protagonist should later undergo redemption or conversion through the agency of some Virtue, the Vice usually ends up still active and determined to take on his next victim, satirically emphasizing the ongoing temptation that he represents to all humans. The mode of the morality play thus establishes a theatrical paradox: The audience members are engaged by the central Vice while being told and shown that they ought to be on their guard against him; his superior perspective, comic duplicity, and inevitable efficiency invite their complicity as spectators, even as they watch the fall of the protagonist who technically mirrors their humanity. The moral labels tell them that they should be on the side of the victim and against the destructive Vice, while the dynamics of the presentation push their emotions in the opposite direction. In the theatrical experience, they find themselves distanced from the witless human and allied with the witty villain. In moral drama, this paradox may well serve the moral purpose of the play, for it suggests indirectly that the audience members are more attached to the Vice of the play than they should be or would willingly admit: "Admired I am of those that hate me most."

To note this pattern and strategy in the tradition of morality drama is also to see that more than Marlowe's prologue is relevant here. The ongoing presentation of his central character, Barabas, is conceived along the lines of the Vice in the morality plays, although by no means restricted to that convention. The Jew's opening monologue celebrates his avarice, and, as the ensuing action unfolds in all its episodic complexity, we discover that avarice is one vice that unites virtually all the factions in the script: Turks, Christians, and Jews are all engaged in measures to exploit one another's wealth. The friars are moved to violent rivalry in their hope to benefit from Barabas' wealth; the bawdy-house couple, Bellamira and Pilia-Borza, conspire with Ithamore to extort money from Barabas; and the Turkish Basso, when asked by the Maltese leaders what wind and purpose have brought him to the island, responds with a salient caption for this avaricious universe: "The wind that bloweth all the world besides, / Desire of gold" (3.5.3–4). Barabas, however, is not engaged in bringing others to moral destruction by the lure of avarice; rather he uses their predisposition to greed to manipulate them into physically destructive situations, feeding his own desire for revenge against those who have done or would do him wrong. Still, his duplicitous way of engineering the destruction of his unsuspecting enemies, above all the constant use of asides and of "partial" asides that finish a sentence with an ironic phrase that reveals his hidden purpose and goes unheard by his interlocutor, reveals his theatrical ancestor, the Vice. So, too, does the remarkable catalogue of present and past secret crimes he gloatingly enumerates to Ithamore, his new slave, in the third scene of Act Two; here he is no longer a personification of avarice, but of delight in destruction:

> As for myself, I walk abroad a-nights,
> And kill sick people groaning under walls:
> Sometimes I go about and poison wells;
> And now and then, to cherish Christian thieves,
> I am content to lose some of my crowns;
> That I may, walking in my gallery,
> See 'em go pinioned along by my door.
> Being young I studied physic, and began
> To practise first upon the Italian;
> There I enriched the priests with burials,
> And always kept the sexton's arms in ure
> With digging graves and ringing dead men's knells:
> And after that was I an engineer,
> And in the wars 'twixt France and Germany,
> Under pretence of helping Charles the Fifth,
> Slew friend and enemy with my stratagems.
> Then after that was I an usurer,
> And with extorting, cozening, forfeiting,
> And tricks belonging unto brokery,

I filled the jails with bankrouts in a year,
And with young orphans planted hospitals,
And every moon made some or other mad,
And now and then one hang himself for grief,
Pinning upon his breast a long great scroll
How I with interest tormented him.
But mark how I am blest for plaguing them,
I have as much coin as will buy the town.
But tell me now, how hast thou spent thy time? (2.3.178–205)

Hyperbole and caricature meet in this outrageous bit of grotesquerie, which is further extended by Ithamore's reply in kind. The catalogue of evils may be Vice-like, but, taken out of the abstract context of morality drama and presented as a character's autobiography (albeit an emblematic character who embodies all the worst traits associated with the popular myths of Jewish and Machiavellian evil), it assumes the flavor of comic monstrosity. The last line's equation of all those sadistic activities with ways to spend time is one of the clearest indications of the play's "black comic" edge, its ability to transform horrid destruction into something like farce.

This is the point where nearly every modern commentary on the play invokes the sagely acute observation by T. S. Eliot in 1919 that *The Jew of Malta* is not so much a tragedy as a farce "of the old English humour, the terribly serious, even savage comic humour," instanced in Ben Jonson and, much later, in "the decadent genius of Dickens" (Eliot [1919] 1950, 105). We can understand more clearly what Eliot meant if we trace the development of this judgment in his essays on Jonson and other Jacobean playwrights. Eliot called Jonson "the legitimate heir of Marlowe" (Eliot 1950, 133), pointing particularly to *Volpone* as a work that reconstituted many of the elements in *The Jew of Malta*. He laid greatest stress on two aspects of this inheritance: the drawing of character and the drawing of the world in which the character lives. The process of characterization common to both actions involved "simplification" by reduction of detail and conformity to a particular setting; the effect is that of "a flat distortion"—"it is an art of caricature, of great caricature" (Eliot 1950, 138). Eliot likened this mode of representation to the satiric effects of François Rabelais, an intentionally exaggerated art that draws a world to suit such characters and vice versa, producing a world and characters with a logic of their own: "this logic illuminates the actual world, because it gives us a new point of view from which to inspect it" (Eliot 1950, 136).

The key to what is "serious" about this kind of farce lies in that last phrase; the more familiar modes of farce release us from connections to the real world, but this mode illuminates our world by providing a new perspective from which to "inspect" it, presumably to discover in it what those artificially flat distortions and caricatures evoke. In the case of Marlowe's play, we may be led in several directions: It is not just greed and extortion that make the world go round but a greed that likes to dress itself in self-righteous superiority, even religiosity.

The hypocritical mask, of course, is the Machiavellian trademark. In this play, it is worn not only by Barabas, who uses deception—even the deception of a religious conversion—to attain his vindictive ends, but also by the friars, whose religious habits barely cover their competitive greed and secret lechery, and by the opportunistic Ferneze, Governor of Malta, whose invocation of divine providence at the close of the play cloaks in a pious formula the actual efficacy of his own capacity for double-dealing. Marlowe persistently exposed self-aggrandizement as the common denominator motivating the actions of virtually all his characters, save Abigail. Implemented as it is through a tone of cynical mockery, this exposure flows directly from the implications of Marlowe's knowing prologue. It is also tied to Machiavelli's observation in *The Prince* that prudent rulers ought not to keep faith when that would harm their interests: "If men were all good, this precept would not be a good one, but as they are bad, and would not observe their faith with you, so you are not bound to keep faith with them" (Machiavelli 1940, 64). Barabas' motto—"*Ego mihimet sum semper proximus*" (which the modern world translates into "looking out for Number One")—is the law of the Machiavellian land.

And yet, that law does not provide an entirely satisfactory rationale for the raw energies of the script, the more farcical dimensions of this savage farce, which, despite its clear exploitation of morality play devices and its satiric implications about the universality of Machiavellian hypocrisy, consistently spills its colors outside those lines. As we watch Barabas in action, we discover a figure whose energies and delights are not all comprehensible as those of a Machiavellian Vice, for the end that justifies Barabas' means is not the acquisition of power. Indeed, when his compound betrayals lead to the overthrow of Malta by the Turks, who then reward him with the governorship, he quickly reveals his distrust of political power and plots chiefly to use his status as a means of exchange to increase his wealth, conspiring with his old enemy Ferneze to destroy the Turks. Taking another Machiavellian into his confidence, of course, proves his ironic undoing, just as it violates his usual principle of trusting no one. But more than that, this choice seems to stem from a still more urgent principle underlying most of his actions: to take delight in his own intricate and deceptive manipulations for their own sake. Watching Barabas at work, whether baiting and overseeing the mutually destructive duel of his daughter's suitors, preparing the poisoned porridge for the nunnery, luring the envious friars to their destruction, disguising himself as a musician to counterplot against Ithamore and his bawdy-house allies (see Illustration 9), or busily hammering away at the trapdoor and pulley engineered to destroy Calymath, we see someone who enjoys the means for their own sake, rather than a true Machiavellian, for whom a particular end justifies the means. It is the clever *doing* that counts, not the fruits of the process, both for Barabas and for the audience. No matter that his actions are always egregious in their destructive carelessness of who or how many are slain in his effort to get back at an enemy. Marlowe, in focusing on Barabas' contortionist skills and in keeping most of his victims either flat or downright unsympathetic, induced the audience to share in the delights of cunning villainy. The fact that most of Barabas' schemes are themselves speedy improvisations, in response to challenges and chances that he could neither plan nor predict, is a further sign of their distance from the carefully premeditated plotting of political maneuvering and one-upmanship. Marlowe's plot is an implausible concatenation of surprising situations and reversals—the backbone of farcical structure—that test the mettle of Barabas as a tactician rather than as a strategist, for all his pride in "stratagems." There is a related lack of concern on Marlowe's part for providing Barabas with a dominating motivation or quest that might lend coherence to his destructive escapades. The stereo-typical delight in acquiring wealth with which Barabas begins the play does not really explain the perverse mode of revenge he undertakes against Ferneze or his wholesale poisoning of the nuns. His hostility toward the friars and Ithamore's new cohorts is spurred by their threats of blackmail, a nearly mechanical defensive reaction, while his alliance with the Turkish marauders is the product of sheer happenstance. By the time that moment comes, however, the audience is not looking for plausible motivations but is more likely wondering what the miraculously resurrected Barabas will offer next in the vein of new outrages. The dizzy display of his bravura deceptions and the sheer excess of his destructive energy and ingenuity have become the focus of attention. Even as the mayhem escalates in its range, intensity, and pace, we realize that the play is not forcing us to count the corpses or taste the blood. The climate of farce, where destructive consequences are muted or disregarded, begins to shape our responses. Ithamore, before he turns against Barabas, serves as a kind of comic cheerleader, joining in his relish and providing reinforcement for the absurd

Illustration 9. 1965 Royal Shakespeare Company production of *The Jew of Malta*. The farcical mode in tragedy: Barabas (Eric Porter), in disguise as a musician, serenades Bellamira (Patsy Byrne), Ithamore (Peter McEnery), and Pilia-Borza (Timothy West) in the Royal Shakespeare Company production at Stratford-on-Avon, directed by Clifford Williams. (Photo courtesy of the Shakespeare Centre Library: The Tom Holte Theatre Photographic Collection.)

contours of this behavior. This is a world closer to that of Rabelais than to the world of Seneca's more luridly violent scenarios; it is a world of the medieval "comedy of evil" run amok, where demons indulge in grotesque practical jokes and vices cavort around their easily duped victims. Even as Barabas stews in his own emblematic cauldron, cursing his last and proudly proclaiming his secret recent crimes, the irony of the spectacle seems more grotesquely amusing than morally satisfying, and the smug verdict of Ferneze brings us back to the mood of cynicism that the prologue initiated.

To entitle this play a tragedy is to stretch even the broad Elizabethan definition of the genre. Death and destruction are here, but they are not rendered in a mode that emphasizes their horror or complicates the issues of justice and injustice, fate and individual responsibility, fortune and will. Even the paradigm of the over-reacher destroyed by his own excesses, employed by Marlowe in *The Massacre at Paris* and schematically present here as well, does not seem to have its usual paradoxical bite. Dominating the mood of this caricatured display of evil is the Mask of Mockery, which contorts the response to malice and violence out of its usually somber emotional shape into an attitude of cynical amusement. The farce is savage, not merely because of the sheer brutality of the destruction displayed, but also because of the implication that these monstrosities proceed from universal promptings common to Christian, Turk, and Jew—"infidels" all. Here, glimpsed in absurdly hideous exaggeration and offered insidiously as amusing rather than horrifying acts, the monstrosities are posed as distorting mirrors of the audience's own "Machiavellian" affinity for pragmatically triumphant hypocrisy and deceit.

Whether Elizabethan audiences actually saw themselves in those distorting mirrors or preferred to identify the distortions with a safely distanced Other is not easy to discern. We do know from Henslowe's records that the play was a popular success when Lord Strange's company performed it between February 1592 and 1593, as well as when it was revived by other companies playing at Henslowe's theatre between February 1594 and June 1596. Barabas became one of Alleyn's most memorable roles, and the play was revived in 1601 and again—both at Court and at the Cockpit—closer to 1633, when the only extant printed edition was published. (We do not know when Marlowe wrote it, although the prologue's reference to the death of Guise would place it after December 1588.) Clearly, Marlowe's vindictive Jew was an important model for Shakespeare's *Merchant of Venice*, although it is notable that Shylock's villainy unfolds in a very different kind of world from that of Marlowe's Malta, and in a very different genre. Eliot, as noted above, pointed to Jonson's

Volpone—a satiric comedy—as another direct descendant of Marlowe's model. But there was another line of descent as well, in a mode of tragedy that indulged in caricature and satire, which blended traits of sensationalistic violence and emotional rant, apparent in such popular plays as Thomas Kyd's *The Spanish Tragedy*, with the detached, cynical irony of Marlowe's *Jew. The Revenger's Tragedy* and John Webster's *The White Devil* stand out in this line, both using a central figure to comment on the moral depravity of their worlds while engaged in actions that contribute to that depravity. While setting their action in a grotesquely exaggerated Italianate court that is characterized by deceit, intrigue, and corruption of every kind, these plays also have a quasi-allegorical edge that suggests that the evil exposed is neither tied to locale nor determined by peculiar psychological makeup. Finally, like Marlowe's play, they draw the audience into a fascination with how well and how wittily the game of deceit and counter-deceit is played, even when the players are manifestly evil. This line of tragedy reveals a new dynamic not encountered in the Senecan tradition of lamentation and tirade, interspersed with moralizing choral commentary. This new kind of tragedy may overlap certain Senecan themes and motivations such as revenge. Nevertheless, the knowing, observant perspective, the emphasis on amusing ironies and surprising reversals that evoke ingenious improvisation instead of emotional set speeches, and the subversive insistence that the monstrosities displayed are somehow symbolic of a broadly shared penchant for evil that even the audience may recognize as their own all point to a new set of conventions and expectations for tragedy in the English Renaissance. Marlowe's *Jew of Malta*, with its odd combination of farce, savagery, and allegorical suggestiveness, was clearly helping to open up new directions for both comedy and tragedy.

Chapter 6

Edward II:
Tragedy in the *De Casibus* Tradition

Marlowe's penchant for the emblematic scene provides a key to his central emphases in defining the tragic in his English history play, *Edward II*. Two such scenes late in the drama are further marked for us by Latin quotations captioning the visual moment: the arrest of the fugitive King at Neath Abbey (4.6) and the self-lauding soliloquy of Mortimer just after he has ordered Edward's assassination (5.4.47–71). Taken together, these two scenes form a diptych that parallels the "double subject" announced in the title of the printed play: *The Troublesome Reign and Lamentable Death of Edward the Second, King of England; with the Tragical Fall of Proud Mortimer*.[27]

In the first of these scenes, Edward, whose forces have been defeated by the barons in league with the Queen and Roger Mortimer, is discovered in the Welsh abbey where he has sought secret refuge. He is apparently cloaked in either a monk's habit or some common garb assumed to help disguise himself, as indicated by his exclamation and gesture late in the scene: "Hence, feigned weeds, unfeigned are my woes" (4.6.96). Before his adversaries come upon him, however, his words and actions portray his fallen condition: miserably distressed, anxious about possible betrayal, and, for a flickering moment, uncharacteristically attempting a Boethian response to adversity with the consolation of philosophy:

> Father, thy face should harbour no deceit;
> Oh hadst thou ever been a king, thy heart

> Pierced deeply with sense of my distress,
> Could not but take compassion of my state;
> Stately and proud, in riches and in train,
> Whilom I was powerful and full of pomp,
> But what is he whom rule and empiry
> Have not in life or death made miserable?
> Come Spencer, come Baldock, come, sit down by me,
> Make trial now of that philosophy,
> That in our famous nurseries of arts
> Thou suckedst from Plato and from Aristotle.
> Father, this life contemplative is heaven,
> Oh that I might this life in quiet lead;
> But we alas are chased, and you my friends,
> Your lives and my dishonour they pursue;
> Yet gentle monks, for treasure, gold nor fee,
> Do you betray us and our company. (4.6.8–25)

The fear of betrayal that frames this speech and ultimately extinguishes the glimmering hope of meditative peace is further aggravated by Baldock's naming of their arch-enemy, Mortimer. Edward, who cannot bear to hear that name without feeling wounded, lapses now into despairing passivity, which Marlowe underlined by having him collapse against the abbot:

> Good father, on thy lap
> Lay I this head, laden with mickle care,
> Oh might I never open these eyes again,
> Never again lift up this drooping head,
> Oh never more lift up this dying heart! (4.6.39–43)

This is the picture of the king—eyes closed, nearly prostrate, wishing for death—that greets the intruding adversaries, the Earl of Leicester and Rice ap Howell. This is the emblematic moment of Edward's defeat, "frozen" for the space of a few lines uttered aside by Leicester, who feels spontaneous pity for the ironically vulnerable king:

> Alas, see where he sits and hopes unseen
> T'escape their hands that seek to reave his life;
> Too true it is, *quem dies vidit veniens superbum,*
> *Hunc dies vidit fugiens iacentem.*
> But Leicester, leave to grow so passionate . . . (4.6.51–55)

The Latin caption, a quotation from Seneca's *Thyestes* (613–614), adds a formal flourish to the ironic situation of fallen pride and might ("He whom the beginning of the day saw high and mighty, the end of the day saw cast down"). Less formal but even more effective in its foreboding implications is the presence in the concluding part of this scene of the Mower (that "gloomy fellow in a mead below" as Spencer describes him [4.6.30]), who has led the enemy to their quarry: as Clifford Leech noted long ago (1959, 193), this figure must be identified by his scythe, which in turn transforms him, within such a context, into an emblem of Death.

Edward still has much more to suffer before the time of his terrible death, but this emblematic scene of his defeat stands as a verbal and visual reminder of one simple kind of tragic paradigm familiar to Elizabethans: the fall of the mighty, the potentate rendered powerless, or, in the phrase of Shakespeare's Richard II, "sad stories of the death of kings." The paradigm predated the development of tragic Elizabethan history plays. It went back, in fact, to the nondramatic narrative tradition of tales depicting the downfall of the great. This tradition is now called "*de casibus* tragedy," in reference to Giovanni Boccaccio's influential Latin model, *De Casibus Virorum Illustrium* ("Concerning the Falls of Famous Men"). Geoffrey Chaucer's "Monk's Tale" is a parodic reflection of the genre, which was more seriously exemplified in works by John Lydgate and, in the Elizabethan period, by the celebrated and influential anthology entitled *The Mirror for Magistrates*, first published in 1559 and often reprinted and expanded until 1610.[28] The explicit goal of the *Mirror* was to apply the format used by Boccaccio and Lydgate to subjects drawn from English history. The full title of the *Mirror*'s first edition expresses the moral bent of these verse tragedies: *A Mirror for Magistrates: Wherein may be seen by example of other, with how grievous plagues vices are punished and how frail and unstable worldly prosperity is found, even of those whom Fortune seemeth most highly to favor.* Marlowe's depiction of Edward's arrest accentuates the latter part of this title. Likewise, the Latin caption provided by Leicester points to the irony implicit in such tales, as do Edward's self-captioning lines:

> Stately and proud, in riches and in train,
> Whilom I was powerful and full of pomp,
> But what is he whom rule and empiry
> Have not in life or death made miserable? (4.6.12–15)

These clearly express sentiments echoed monotonously throughout the pages of the *Mirror*. And, in Marlowe's climactic presentation of Mortimer, we find a complementary facet of *de casibus* tragedy, the emphasis on tyrannical pride that provokes eventual punishment.

After Mortimer has sent Lightborn to execute the deposed and imprisoned Edward, immediately before the coronation of young Prince Edward, Mortimer gloats over his new power in a soliloquy:

> The prince I rule, the queen do I command,
> And with a lowly congé to the ground
> The proudest lords salute me as I pass;
> I seal, I cancel, I do what I will;
> Feared am I more than loved, let me be feared,
> And when I frown make all the court look pale. . . .
> Now is all sure, the queen and Mortimer
> Shall rule the realm, the king, and none rule us;
> Mine enemies will I plague, my friends advance,
> And what I list command, who dare control?
> *Maior sum quam cui possit fortuna nocere.* (5.4.47–52, 64–68)

The function of this speech is sheer self-characterization; we learn nothing from it about actions yet to come. It underscores the egocentric delight in sheer power that has fully overtaken Mortimer and corrupted his earlier motivations for the country's welfare. The insistent repetition of "I" that punches out the rhythm of egomania leads finally to the Latin boast ("I am greater than anyone Fortune can harm"), which is drawn, ironically enough, from Ovid's tale of Niobe—whose boast led to the wholesale destruction of her extensive family. Mortimer has no "family" to lose, but he is poised in absolute confidence on the brink of his own reversal, his own "tragical fall." Marlowe used the soliloquy not to tell us what is coming but to underscore Mortimer's sublime self-delusion about what he thinks he can get away with. The audience, wise with historical hindsight, knows better than he the secret message of destruction that lies hidden in the Latin boast (a perception rendered doubly ironic in that Mortimer has just taken special care to send an ambiguous Latin "execution-message" to Edward's jailers). The moment is emblematic of the tyrant whose consummate pride cannot see his vulnerability, the magistrate who has no mirror warning of mutability and of the punishment of vice in high places. Modern audiences are not inclined to think of the villainous Mortimer as tragic, but for the Elizabethans, as we have seen, there were no moral criteria for tragic figures. "Proud Mortimer" is clearly eligible for a tragic downfall in the *de casibus* vein. Thus, Marlowe enlisted both protagonist and antagonist in the tragic paradigm adapted in this play and provided a capstone emblematic scene—as grotesque as it was unhistorical—in his finale to clinch their mutually destructive relationship. At the final exit, the young King Edward III in mourning cloak accompanies his father's hearse off the stage, while on that very hearse rests in token of revenge the head of the executed Mortimer.

To discover in the *de casibus* tradition certain coordinates for Marlowe's definition of the tragic dimensions in English history does not imply that the playwright was merely adapting a narrative genre to the stage. As with all his adaptations of native and classical traditions, Marlowe's single excursion into English history reveals a blending of the conventional with unexpected innovation. In *Edward II*, he not only succeeded in writing a history play with a tighter structure (in the traditional sense of providing a unifying line of action held together by cause–and–effect linkages and strongly etched character conflicts) than anything seen on the English stage before, but he also managed to define that structure along lines that were shaped by tragic paradigms derived from *de casibus* writing but worked into ironic implications peculiarly his own. While he did not find the case of Edward II among those treated in *The Mirror for Magistrates*, he did find in Raphael Holinshed's *Chronicles* certain interpretive hints that suggested that both Edward and Mortimer "belonged" among those careers exemplary of tragedy. He did so well before Michael Drayton's verse narratives, *Peirs Gaveston* (1594) and *Mortimeriados* (1596), as well as before Richard Niccols' 1610 addition of Edward's career to the *Mirror*. His turning to the more contentious chapters in England's history for theatrical material may well have been inspired by the success of Shakespeare's forays into the reign of Henry VI, but Marlowe seems to have been the first to find a formula to provide some tragic unity to such material, in character as well as in incident.[29] Shakespeare clearly saw the virtue in Marlowe's achievement and built upon it in developing his conception for *Richard II*.

The endeavor to mold historical matter into tragic shape was hardly a novel one in Tudor drama, but the usual pattern, to judge by the few extant plays of this sort, had involved the studious imitation of Senecan formal techniques. *Gorboduc*, based on Geoffrey of Monmouth's history of ancient Britain and produced at the Inns of Court in the early 1560s, is perhaps the most famous example, notable not only for its innovative use of blank verse but also for the sustained elevation (albeit long-winded and monotonous to the modern ear) of its rhetoric, which Sir Philip Sidney praised as matching the heights of Seneca's style. *Gorboduc*'s long monologues and debates, its choruses and sententious maxims, and even its un-Senecan allegorical dumbshows preceding each act all point clearly to the self-conscious effort to merge the thematic motifs of political ambition, revenge, and civil chaos with the inherited forms of classical tragedy.[30] A generation later, when Marlowe and Shakespeare, along with several anonymous authors, took up the challenge, it was clear that the "classical" pattern would no longer serve. That there was a taste for "historical" plays seems amply demonstrated by titles in the Admiral's Men's repertory in the 1590s, but most of these have been lost, and those few that have survived suggest a major reliance on sensational acts of treachery and violence.

Shakespeare's *Henry VI* plays dynamically exploited the chaotic see-saw contentions of the Houses of York and Lancaster, presenting a kaleidoscopic panorama of political rivalry, reversals, and revenge, and amply demonstrating the victimization of the commonwealth as well as the capacity of both sides to behave brutally. In Part Three, the devout but ineffectual King Henry is given a lamenting choral voice to decry the destruction of the kingdom that is out of his control, but his role in the major conflicts is so passive that it seems virtually peripheral. He is not "centered" as a tragic protagonist within the events; his motivations do not precipitate the conflicts and calamities that beset the nation. Indeed, the word "tragedy" does not appear in the titles of Shakespeare's histories until the publication of *Richard III* and *Richard II* in 1597; the first centers on the rise and fall of a Machiavellian tyrant; the second, clearly following Marlowe, centers on the fall of a monarch whose arrogant willfulness precipitates political resistance and ultimate calamity. A new formula for historical tragedy was in the making. At the thematic or conceptual level, it matched character with destiny in an ironic network of self-destruction; at the formal or stylistic level, it reserved the elaborated rhetoric of the set speech for special moments within the scenario, "tuned" the expression in such speeches more precisely to match their speakers, and worked out new ways of suggesting mood and meaning by the orchestration of character interactions and by the interplay of verbal and visual images. The themat-ics of the new formula evolved from the *de casibus* tradition but did not remain within the constraints of that tradition; the new style or form resulted from experiment and innovation with the dimensions of staged performance. Surrounding the total endeavor, of course, was the cultural matrix of political ideology, which was already interwoven in complicated ways within the historical chronicles from which the dramatists drew their material and was often made problematic by more immediate issues in Elizabethan politics.[31]

Marlowe (and Shakespeare) found in Holinshed's *Chronicles* (1577, 1587) not only an account of events but also frequent moral judgments and commentaries on behavior. Edward II and Richard II are both notable in English history for their having been deposed, largely as a result of their abuses of power against the interests of the nobility. In Edward's case, the revolutionary aspect of the unprecedented deposition was somewhat muted by the formal accession of his son, but the event was clearly a disturbing one. Nevertheless, his deposition did not provoke the sort of outraged commentary in the chronicles that one might expect in a sixteenth-century monarchy intent on preserving the sacrosanct inviolability of the crown. Holinshed blamed both the King for his failure to heed any but his selfish favorites and the barons for bringing him down; he even hinted that the misfortunes of the last decade of Edward III's otherwise successful half-century reign might have been punishment for his acquiescence in his father's deposition. Holinshed's sternest reprimand of Edward II's adversaries appears after his account of the captive king's resignation:

Ah, lamentable ruin from royalty to miserable calamity, procured by them chiefly that should have been the pillars of the king's estate, and not the hooked engines to pull him down from his throne! So that here we see it verified by trial, that

———— *miser atque infelix est etiam rex,*
Nec quenquam (mihi crede) facit diadema beatum.
                                    (Holinshed [1577, 1587] 1807, 585)

Even here, the castigation of the barons is couched within sentiments of another sort, the tragic theme of mutability and misery in high places. Holinshed thus gave the impression that, although the nobles were politically at fault, what they brought about was a hallmark illustration of a larger and more pervasive pattern inherent in royal power: "Even kings are miserable and unhappy, for a crown, I believe, makes no one blessed." At another point, he characterized Edward's reign as "the pitiful tragedy of this king's time" (587).

Marlowe also found in Holinshed much stronger words about the King's own behavior in his younger days—above all, in his controversial attachment to Piers Gaveston:

But now, concerning the demeanor of this new king, whose disordered manners brought himself and many others unto destruction; we find that in the beginning . . . he counterfeited a kind of gravity, virtue, and modesty; but yet he could not thoroughly be so bridled, but that forthwith he began to play diverse wanton and light parts.

... For having revoked again into England his old mate the said Piers de Gaveston, he received him into most high favor ... through whose company and society he was suddenly so corrupted, that he burst out into most heinous vices; for then using the said Piers as a procurer of his disordered doings, he began to have his nobles in no regard, to set nothing by their instructions, and to take small heed unto the good government of the commonwealth, so that within a while, he gave himself to wantonness, passing his time in voluptuous pleasure, and riotous excess: and to help them forward in that kind of life, the foresaid Piers ... furnished his court with companies of jesters, ruffians, flattering parasites, musicians, and other vile and naughty ribalds, that the king might spend both days and nights in jesting, playing, blanketing, and in such other filthy and dishonorable exercises. (Holinshed 1807, 547)

For Gaveston himself, Holinshed provided a "memorial" after describing his capture and beheading: "But lo the vice of ambition, accompanied with a rabble of other outrages, even a reproachful end, with an everlasting mark of infamy, which he pulled by violent means on himself with the cords of his own lewdness, and could not escape his fatal fall" (Holinshed 1807, 552).

Thus, even in these few moralizing comments, Holinshed traced the themes that *The Mirror for Magistrates* poets harped upon in their tragic narratives of other English kings: princes abusing their power and bringing destruction to their realm and to themselves. What the poets added to the pattern was to stress the pain of the tragic figure himself as he looked back upon his past and recounted his own fall; the typical form was that of a confessional monologue, combining retrospective narrative with lamentation. Marlowe opened up that dimension in his portrayal of Edward, starting with the scene of his arrest and building upon it in all the subsequent scenes of Edward's imprisonment, torture, and death.

The chroniclers and the *de casibus* poets shared a fundamental premise about tragedy: It is a story of self-destruction. Their interpretations point persistently to individual human will as the cause of personal and political disaster, and, in the poetic laments, the recognition of that fact becomes an added source of grief. In some instances, the familiar trope of Fortune as the suprahuman force that guides individual destinies spurs a counterargument, as in *The Mirror for Magistrates'* poem on Jack Cade:

Now if this hap whereby we yield our mind
To lust and will, be Fortune, as we name her,

Then is she justly called false and blind,
And no reproach can be too much to blame her:
Yet is the shame our own when so we shame her,
For sure this hap if it be rightly known,
Cometh of ourselves, and so the blame our own. (*Mirror* 1938, 172)

In a 1574 addition to the *Mirror* by John Higgins, the character Irenglas echoes this forthright conclusion:

There is no fate whom we have need to blame;
There is no destiny, but is deserved;
No luck that leaves us safe, or unpreserved;
Let us not then complain of Fortune's skill;
For all our good descends from God's good will,
And of our lewdness, springeth all our ill.
                                  (Higgins 1574 [1946], 212–13)

From one point of view, such an insistent focus on the individual's responsibility for adversity may well seem not only a simplistic exaggeration but also antithetical to both ancient and modern notions of tragedy; it clearly ignores the more perplexing problem of suffering that afflicts the innocent. Nonetheless, it is a dominant notion in Elizabethan tragic poetry and helps to explain the decidedly un-Aristotelian convention of tragic protagonists who are morally weak or evil. From still another point of view, the notion of self-destruction invites the elaboration of ironies that can be sensed and defined as tragic: the pursuit of a goal that hides within itself its own sinister negation. Marlowe's rendition of Edward's and Mortimer's self-destructive careers reveals a strong response to such an invitation. It reveals further ironies as well, particularly with respect to the explicitly moralizing dimensions of his historical sources and *de casibus* analogues. As we shall see, Marlowe carefully resisted the convention of having his fallen figures recognize or even decry their own past misdeeds. Not even retributive adversity will shake them from the attachment to their original obsessions.

Marlowe centered what Holinshed called "the pitiful tragedy of this king's time" in personal drives and interpersonal conflicts, simplifying the range and shifting composition of Edward's baronial adversaries by concentrating on the figure of Roger Mortimer of Wigmore as the chief antagonist. His most notable departure from the outline of Edward's reign as provided by Holinshed and John Stow—apart from virtually ignoring the long and complicated hostilities in Scotland, Ireland, and France—was

to give Mortimer a totally unhistorical role in the baronial opposition to
Gaveston that marked the opening years of Edward's reign. He thereby
positioned him from the start not only as a leading political rival but also
as a rival for the Queen's affections. In historical fact, Mortimer first
appeared as an opponent in 1321, nine years after Gaveston's death, when
he and many other barons hostile to the Spencers joined forces in an
attempt to oust these latter favorites of the King. Marlowe's overall
compression of time, moreover, by which Edward's twenty-year reign is
made to seem like only a year or two, complements the effects of continuity
achieved by anticipating Mortimer's participation in Edward's downfall.
But more than continuity is at stake here; the personal rather than political
bases for rivalry are accentuated by Marlowe's making much of two sexual
triangles in the early scenes of the play: The Queen loves Edward, who
prefers Gaveston; Mortimer, seeing the Queen cast off by Edward, sees
also his opportunities with her. And Gaveston, who maliciously plants in
Edward's mind the notion that Isabel has adulterous leanings toward
Mortimer long before either of them has made a move in such a direction,
proves, ironically, to be a prophet. Marlowe seems to have taken some
pains to insinuate erotic and personally vindictive motivations into his
sketch of these relationships, thus expanding and complicating the historical image of the vice-ridden King and his familiar. Gaveston thus not only
leads the King along a path that ends in destruction for them both, but his
presence also serves indirectly to open the way to the liaison between
Mortimer and the Queen. By a kind of invented sexual politics, Marlowe
precipitated the conflicts that destroy all the parties involved.

    For Mortimer and Isabel, the "destruction" takes not just the form of
some ultimate punishment but interim moral degradation as well. Each
begins as an idealist: she, dedicated to her husband, and he, to the good of
the country whose welfare is jeopardized by Edward's infatuation. Each
ends as a tyrannical villain, collaborating in treachery, hypocrisy, and
murder. In his revision of the last stages of this history, Marlowe magnified
and isolated the malicious hostility toward Edward in the roles of Mortimer
and the Queen; Holinshed's account, although very clear about their
liaison and Mortimer's power behind the scenes, had not indicated Mortimer as the leading agent in Edward's death, even though he recorded that
Parliament later charged Mortimer with that crime. His immediate description of the execution command in ambiguously worded Latin attributed it
to the Bishop of Hereford, who had earlier suffered great privations at the
hands of Edward and whose intense vindictiveness allied him with the
destructive wishes of the Queen. Marlowe's reduction of Hereford's role
is not only a tactic of dramatic economy; it also helps to amplify the image

of Mortimer as the supremely (but blindly) confident tyrant who believes himself to be at the top of the mountain when in fact he is poised at the crumbling edge of a cliff.

But it was Edward's trajectory that concerned Marlowe most and that he developed with the most skill and subtlety. Edward's obsession with Gaveston, which Marlowe read about in Holinshed, provided the key: "a wonderful matter that the king should be so enchanted with the said Earl, and so addict himself, or rather fix his heart upon a man of such a corrupt humor" (Holinshed 1807, 549) (see Illustration 10). Although neither Holinshed nor Stow employed the same kind of rhetoric in describing Edward's later attachment to the Spencers, Marlowe was quick to seize on the repetitive quality of the King's behavior in indulging unpopular favorites at the expense of the kingdom. He managed, by a playwright's sleight-of-hand, to include in one scene (3.2) events that were actually separated by more than nine years: the report of Gaveston's death, the immediate investing of Spencer Junior as Earl of Gloucester and Lord Chamberlain to spite his enemies, and the barons' demand that Edward renounce the Spencers. This compression and the corresponding elimination of all the international conflicts that bothered the historical Edward at this time leave the audience with the strong impression that Edward's reign was devoted to one issue and one issue only: the defense of his chosen personal favorites against the peers of the realm. To emphasize the continuity, Marlowe even invented another, historically inaccurate personal link between Gaveston and Spencer Junior as one-time loving companions (2.1.13–15).

That Edward's all-consuming concern for his favorites is to be taken as a destructive weakness rather than a strength is not something the audience must take on the word of the hostile nobles alone. Marlowe's choices in staging are emphatic in their implications. Gaveston's quasi-prologue to the play unabashedly reveals his opportunistic and exploitative outlook on his relationship with Edward. He plans to become a kind of master of the King's revels (elaborated in homoerotic imagery involving boys enacting the voyeuristic myth of Diana and Actaeon) in order to "draw the pliant king which way I please" (1.1.52). His treatment of the would-be servingmen and his secret spying on the quarrel between the King and the nobles creates the impression of a man of cunning and detachment. Marlowe, to be sure, did not present Gaveston's attachment to Edward as hypocritical, but he did establish a marked contrast in the emotional intensity with which the two men treat each other: Edward is the effusive and hyperbolic devotee, while Gaveston remains the more tight-lipped idol. The scene in which the King urges Gaveston to humiliate the Bishop of Coventry, who

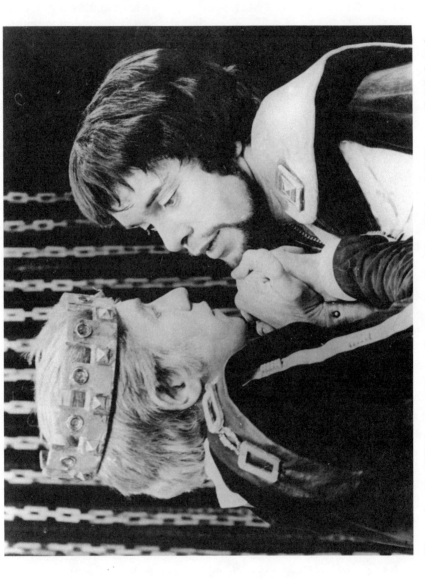

Illustration 10. 1969 Prospect Theatre Company production of *Edward II.* The tragedy of obsession: Edward the King (Ian McKellen, left) consorts with Piers Gaveston (James Laurenson). (Photo courtesy of Mander & Mitchenson Theatre Collection.)

is then arbitrarily stripped of his property and "given" as prisoner to Gaveston to do with as he likes, is marked by sardonic cruelty in both Edward and Gaveston. Edward's humiliating treatment of his wife follows shortly afterward. On more than one later occasion, the play shows Edward's inability to focus on urgent matters of foreign affairs when beset by the more emotionally pressing issue of Gaveston's banishment. Later, even before the King is at the point of welcoming Spencer and Baldock into his service, Marlowe presented the two of them engaged in a cynical discussion of how to move up in the world via flattery and hypocrisy (2.1.1–55).

That Edward's devotion is misplaced and extreme becomes evident enough. Even more important for the pattern of tragic irony is the sense that, in defending that devotion in such arbitrary and aggressive ways, he is creating and expanding the opposition that will one day destroy him. He creates his own enemies. This may well be another reason for Marlowe's ignoring the historical battles with Scotland, where the enemy is not so "constructed" as a direct consequence of Edward's attachment to his favorites. Thus, there is a special irony in one of the ways that Marlowe showed Edward asserting his royal power: the heaping of titles and offices on his friends. With each such measure, he antagonizes and alienates the lords of the realm, indirectly making adversaries as he grants honors to his friends.

Marlowe's definition of conflict between private and public values in the career of Edward II, it should be stressed, is not located, as it would be so often in later tragedy, within the protagonist. Unlike Aeneas (or, indeed, unlike Marlowe's Dido), Edward never conceives of his problem as a choice between conflicting claims of love and duty. Even when he is persuaded to banish Gaveston, it is more a matter of his being browbeaten by his opponents rather than making the hard or self-sacrificing choice. In fact, he himself turns at once to browbeating his wife in order to get Gaveston back. Edward never has the clarity of vision to see that fulfilling his private desires is destructive to the public weal, much less frame the issue as a conflict or choice. He has no internal battles, although he suffers when he has lost the external ones. Marlowe consistently characterized him as one incapable of seeing himself (or part of himself) as his own enemy or his own problem. This incapacity to see what the rest of the play insists that the audience see is still another mark of Marlowe's art in building tragic irony. Historical playwrights habitually rely on the impact of historical hindsight to give edge to their ironic effects; in most cases, irony arises from situations in which the protagonist does not know something that the audience knows lies in his future. But Marlowe stressed

also the protagonist's ignorance of the present, and even of the past—
Edward's *not wanting to see what is happening* as a result of his actions
or to see how his past actions have already led to ill consequences.
Marlowe's tragic protagonists do not try to fashion themselves so much
as they try to fashion their "favorite" worlds, which happen not to
correspond to the worlds in which they must live and die.

Thus, personal obsession drives Edward to his doom, and he does not
see it. Marlowe's telescoped time-frame, which pushes cause and destructive effect closer together than ordinary chronology allows, emphasizes
the point. Pacing and compression, with one scene flowing into the next
with hardly any notice of intervening time, lend a juggernaut quality to
Edward's career and stress the way his assertions of private will ironically
backfire. And, although we are told that the kingdom suffers, the play
comes to its climax by stressing what the King suffers.

The scene of Edward's deposition (5.1) immediately follows the scene
of his arrest. In it, Marlowe gave Edward fullest rein to vent his grief,
anger, and frustration at the loss of power. Holinshed noted, tersely
enough, that when the King first heard the request that he formally resign
his crown in order to ensure the accession of his son, "The king being
sore troubled to hear such displeasant news, was brought into a marvelous agony; but in the end, for the quiet of the realm and doubt of further
danger to himself, he determined to follow their advice" (Holinshed
1807, 585). That "marvelous agony" was Marlowe's cue for a brilliantly
orchestrated emotional display, quite in contrast to the preceding abbey
scene where Edward's thoughts wandered briefly to philosophy and the
contemplative life, where even his own sense of self-pity was expressed
with recumbent posture and closed eyes. Here, to use his own simile,
Edward grieves like the wounded "imperial lion," mounting up in wrath
against his affliction. Moved by "outrageous passions," he roars out his
"rancour and disdain" for his adversaries, "ambitious Mortimer . . . and
that unnatural queen, false Isabel," upon whom he imagines revenge.
Marlowe built to that wrathful climax in twenty-five lines, and then,
suddenly, undercut its power with Edward's quiet, pained realization of
his actual impotence:

> But what are kings when regiment is gone
> But perfect shadows in a sunshine day? (5.1.26–27)

He is brought back to the agenda of the moment—the resignation of the
crown—and launches into another tirade, cursing "usurping Mortimer,"
whose name rings ten times over in Edward's speeches throughout this

scene as a self-torturing refrain; here Edward's imprecation reaches for mythology (a tactic Marlowe used sparingly in this play) to amplify its intensity:

> But if proud Mortimer do wear this crown,
> Heavens turn it to a blaze of quenchless fire,
> Or, like the snaky wreath of Tisiphon,
> Engirt the temples of his hateful head. (5.1.43–46)

Edward's passionate outburst is immediately undercut by the coaxing, matter-of-fact comment by Leicester, "My lord, why waste you thus the time away?" Edward again tries to come back to the business at hand. With an uncharacteristic line of sufferance—"But what the heavens appoint I must obey"—he removes his crown and offers it to the commissioners, only to reverse himself in another second:

> But stay awhile, let me be king till night,
> That I may gaze upon this glittering crown. . . .
> Continue ever thou celestial sun,
> Let never silent night possess this clime;
> Stand still you watches of the element,
> All times and seasons rest you at a stay,
> That Edward may be still fair England's king. (5.1.59–68)

This desperate plea, or command, parallels what Marlowe did at the start of the famous final soliloquy in *Doctor Faustus*, where Faustus is trying, like Edward, to stop time so that he will not meet damnation. And like that scene, this one too moves from the impossible wish to the acknowledgment of reality:

> But day's bright beams doth vanish fast away,
> And needs I must resign my wished crown. (5.1.69–70)

But not quite. Marlowe was intent on putting that very symbolic prop to further use in this emblematic scene, and decided to let Edward continue to use it as a stimulus for a succession of contrasting emotions: indignant fury at those who have come for the crown ("Inhuman creatures, . . . Why gape you for your sovereign's overthrow? . . . See, monsters, see, I'll wear my crown again"); self-pity at his impotence before them; child-like begging to let him "wear it yet awhile"; lunatic raving ("The King rageth," notes the stage direction) and absolute denial of their request; and, as they turn to go, deflated acquiescence that is suddenly converted to sardonic indictment:

> . . . here receive my crown;
> Receive it? no, these innocent hands of mine
> Shall not be guilty of so foul a crime;
> He of you all that most desires my blood
> And will be called the murtherer of a king
> Take it . . . (5.1.97–102)

No one does, for no one dares, in the context of such an invitation. Moreover, Edward's next question ("what, are you moved? pity you me?") and the following lines imply that some of them now show visible signs of grief at Edward's plight. As they turn once more to go at Edward's sarcastic suggestion that they send the pitiless Mortimer and Isabel to take the crown, the King finally relents, yields it to them, urges that they protect his son, and asks that they bear his handkerchief, "Wet with my tears," as a token to the Queen.[32]

A histrionic scene, to be sure, but one of enormous emotional range and intensity for any actor with the talent to meet its demands. Here, Marlowe has moved far beyond the grandiloquent set speeches of *Tamburlaine*, showing a cannier sense of how to vary tone and to play the key speaker off against his on-stage audience by shifts in mood, tempo, and staged gesture. The sudden twists and turns take one constantly by surprise; beyond the obvious expression of frantic grief, there is the ever-present psychological sparring with the enemy, both those in the scene and those behind the scenes. No wonder that Shakespeare borrowed so many of its elements to craft his own deposition scene in *Richard II*. As a major "aria" in King Edward's tragedy, it is also indicative of the consistent line of characterization that Marlowe has been developing for the King. Now that he is about to lose his crown, it has come to take on great meaning for him—not just as the conventional symbol of royal power, but, more deeply, as the symbol of his own identity. Without it, he lacks a sense of self, a reason to live. He knows instinctively that the next step will be death.

With respect to his understanding of how he has come to this pass, however, this scene defies both the conventions of *de casibus* tragedy, which typically calls for the tragic figure to recognize his crimes, and the report of Holinshed that:

> he answered that he knew that he was fallen into this misery through his own offenses, and therefore he was contented patiently to suffer

it, but yet it could not (he said) but grieve him, that he had in such
wise run into the hatred of all his people: notwithstanding he gave
the lords most hearty thanks, that they had so forgotten their received
injuries, and ceased not to bear so much good will towards his son
Edward, as to wish that he might reign over them. Therefore to satisfy
them, since otherwise it might not be, he utterly renounced his right
to the kingdom, and to the whole administration thereof. And lastly
he besought the lords now in his misery to forgive him such offenses
as he had committed against them. (Holinshed 1807, 585)

Marlowe's Edward makes only one apology to the commissioners—for
his angry words directed at them previously in this scene, words that he
attributes to grief-induced lunacy. The crimes he recognizes most vividly
are those of Mortimer and Isabel; he calls his own life "guiltless," his own
hands "innocent," and his farewell asks the lords to commend him to his
son:

> and bid him rule
> Better than I; yet how have I transgressed
> Unless it be with too much clemency? (5.1.121–23)

Edward is unwilling or unable to see in his earlier attachments the cause
of his downfall. Marlowe's stress on the king's belief in his own virtue is
absolute, so much so that, in the later scene of the humiliating shaving
with ditchwater, he gives Edward the self-comforting thought that he now
suffers as a martyr for love:

> Oh Gaveston, it is for thee that I am wronged;
> For me both thou and both the Spencers died,
> And for your sakes a thousand wrongs I'll take. (5.3.41–43)

Mortimer, too, when meeting his final retribution, refuses to draw the
usual conclusion about why or how he earned it. True to his own pride, he
says that since he had reached the highest point on Fortune's wheel and
"there was no place to mount up higher / Why should I grieve at my
declining fall?" (5.6.62–63). No *Mirror* lamentations for him!
Marlowe's resistance to the more conventional self-accusation may well
be the result of his impatience with easy pieties and moralizing. Indeed,
he illustrates such impatience elsewhere in the play, such as the opening
of the scene after the Queen's landing in England, where her public
sermonizing on Edward's misgovernment of the realm is cut short by

Mortimer's pragmatic words, "Nay, madam, if you be a warrior / Ye must not grow so passionate in speeches" (4.4.15–16). Even Baldock's sententious stoicism in the face of death (4.6.110–11) is undercut by Rice's prose response: "Come, come, keep these preachments till you come to the place appointed." But, in the instances of Edward and Mortimer, where the play's plot has so patently demonstrated their flaws, the lack of moral self-recognition may be seen as instrumental in achieving Marlowe's more disturbing ironies about those who fall tragically. Such ironies insist that character is destiny, that neither man can be expected to change for the better, that the obsessive aspiration to have the world respond comfortably to the arbitrary enactment of personal desire is a destructive delusion—and one that men hold on to even in the face of destruction itself. Shakespeare, who did not flinch from the convention of self-accusing moments (especially in *Richard III*), followed Marlowe's mode in elaborating the character of Richard II, who also refuses to acknowledge fully his own measure of responsibility for his downfall.

Marlowe's sense of historical tragedy, for all its final emphasis on the suffering of the fallen King, focuses far more attention than does *de casibus* poetry on the particular psychological process of that fall and its ironies. The conventional lament of a victim in *Mirror* anthologies is that he has been cast down. The irony nearly always points in the same direction: The mighty one is no longer mighty because his vice has brought him retribution. The form of first-person retrospective lament invites such an emphasis. But a dramatic form that relies on the swift unfolding of events in progress and that ties those events together by cause and effect (or action and reaction) can produce ironies of another kind, such as those of Edward's excesses intensifying the opposition even as he believes they are assertions of his power. That he remains oblivious to the damage he is doing, not only to others but ultimately to himself as well, is the critical dimension in this kind of irony.

Furthermore, Marlowe's consistent stress on how the problems of state arise from quite personal conflicts, rivalries, and animosities adds still other ironies to the picture, turning the overall conflict into one energized by private ambitions and vendettas, rather than by political causes based on loyalties to class, nation, or principle. One need only reflect on how exceptional Kent's attitudes and reactions are throughout the play. Even though he finds himself on different sides at various times, Kent is always given an explicit rationale for his movements, a rationale that tries to measure the relative weight of conflicting public values. He is the only figure, with perhaps the exception of the young Edward III (who seems to act more on the basis of decent instinct rather than reasoned grounds), who shows signs of having a conscience. By contrast, the others are all too sure of their own positions, and all too eager to goad their opponents into further conflict. Marlowe frequently added a dimension of cruel enjoyment to their hostile interactions. This is strikingly evident in the physical attack by Edward and Gaveston on the Bishop of Coventry (1.1), in the gloating of Edward before his outraged nobles when they find Gaveston sharing the royal throne (1.4), in the nobles' allegorical banners or "devices" that bear symbolic insults to Gaveston (2.2), in the more direct insults that opposing leaders fling at one another, in the smug delight of Mortimer and Isabel over her feigned concern for the imprisoned Edward (5.2), and in their defiance of Kent's attempts to influence the prince by Mortimer's physically carrying young Edward off stage (5.2). These nasty and contentious moments, marked by theatrical details of the playwright's own invention, are hardly ever graced with professions of the political ideals supposedly championed by such actions; they are instead presented as a kind of raw personal aggression. Thus, the process of both fighting and falling is dramatized as something radically private, much more so than is the case in *The Massacre at Paris*, where the much more visible parade of violence marches under the banners of opposed ideologies. That the good of the state should, in such a perspective, be so vulnerable to the power of personal animosities and obsessions is part of the tragic vision that Marlowe's play offers us. It reminds us of the broader reference in Holinshed's phrase, "the pitiful tragedy of this king's *time*."

The pathos of Edward II's last days, as well as the physical indignities and tortures inflicted upon him, including the grotesque means of his execution, were noted by the chroniclers Holinshed and Stow (who supplied the incident of the puddle-shaving). Marlowe added one major innovation in depicting Edward's death (the first death that actually takes place on stage in this play): Lightborn. His presence turns the murder scene into an altogether unexpected sort of experience, a cruel and gratuitous game of cat-and-mouse in which manifold ironies reveal themselves. Past critics have pointed to this character's name, an Anglicized form of "Lucifer," as an indication of his symbolically diabolic quality; they have also suggested a link between the diabolic hint and the mode of the murder, which takes on an allegorically retributive overtone with respect to Edward's homosexual past, outdoing Dante in matching hellish punishment to a particular sin. More immediately evident, however, is another aspect of Lightborn's role in setting a mood, in establishing a visual perspective for our last view of King Edward II, and, above all, in drawing the audience into the action in peculiarly discomfiting ways. Lightborn is a hired assassin, especially skilled in the art of murders ingeniously executed to leave no trace of the means of death. In his scene with Mortimer, he keeps the "secret" of how he will dispense with Edward to himself, leaving at least that part of the Elizabethan audience unfamiliar with the history in a particular kind of suspense. Edward's death is inevitable; *how* he will be killed becomes a special question for the viewer. What is Lightborn's "braver way"?

It certainly is not brave in the sense of courageous, for the weakened and desolate Edward is unable to offer any physical resistance at all, no matter what the threat. Lightborn implies rather that his murder will be admirably stunning in its ingenuity and "artistry"—something that will deserve not just a salary from Mortimer but a "bravo" from an audience. In fact, he asks for that response from Matrevis and Gurney in his last line: "was it not bravely done?" What he receives, of course, is his own death. But, in the meantime, Lightborn has also been asking us, the audience, to "appreciate" his artfulness. As Matrevis and Gurney leave him with the lantern so that he can see Edward in the dungeon, Lightborn confides to us: "ne'er was there any / So finely handled as this king shall be." He exudes a pride and delight in destruction, not exactly for its own sake, but for the sake of its performance.

Face to face with Edward, who distrusts him from the start, he pretends to be a friend, to bring comfort and joyful news. Indeed, he even goes so far as to shed tears of pity for Edward's wretched state. This bundle of behavior is hardly essential to the basic task at hand. In fact, it is a throwback to the dramaturgical behavior of the morality play Vice, who typically invited the audience to share his delight in mastery over his human victim and who pretended to be the opposite of what he really was, often by showing sympathy in the form of crocodile tears. For audiences familiar with those conventions, Lightborn, like Barabas, thus takes on some of the qualities of incarnate or allegorical evil. For all audiences, his manner exhibits a deeply ironic cruelty, a sadistic pleasure not so much in the physical pain he is about to inflict on Edward as in his absolute power over him.

It is in this latter regard that Lightborn's ironic role is most important, especially as the scene moves toward its horrific climax. After Edward's pitiful attempt to bribe Lightborn with the gift of his last jewel, Lightborn urges the king to "lie down and rest." Edward, still troubled, does so; he even bids Lightborn to stay with him as he does. There is a remarkable moment of hideous "peace," as the recumbent Edward falls quiet, his eyes closed. The visual picture mirrors the scene at Neath Abbey, where Edward, fearful and in need of protection, rested his head in the abbot's lap and closed his eyes. Here, as Edward drowses, Lightborn exclaims to

the audience, with what must be infinite self-confidence and self-congratu-
lation, "He sleeps." Edward will quickly start up from that sleep, as though
from a bad dream, and have to meet the nightmare of his execution. But,
in that strange moment of rest, with its replication of an earlier emblematic
scene of vulnerability and downfall, Marlowe summed up the irony of
Edward's life—a man lulled into false security by those who befriend him
in order to control him.

Even more disturbingly, Lightborn's invitation to us as spectators to
admire his art and power bears perhaps still another irony, no longer about
the history itself but about the artist and ourselves. Is his invitation to an
extraordinary execution the model of the tragic artist's more cynical side,
suggesting that we are all keenly interested in watching destruction and
violence? Do we approach what is to come—the repulsive, the gratuitously
cruel—as a fascinating work of art? Marlowe has offered us, through his
artful deceiver and destroyer Lightborn, as he has done through *Doctor
Faustus*, the fascination of what is damnable.

Chapter 7

Doctor Faustus:
Tragedy in the Allegorical Tradition

The Tragical History of Doctor Faustus is not only Marlowe's best-known
play but also the most often produced non-Shakespearean Elizabethan
drama in English professional theatre of the last century.[33] In textbooks
and anthologies of drama, it stands conventionally as the most notable
"bridge-piece" between the theatrical modes of medieval drama and the
more modern developments associated with the Renaissance stage. The
play's subject and theme have also earned for it a pivotal place in literary
and cultural history, marking as it does an important threshold between
images of medieval and modern man. Finally, it represents one of several
artistic achievements in the Western tradition that have explored and
re-explored the symbolic implications of the Faust legend, a legend that
has assumed, largely because of versions such as those created by Marlowe
and Goethe, the resonant proportions of myth.

Yet only the privilege of hindsight allows such a mapping of this play's
significance. Not many Englishmen of the early eighteenth century, for
example, would have or could have understood it in these terms. For them,
the fantastic adventures of the legendary German conjuror were most
familiar from the popular pantomime farces that drew London audiences
to the rival theatres of Drury Lane and Lincoln's Inn Fields in the 1720s;
there John Thurmond's *Harlequin Doctor Faustus* and John Rich's *Harlequin Necromancer* contrived to outdo one another in slapstick, music,
dance, and spectacular special effects. This was the culmination of a
theatrical tradition that had overtaken and swallowed up Marlowe's script

in the 1680s, when the popular appeal of Harlequin and Scaramouche on the English stage led William Mountfort to incorporate their antics into *The Life and Death of Doctor Faustus, Made into a Farce*. Both Alexander Pope and William Hogarth satirized this trend as a vulgar degradation of taste, the former amid his *Dunciad* (III, 229 ff.) and the latter in an engraving, *A just view of the British Stage*, which includes a bust of the Muse of Tragedy, her face plastered over with a playbill bearing the legend *Harlequin Doctor Faustus* (Butler 1952, 62).

From the strict vantage point of English theatrical history, then, it is also the case that Marlowe's *Doctor Faustus* stands on still another threshold, a narrow one, where somehow, for the space of one theatrical generation, a tragic rendering of this legend emerged from the traditions of homiletic chapbooks and morality drama, only to disappear into the contortions of farce and pantomime. The renewal of English interest in Faustus as a tragic figure would have to wait until the nineteenth century, when the reputation of Goethe's *Faust* called forth comparisons and contrasts with Marlowe's neglected Elizabethan play.[34]

A major difficulty in discussing *Doctor Faustus* is its problematical textual history. The earliest extant edition (of which only one copy survives) is dated 1604; this version is considerably shorter than the 1616 edition, in which the subplot activities of Wagner, Robin, and Ralph, incidents involving the hostile knight (there named Benvolio), and the spectacular appearances of the devils are all extended. Scholars have argued in the last half-century over which of these versions may be closer to Marlowe's original. Besides the usual problem of textual variants of individual lines, these scholars have addressed the issue of the larger structural contrast, with opposing results. For some, the shorter version is seen as a stripped-down alteration of a prior, longer, and more coherent scenario that is preserved in the 1616 edition; for others, the shorter version is seen as prior and the longer one as an extended adaptation resulting from non-Marlovian additions. Although certainty remains elusive, opinion in the last decade has shifted in favor of the earlier edition of 1604. We do know with certainty that, in 1602, the theatre manager Henslowe paid two other writers, William Birde and Samuel Rowley, for "additions" to the play, thus complicating the question of the extent of Marlowe's authorship in either of the extant printed versions. It is also difficult to specify when Marlowe first wrote the play. His major source for the story, an English adaptation and translation of a German prose tract (now called the "Faust Book") that was first published in 1587, survives (again in a single copy) in an edition dated 1592; its title page attests that it includes "newly amended" matter, a probable indication of an earlier (now lost) edition.

Henslowe's *Diary*, which begins in 1592, does not mention the play until September 1594.[35]

In order to appreciate the transforming achievement of Marlowe's play, we need to have some sense of the material from which he drew his story. The German Faust Book of 1587 was printed by Johann Spies, a conservative Lutheran who specialized in publishing theological treatises, sermons, jurisprudence, and official documents. Among these works, the Faust Book stood out as a virtual best seller, going through several printings in its first year; by 1600, translations had appeared in English, Danish, Dutch, and French. This widespread popular interest in the legendary sorcerer, about whom various anecdotes had been circulating throughout the sixteenth century, coincided not only with the height of the general European belief in witchcraft as a punishable heresy, but also with the efforts of churchmen in Germany to denigrate the attachment of folk culture to superstitious beliefs in spell-casters, fortune-tellers, and occult practices (Strauss 1989, 32).

The moralistic aim of the anonymous prose narrative is patent in its full German title: *The History of Dr. Johann Faustus, the World-Famous Sorcerer and Black Magician, How He Contracted Himself to the Devil for a Certain Time, What Strange Adventures He Saw and Pursued during This Time, Until in the End He Received His Just Reward, Compiled and Printed, Mostly from His Own Writings, as a Dreadful Example, Ghastly Case Study, and Faithful Warning to All Ambitious, Curious, and Godless Men.* The English translation reduces this to the terse *History of the Damnable Life and Deserved Death of Doctor John Faustus*, but it carries over in its narrative the unremitting emphasis on the career of Faustus as a negative example from start to finish. Its sixty-three chapters are divided into three parts. The first recounts Faustus' parleys with Mephistopheles concerning hell and devils, both before and after the signing of the pact; the second examines the growth of Faustus' regrets about his damnable situation and how Mephistopheles counters these, first with the threatening appearance of devils and then with the distracting wonders of world travel; the third catalogues a number of magical feats performed by Faustus at court and elsewhere, concluding with an account of his final despair and mysterious death by dismemberment. In each section, Faustus is revealed as alternately swept up in his speculations and activities, on the one hand, and depressed and frightened by his spiritual condition, on the other. The number and variety of Faustus' activities is extensive, ranging from forecasting weather and making astrological predictions, through performing practical jokes and magical illusions, to indulging in brigandage and sexual excess. Oddly, given the contemporary attribution of violent and fatal events to witches and devils, Faustus never causes anyone's death. Although he does once ask his diabolic servants to kill a pious old man who had admonished Faustus to repent his sins, the old man comes to no harm. The history is intent rather on the self-destructive aspects of Faustus' career. The homiletic voice of the narrator persistently points out the dreadful mistakes Faustus makes and the delusions to which he falls victim. Indirect sermons are also woven into the discourse, not only in the admonitions of the virtuous old man but also in comments by Mephistopheles and in a final exhortation by Faustus to his own students.[36]

Marlowe's play, while necessarily condensing much of the material in his eighty-page source, remains fairly close to the Faust Book's basic outline of Faustus' career. Certain theatrical elements from the medieval tradition of morality drama are added (such as the Good and Evil Angels, the Seven Deadly Sins). In line with the subplotting practices of much Tudor drama, the play also adds a level of comic action in which servants (Wagner, Robin, and Ralph) unconsciously parody the actions and motives of the protagonist. Most important, Marlowe invented opening and closing scenes that reveal the inner depths of Faustus' desires and fears, defined in ways unmatched in the Faust Book. Still, Marlowe did not invent any new feats for Faustus or new requests to make of his servant devil once the pact is made. The thwarted request for a wife, the travels (including the slapstick disruption of the Papal banquet), the appearances of Alexander and Helen of Troy, the horns grown on the insulting knight, the grapes brought to the Duchess, the swindling of the horse-courser—all these deeds are replicated from the Faust Book. Marlowe's originality lies in redefining the internal qualities of Doctor Faustus, in providing him with a set of motives and attitudes, both at the start and end of his magician's career, which develop the tragic potentiality in his story.

The germ of that tragedy lies in the Faust Book's focus on the irony of self-destruction, on the paradox of a learned doctor of divinity trading his eternal soul for twenty-four years of the devil's service. The extreme exemplar for this "worst corruption of the best" is, of course, Lucifer—the brightest of angels, whose pride, religious tradition taught, led him to attempt to displace God and thence to his eternal punishment and enmity with God. More than once, the Faust Book narrator comments on the parallel between the fall of Lucifer and that of Faustus. When Faustus hears that Mephistopheles serves Lucifer, the narrator states that the Doctor is so taken with the notion of commanding such a powerful spirit that:

he forgot the Lord his maker, and Christ his redeemer, became an enemy unto all mankind, yea, worse than the Giants whom the poets

feign to climb the hills to make war with the gods: not unlike that
enemy of God and his Christ, that for his pride was cast into hell: so
likewise Faustus forgot that the high climbers catch the greatest falls.
(Palmer [1936] 1965, 142)

The allusion to the Titans of classical mythology, allegorized in the Faust
Book as evil rebels, is a rare instance in this writer's style; Marlowe, as
we shall see, surrounded his Faustus with several telling mythological
allusions. Later, Mephistopheles recounts the fall of Lucifer and flatters
Faustus that he is "one of the beloved children of my Lord Lucifer,
following and feeding thy mind in manner as he did his" (Palmer 1965,
148). Faustus finally draws his own self-condemning parallel a few
chapters later, in the midst of one of his remorseful meditations (Palmer
1965, 151). The figure is fixed: Faustus repeats the sin of Lucifer in
aspiring to godhead; his fall is the fall of the mighty in intellectual and
spiritual endowments—and hence tragic by one mechanical definition of
that term.

Marlowe's incorporation of this motif is managed with considerably
more sophistication and irony. He invoked it first in the mythological
imagery of the opening Chorus:

> —shortly he was graced with doctor's name,
> Excelling all whose sweet delight disputes
> In heavenly matters of theology;
> Till, swoll'n with cunning of a self-conceit,
> His waxen wings did mount above his reach,
> And melting heavens conspired his overthrow. (17–22)

The immediate allusion is to Icarus, who, in Ovid's retelling of the myth
in *Metamorphoses* (III, 180–230), fails to heed his father's warning not to
fly too high with his artificial wings, whose feathers are held on by wax
that eventually melts from the heat of the sun. Icarus is heedless, rather
than proud, but Marlowe's yoking of the image with "self-conceit" and
with Faustus' place of excellence in "heavenly" theology prepares us for
the eventual parallel with Lucifer.

Marlowe next wove this idea into the pattern of rationalization whereby
Faustus, in his opening soliloquy, rejects the usual intellectual and professional pursuits—a process not presented in the Faust Book. Philosophy
(or logic), aimed at disputing well, is rejected as affording "no greater
miracle." That Faustus is aiming at working miracles is confirmed by his
dissatisfaction with medicine:

Wouldst thou make man to live eternally?
Or, being dead, raise them to life again?
Then this profession were to be esteemed. (1.1.24–26)

Faustus, frustrated by the limits of his humanity ("Yet art thou still but
Faustus and a man"), yearns for God's powers, and his speech moves
inexorably to the rejection of theology—"Divinity, adieu!"—and to his
sense of the final goal of magic:

A sound magician is a mighty god.
Here, Faustus, try thy brains to gain a deity. (1.1.64–65)

Faustus turns his back on God in order to become his own god. When,
after conjuring Mephistopheles, he asks how Lucifer became prince of
devils, he receives the laconic answer:

O, by aspiring pride and insolence,
For which God threw him from the face of heaven. (1.3.69–70)

Marlowe's Faustus, unlike his Faust Book model, does not make the
connection, but Marlowe provided the audience with the perspective from
which they can see the parallel to which Faustus himself is ironically blind.
There is additional irony, of course, in a doctor of divinity's needing to be
told about Lucifer in the first place, since Lucifer's traditional image is
derived from the passage in Isaiah 14:12–15: "How art thou fallen from
heaven, O Lucifer, son of the morning. . . . For thou hast said in thine
heart . . . I will ascend above the heights of clouds; I will be like the most
High. Yet thou shalt be brought down to hell." Marlowe wove the
archetype of self-destructive aspiration so central to this imaging into a
more complex configuration of motifs involving a wide range of goals
for human activity and achievement. He also merged this seeking into
an intellectual process that embodies the paradox of man's using the
power of reason to choose a course of ruin.
    We need to look at that process first, if only because our contemporary
sense of reason in an age of computerized artificial intelligence, on the one
hand, and of supersensitivity to the force of the irrational and the uncon-
scious, on the other, is so remote from the Renaissance perspective on
reason and its value. In the "psychology" of Marlowe's time, reason is the
intellectual faculty or power that defines what is human and not merely
animal, that provides a basis for human dignity and morality. Both Shakespeare's Hamlet, who calls reason "god-like," and John Donne, who terms

it as God's "viceroy" in one of his "Holy Sonnets," allude to the notion that reason is a gift from and a reflection of the creator. Reason gives human beings the power to discern, as will gives them the power to choose and to act on the basis of what they know and discern. Taken together, reason and will form the basis for moral responsibility.

This perspective allows us to see in Faustus' opening soliloquy further ironies. The orderly process by which a man of uncommon intellectual attainments examines each academic discipline by reflecting on key texts drawn from an authoritative book in the field seems appropriate enough, even if, as noted above, the discipline is discarded on grounds that have little to do with its own purposes. When Faustus moves to the Bible, however, his reflection takes the shape of a syllogism. He conjoins two partial quotations—"the reward of sin is death" and "if we say that we have no sin we deceive ourselves"—as major and minor premises. He then concludes from them that we are doomed to sin and death. This vision of a predetermined and inevitable doom he finds too fatalistic ("What doctrine call you this—*Che serà, serà?*"), and, on this basis, he discards Divinity. Faustus' logical skills, however, are manifestly mocked by his selection of premises—each a familiar New Testament quotation, but each of which he has truncated, leaving out the "good news" in the completion. The first, from Romans 6:23, continues, "but the gift of God is eternal life through Jesus Christ our Lord." The second, from 1 John 1:8, adds: "If we acknowledge our sins, He is faithful and just to forgive us our sins and to cleanse us from all unrighteousness." The full quotation from John was in fact part of the opening of one of the official sermons promulgated in Elizabeth's reign to be preached each year throughout the realm.[37] Marlowe thus presented us with a logician exercising his rational skill with half-truths and faulty premises, a doctor of divinity turning scriptural texts into pretexts for abandoning theology.

There is more than irony here. From the perspective of Renaissance thought, this mode of turning away from God, through the exercise of reason rather than through sensual inclination or passion, was judged to be more reprehensible than other sins, even more obviously violent and destructive ones, precisely because it was an abuse of rational intelligence. John Donne expressed this judgment in one of his sermons:

Whilst we sin strongly, by oppressing others that are weaker, or craftily, by circumventing others that are simple, this is but *leoninum* and *vulpinum*, that tincture of the lion and of the fox, that brutal nature that is in us. But when we come to sin upon reason and upon discourse, upon meditation and upon plot, this is *humanum*, to become the Man of Sin, to surrender that which is the form and essence of man, reason and understanding, to the service of sin. When we come to sin wisely and learnedly, to sin logically, by a *quia* and an *ergo*, that, because God does thus, we may do as we do, we shall come to sin through all the arts and all our knowledge. (Donne 1953–59, 1:225)

This is not a notion that modern readers and audiences are likely to have in the back of their minds as they respond to the career of Dr. Faustus, especially since, in the course of his career as magician, he seems not to cause any serious harm to others. The penalty of damnation seems somehow excessive, given that relatively harmless record. But to interpret the evil of destruction in such pragmatic terms is to miss the more serious point about self-destruction made in the play and in reference to the theological outlook of its times. What Faustus destroys *in himself* is what terrifies here; what man does to the source of dignity within him—his reason—is the issue.

The image of Faustus as scholar and intellectual has still further repercussions in Marlowe's presentation. Faustus sees his choice of magic as superior not only to Divinity, but also to other applications of the human intellect in philosophy, law, and medicine. His grounds for doing so, however, are centered not in these disciplines' limitations as sources of knowledge or truth, but as sources of power. Even his rejection of Divinity is provoked by scriptural texts that seem to insist on the powerlessness of man to escape a sinful and mortal condition. When he finally turns to the "heavenly" books of magic, his most insistent desires and goals are clear:

> O, what a world of profit and delight,
> Of power, of honour, of omnipotence,
> Is promised to the studious artisan!
> All things that move between the quiet poles
> Shall be at my command. Emperors and kings
> Are but obeyed in their several provinces,
> Nor can they raise the wind or rend the clouds;
> But his dominion that exceeds in this
> Stretcheth as far as doth the mind of man. (1.1.55–63)

Power, omnipotence, command, dominion—the pulse of Faustus' life-blood is felt in these words as the verse hammers home. There is no precedent for this in the Faust Book, nor for the expansion of this motivation that is provided by further monologues in which Faustus envisions what he will do with magical power and by the encouragements of Valdes and Cornelius. How far do the minds of these men stretch? Even before the others join him, Faustus begins to imagine his agenda, cued by the promptings of the Evil Angel to discover "all nature's treasury" and to become "Lord and commander of these elements" (1.1.77–79):

> Shall I make spirits fetch me what I please,
> Resolve me of all ambiguities,
> Perform what desperate enterprise I will?
> I'll have them fly to India for gold,
> Ransack the ocean for orient pearl,
> And search all corners of the new-found world
> For pleasant fruits and princely delicates. (1.1.81–87)

The intellectual's goal of resolving ambiguities is smothered by the more exciting prospect of global treasure-gathering, a temptation pointedly attuned to the ambitions of the age of Renaissance world exploration. The speech continues in a more haphazard way, moving beyond the satisfaction of personal desires for exotic wealth and for hearing "strange philosophy" into a series of imagined projects to benefit Germany: Faustus will gather the "secrets of all foreign kings," build a brass wall around the entire country, divert the Rhine to circle Wittenberg, dress students in silk, raise armies to rout the Prince of Parma, invent strange military weaponry, and—bringing it all back to himself—"reign sole king of all our provinces." This is the last we ever hear or see of Faustus' agenda for Germany; by the time he has first conjured up Mephistopheles, he is dreaming of becoming "great emperor of the world" and linking continents by miraculous engineering.

The grand political schemes are temporarily eclipsed, however, when Valdes and Cornelius amplify the theme of personal wealth amassed from around the world by their serving spirits. Valdes sees them bringing in "huge argosies" from Venice (the mercantile capital of Renaissance Europe) and a veritable "golden fleece" from America; Cornelius adds that the spirits:

> can dry the sea
> And fetch the treasure of all foreign wrecks—
> Ay, all the wealth that our forefathers hid
> Within the massy entrails of the earth. (1.1.146–49)

A less materialistic but no less exotic vision accompanies these imagined projects in Valdes' evocation of the varied forms in which spirits will serve them:

Like lions shall they guard us when we please,
Like Almaine rutters with their horsemen's staves,
Or Lapland giants, trotting by our sides;
Sometimes like women, or unwedded maids,
Shadowing more beauty in their airy brows
Than in the white breasts of the Queen of Love. (1.1.126–31)

The three-way conversation is a choral adaptation of the kind of poetic rhetoric distilled in Marlowe's lyric "Come Live with Me and Be My Love." It is a mutual seduction piece, in which fantasy paints a rainbow picture of exotic wealth and of spirits parading in fairy-tale shapes.

Nothing so grandiose or fanciful is dreamt of by Faustus in the Faust Book, nor do any of his fabled adventures recounted there match these anticipated "miracles that magic will perform." Marlowe has his own way of defining unbounded aspiration, as well as his own purpose in framing Faustus' career with such visions. It is now a critical commonplace that the structure of his play, with its emphasis on the illusory and sometimes farcical tricks of Faustus' career, offers an indirect comment on how the actual exercise of diabolic power trivializes and degrades. In other words, Faustus' actual achievements are a parody of his original ambitions, and the subplot's demonstration of the ridiculous uses that magic power comes to in the minds of the servants is a further parodic reflection of the same theme. What has been less noticed is the declension of aspiration visible even in the earliest scenes of the play, the modulation of desire from the level that seeks god-like dominion, miracles of resurrection, and life everlasting, to the level that seeks magical command of nature's elements to promote political power through miracles of engineering, diplomatic intelligence, and warfare, and down again to the level that seeks untold wealth from around the world, sauced with the companionship of apparitions that comfort the magician and frighten others. "The mind of man" disclosed in this fantastic stretching exercise already reveals its retrograde limitations, its material and self-centered direction. Bursting all boundaries, daring its utmost, the human mind formulates an agenda of cosmic self-aggrandizement, settles for much less than that in the offing, and, in the process, loses its dignity and its soul without ever noticing.

Here is Marlowe's metaphysical tracing of the hidden corrupting process of even the imagination of power. His depiction moves the archetype of Lucifer into a less literal context, in which the self-limiting and self-destructive aspects of aspiration are defined and felt in more human terms, spelled out in a pattern of deviant reason and will. The human image tragically defaces itself in the quest for the superhuman. The Renaissance image of man enshrined in the writings of the learned Florentine, Pico della Mirandola, provides a potential blueprint for this formula for tragedy, placing man so powerfully and, at the same time, so precariously within the cosmos. In his *Oration on the Dignity of Man* (1486), Pico imagined the Creator's address to Adam:

> The nature of all other beings is limited and constrained within the bounds of laws prescribed by Us. Thou, constrained by no limits, in accordance with thine own free will, in whose hands We have placed thee, shalt ordain for thyself the limits of thy nature. We have set thee at the world's center that thou mayest from thence more easily observe whatever is in the world. We have made thee neither of heaven nor of earth, neither mortal nor immortal, so that with freedom of choice and with honor, as though the maker and molder of thyself, thou mayest fashion thyself in whatever shape thou shalt prefer. Thou shalt have the power to degenerate into the lower forms of life, which are brutish. Thou shalt have the power, out of thy soul's judgment, to be reborn into the higher forms, which are divine. (Cassirer 1948, 225)

As Marlowe defined him, Faustus, frustrated with the limits of his humanity, seeks to extend those limits, but, with each step that he takes "upwards," he exemplifies and at times experiences an ironic sinking. That pattern continues throughout the play, stressed by several additional ironies: the refusal of Faustus to acknowledge the witness of the devil he has called upon to provide answers to his questions about hell; the devil's refusal to fulfill certain requests (such as for a wife, or to answer the question about who made the universe); the reversal of master and servant roles that occurs whenever Faustus, tempted to repent, is browbeaten into submission by the demons; and the double-edged imagery in which Faustus' most ecstatic moments are couched, so as to reveal simultaneously their self-destructive implications. Many of these ironies were already present in the Faust Book, but, in nearly every case, Marlowe added his own twist to sharpen their effect and to expose more trenchantly the weaknesses and self-delusions of the mind that has given itself over to unlimited desire. Pico della Mirandola saw in the human capacity to make of itself what it wished the basis of human dignity; Marlowe placed the literal motif of shape-changing into his scenario at a very ironic moment. After Faustus' repeated thoughts of repentance have been met with the terrifying appearance of Lucifer and Beelzebub, and when he is frightened into making promises of obedience to them, he is rewarded with a comic pageant of the Seven Deadly Sins. His response, "O, this feeds my soul!" (2.3.166), is hardly in keeping with his earlier visions of unbounded greatness, no more than his cowering before the demons matches his original thirst for god-like power. This is the moment when the departing Lucifer bestows on the grateful Faustus yet another reward—a book: "Peruse it thoroughly," Lucifer bids, "and thou shalt turn thyself into what shape thou wilt" (2.3.171–73). The change has already begun.

The episode of the Seven Deadly Sins is one of those allegorical devices, along with the Good and Evil Angels, that Marlowe added to his retelling of the Faust story. On the face of it, these are derived from the theatrical tradition of morality drama, which had been a part of English theatrical practice since the fifteenth century and had survived, albeit in much altered forms, into the Tudor age. The earliest examples presented the universal paradigm of temptation, fall, and redemption in the form of homiletic allegory: An abstract Mankind or Everyman figure is tempted by some personified Vice or Vices (always disguised as something more pleasant) and recovers from his fall with the aid of personified Virtues. In several early instances (such as *The Castle of Perseverance*), the human protagonist is relegated to a relatively passive role, as Vices and Virtues contend directly with one another in vigorous exchanges and emblematic battles. When devils have a part in the action, they are typically "invisible" to the humans, preferring to work their wiles through the agency of the Vices. By the sixteenth century, the thematic focus of morality plays had narrowed to more specialized issues; the universal problem of sin and redemption had given way to moral lessons in good and bad government, for instance, or good and bad habits of study.[38]

Thus, when Marlowe's play introduced allegorical figures with such patently theological labels, he was not reflecting the typical conventions of the Tudor morality play or interlude. Moreover, Marlowe's use of those "throwback" figures differs substantially from late medieval practice as well, so that it is not in fact accurate to see his play as a step along some evolutionary path leading from medieval theatrical forms to more modern, realistic ones. The core of the Faustus story derives from the Faust Book, rather than from a theatrical tradition. Indeed, it is quite possible to imagine a production of Marlowe's play without the Angels or the Deadly Sins. Their presence merely reinforces, rather than reconfigures, the issues at stake in Faustus' self-destructive career.

In the case of the Seven Deadly Sins, for example, Marlowe has provided a self-contained episode; these sins have no conventional medieval role as disguised tempters of the human protagonist. Faustus has already fallen, and, even in the contested moment of possible repentance, they play no part in influencing his submission to Lucifer. They have been transformed into an entertaining show. The irony is not the usual one, which stresses the evil "hidden" under some more attractive disguise, but a new one, which stresses their comically self-confessed evil to which Faustus responds with delight. Marlowe gave Faustus the "transforming power" of putting heavenly labels on grotesque shapes: "This sight will be as pleasing unto me as paradise was to Adam" is his comment.[39] The self-deluding aspect of this kind of transformation is paramount. (See Illustration 11.)

The Faust Book's treatment of this episode helps us to see more clearly Marlowe's new direction. Lucifer and a whole host of devils appear in monstrous, animal-hybrid forms to terrify Faustus; Lucifer bids all but seven to depart. Then, with no intervening action or explanation, the others disappear as well. Mephistopheles shows up as a fire-spitting dragon before changing back to his friar's shape, prompting Faustus to ask if he might do the like. Lucifer gives Faustus a book, which the Doctor uses immediately to change himself into a hog, a worm, and a dragon—"and finding this for his purpose, it liked him well" (Palmer 1965, 165). There is an insistent literalism in the detailed description of these monstrosities, even though the author is also making the point that Faustus is only identifying himself more closely with the devils as he secures this new magical power to make himself over into "filthy forms." Marlowe's adaptation of the scene shows the transformation primarily in Faustus' mind and attitude—his happy self-delusion is perhaps prophetic of Milton's Satan, who is confident that the mind can make a hell of heaven and a heaven of hell.

What is going on in Faustus' mind is also the key to Marlowe's handling of the Good and Evil Angels. They do not initiate options for Faustus, as strictly external forces in a conventional morality drama might do; rather, they appear in response to what Faustus has already been thinking about. Their first appearance follows his rejection of religion, and the Evil Angel's exhortation at that point is an echo of Faustus' own conception of what magic can do. They appear again at the first indication that Faustus has second thoughts about the venture he has proposed to Mephistopheles but which has not yet been contracted. Before their entry, Faustus wavers back and forth, but he ends for the moment on the side of evil, vowing even devil-worship and human sacrifice:

Illustration 11. 1968 Royal Shakespeare Company production of *Doctor Faustus.* Faustus (Eric Porter) enjoys the bizarre spectacle of the Seven Deadly Sins in the production directed by Clifford Williams. (© Photograph by Douglas H. Jeffery.)

The god thou servest is thine own appetite,
Wherein is fixed the love of Beelzebub.
To him I'll build an altar and a church,
And offer lukewarm blood of new-born babes. (2.1.11–14)

When Faustus, in their presence, asks, "Contrition, prayer, repentance—what of them?" the Evil Angel's response—"illusions, fruits of lunacy"—echoes Faustus' own image for thoughts of God and heaven as "vain fancies." The same principle operates in the Angels' third appearance, when Faustus' observation of the heavens turns his mind again to God and to thoughts of repentance, even in the presence of Mephistopheles. The Angels embody and dramatize more vividly the see-saw conflict that originates in Faustus' own mind—they never interact directly with one another, as is conventional in morality drama.[40] More important, they never force a conclusion; Faustus makes up his own mind. Their constant intrusions, nonetheless, are vivid indications that Faustus does have the option to change his course, that even his contract signed in blood has not sealed his doom. The degree to which the other devils continually work at threatening and distracting Faustus is another such indication, although that role was already theirs in the Faust Book. Marlowe's dramaturgy enhances that pattern. In doing so, it stresses the theme that Faustus chooses his self-destructive path over and over again, forging his own painful destiny, even at later moments in his career when some of the initial glamour of wielding diabolic power has been tarnished by certain frustrations. When, in his last hour, blatant fear moves him to thoughts of repentance and he seems powerless to act, the cumulative force of all his earlier choices strikes with ironic insistence. He is his choice, forever.

We have seen how the Evil Angel picks up on images and ideas that are already energizing Faustus' thoughts and wishes, cheering him along, as it were, in the direction that they both want for different reasons. In the early interactions between Faustus and Mephistopheles, by contrast, Marlowe presented a curiously opposite dynamic. Mephistopheles says things that Faustus does not want to hear, much less believe. He gives witness to aspects of his own reality that Faustus, in redefining the limits of human potentiality, prefers to abolish, especially hell and damnation. The Faust Book presents part of the paradox, insofar as it exhibits a man who, while trafficking with the devil in a very literal and explicit way, at the same time does not believe "that there was a God, hell, or devil: he thought that body and soul died together, and had quite forgotten divinity or the immortality of his soul" (Palmer 1965, 146). The comment comes after the contract and the first Epicurean delights provided by Mephistopheles—rich food, wine, and sumptuous apparel stolen from the best houses of Germany. Marlowe chose to highlight the paradox at a much earlier moment, in the initial interviews between Faustus and Mephistopheles, when Faustus seeks to know more about this devil and his origins. When Mephistopheles replies that he is damned in hell with Lucifer, Faustus prods, "How comes it then that thou art out of hell?" Mephistopheles provides a most unexpected answer:

> Why, this is hell, nor am I out of it.
> Think'st thou that I, who saw the face of God
> And tasted the eternal joys of heaven,
> Am not tormented with ten thousand hells
> In being deprived of everlasting bliss?
> O Faustus, leave these frivolous demands,
> Which strike a terror to my fainting soul! (1.3.78–84)

This is an astonishing exclamation in more ways than one. The most obviously surprising thing about it, given the traditional lore about the tempting and deceiving roles of the devil, is its emotional exhortation that Faustus stop his damnable quest. Moreover, his definition of hell's pain as the psychological torment of having lost God (echoing a long-standing theological teaching about the worst pain of damnation) is never found in the Faust Book, which dwells in hideous detail on a multitude of physical torments. The notion is tied to the theme of self-deformity that pervades Marlowe's handling of the Faust story; Milton re-orchestrated the same theme in his depiction of the Satan who discovers "Myself am Hell." Marlowe's Faustus, however, hears the passionate outcry but scoffs it away, urging Mephistopheles to learn "manly fortitude" from him and "scorn those joys thou never shalt possess" (1.3.87–88). The blind arrogance of this response is in line with Faustus' ironic blindness to his own parallel with Lucifer, evoked earlier in the same scene. Nothing, not even a devil who reverses his tempter's role, will stop Faustus from seeing only what he wants to see. He needs no tempting, for he has already made up his mind, already drafted his contract.

The irony is, of course, compounded when Faustus decides to learn more about hell just *after* he has signed his compact. The Faust Book's extensive version of this episode (which does not come as Faustus' initial request) paints a ghastly picture of hideous torments familiar in medieval art, complete with devils tossing human carcasses back and forth with muckforks amid the fire and stench (Palmer 1965, 156). Marlowe's Mephistopheles, by contrast, repeats what he had said before: "Hell hath no limits, nor is circumscribed / In one self place, for where we are is hell" (2.1.124–25). Faustus still does not get it; "I think hell's a fable," he says, despite Mephistopheles' insistence that he is an instance to prove the contrary. Faustus, who will readily understand the later threats of devils to tear him into pieces, cannot understand a state of suffering defined as an inner sense of loss and isolation from God—until it is too late.

What we see in Marlowe's transformation of the Faust Book material, again and again, is a consistent deepening of psychological insight into the habits of mind, imagination, will, and desire that forge the protagonist's tragic destiny. He has reshaped the magician's fundamental motivation from the source's combination of random curiosity and Epicurean self-indulgence into a metaphysical restlessness with the constraints of the human condition, an obsessive thirst for superhuman power that swiftly and ironically diminishes its visionary scope at the very moment that it touches the "forbidden fruit" of diabolic agency. The same man who intoxicates himself with the grand vision of unlimited material possibilities refuses to acknowledge the realities of self-deforming and self-destructive pain in the spirits who serve him. That measure of ironic blindness is amplified immediately after the contract is signed by the sequence of requests that Marlowe's Faustus initiates. The very first piece of new information that the ex-doctor of divinity requests concerns the nature of hell—which he rejects as soon as it is proffered. Having sold his soul to the devil for the promise of having his every wish granted, the visionary who wanted world empery now asks for a wife! More ironically still, he cannot have one, since Mephistopheles cannot supply a participant in an institution created by God. He can promise whores galore, and he can provide instantly a grotesque spectacle to impress Faustus. The pattern of settling for less and of indulging in illusory spectacle is thus established as the pattern of Faustus' magical career. To it will be added a trivial delight in playing practical jokes with the help of illusions, as in the farcical scenes with the Pope, with the insulting knight, and with the horse-courser. These are all lifted from the Faust Book, but their ironic banality has been amplified by their contrast with the earlier grand visions of Marlowe's invention. The defiantly untrammeled mind, left to its own devices, ironically becomes satisfied with the role of international court entertainer.

Even that measure of satisfaction is shadowed by Faustus' recurring conflicts of conscience, as punctuated with his Good and Evil Angels. The resolution of those conflicts, effected by the devils' combination of physical threats and sensational treats, further diminishes Faustus' stature by revealing the extent to which he becomes servile to the forces that he supposed would serve him. Moved by very primal instincts of pleasure and pain, the man of extraordinary intellectual prowess and unbounded individual aspiration gradually cedes control of himself to the destructive demons.

Faustus' fall is thus not a matter of physical affliction and death, but an interior diminishing of the spirit, a narrowing of imagination and purpose, and a self-blinding immersion in delusion. His ironically climactic liaison with the spectral form of Helen of Troy stands as an ultimate ironic emblem of that process. There, Faustus' rapturous celebration of antiquity's most famous *femme fatale* is expressed in imagery that, taken in context, reveals to the audience the destructive opposite of the transcendent glow that Faustus casts upon the moment. We know from the earliest instance of necromancy, when Faustus explained to the emperor that the apparitions of Alexander and his paramour were spirits in the shape of the ancient figures, that his magic is limited to these "insubstantial" resurrections (another ironic contrast with his initial monologue's wish that medicine might bring the dead back to life). The eerie silence attendant upon those apparitions, which is repeated in the first Helen scene and again in this one, is a reminder of the spectral and demonic quality of her presence. There is another relevant repetition, too, in how this last request that Faustus makes of Mephistopheles mirrors his first request for a wife. Then he had asked for "the fairest maid in Germany, for I am wanton and lascivious" (2.1.144); now he seeks "heavenly Helen" as his paramour "to glut the longing of [his] heart's desire" (5.1.83) and to blot out the thoughts of heaven inimical to his fealty to Lucifer. The roots of his erotic yearnings are revealed in what one would hardly call a romantic way. Still, his poetic address to Helen soars and waxes above his confessed need for a sexual opiate:

> Was this the face that launched a thousand ships
> And burnt the topless towers of Ilium?
> Sweet Helen, make me immortal with a kiss.
> Her lips suck forth my soul. See where it flies!
> Come, Helen, come, give me my soul again.
> Here will I dwell, for heaven be in these lips,
> And all is dross that is not Helena. (5.1.91–97)

The ironic spectacle of Faustus clasping this demonic apparition in his arms, asking her to bestow "immortality" upon him, imaging the loss of his soul in her kisses and heaven in her lips, is matched in its trenchant double meanings by what Marlowe provided in the remainder of the speech. Here Faustus fantasizes replaying the heroic role of Paris, battling

Menelaus and Achilles while wearing Helen's colors on his "plumed crest"; what he crowds out of the image is the destruction that Paris met with as the ultimate result of his abducting Helen. Similarly, with the next hyperbolic simile drawn from mythology—"Brighter art thou than flaming Jupiter / When he appeared to hapless Semele" (5.1.106–07)—Faustus places himself in the role of the human lover whose closeness to the fiery god resulted in Semele's incendiary death. Transcendent aspiration, self-delusion, the willful inversion of heaven and hell, self-destruction— all these elements in Faustus' career intersect in this deeply ironic tableau. It is one of the finest instances of Marlowe's ability to make the most of his poetic lyricism within a theatrical context where every image and every gesture convey a double-edged significance.

Ironies abound as well in the admirably orchestrated final soliloquy of Marlowe's Faustus, which seems consciously and carefully designed as the antithesis to the early soliloquies, with their dreams of miraculous power. Faustus' dreams are now nightmares, as he seeks through the force of his imagination to change or to delay his destiny. He is discovering that he cannot change the self that he has remade in the continual rejection of God's image. He is discovering to his dismay that where he is, transformed by his persistent will, is hell. Death will not end it. His frantic last commands convey an ironic wish to destroy his own humanity, to disintegrate himself into elements, to become nothing. But just as he is impotent to stop time, he is also impotent to stop his being. It is not death that frightens him now, not the prospect of being torn into pieces, but the permanence of his soul, his immortality.

Marlowe achieved some miracle-working of his own in distilling some poetic gold from the extensive dross found in the Faust Book's treatment of the last thoughts of Faustus. The narrator of the book actually provided no view of the magician's feelings after he bids his desperate farewell to the students, but before that disconsolate last banquet, which is highlighted by a lengthy sermon by Faustus admonishing them to avoid his foul example, the Faust Book devotes several pages to the magician's lonely lamentations during the final month of his life. Just a taste or two should be enough to indicate its bathos:

Oh poor, woeful and weary wretch; oh sorrowful soul of Faustus, now art thou in the number of the damned, for now must I wait for unmeasurable pains of death, yea, far more lamentable than ever yet any creature hath suffered. Ah, senseless, willful and desperate forgetfulness! O cursed and unstable life! O blind and careless wretch, that so hast abused thy body, sense and soul! O foolish pleasure, into what a weary labyrinth hast thou brought me, blinding mine eyes in the clearest day! . . . how happy wert thou if as an unreasonable beast thou mightest die without soul, so shouldst thou not feel any more doubts. But now the devil will take thee away both body and soul, and set thee in an unspeakable place of darkness, for although others' souls have rest and peace, yet I, poor damned wretch, must suffer all manner of filthy stench, pains, cold, hunger, thirst, heat, freezing, burning, hissing, gnashing, and all the wrath and curse of God. (Palmer 1965, 224–25)

To be fair, there are hints here and there that Marlowe chose to develop, such as the "unreasonable beast" wish above, and others: "Time ran away with Faustus as the hour glass" (Palmer 1965, 223); "Would God that I knew where to hide me, or into what place to creep" (Palmer 1965, 224); "and for a soul to Godwards that have I not, for I shame to speak unto him; if I do, no answer shall he make me, but he will hide his face from me" (Palmer 1965, 225). Marlowe changed the hour glass to a striking clock, but, more significantly, he shifted the blubbering and self-pitying mode of the Faust Book's complaint into a more dynamic and theatrical pattern of increasingly frantic commands that receive no response. The magus who wished to become "lord and commander of the elements" first orders the "ever-moving spheres of heaven" to stand still, "that time may cease and midnight never come"; then he bids the sun rise again to provide more light and more time for him to repent. He caps this inevitably frustrated demand with a Latin tag (always the scholar!) from Ovid's *Amores*, a line beseeching the horses of the night to run slowly, slowly. For those who recall its context in Ovid's poem, where the plea is that of a lover who does not want to leave the arms of his mistress, there is a special irony. But, as Faustus looks up and sees the stars still moving, he knows his magic power cannot work this miracle: "Time runs."

In the next section of the speech (5.2.77–85), which starts with a Godward impulse—"I'll leap up to my God!"—the sense of powerlessness is intensified by movements and gestures that suggest the invisible hand of the devil inflicting physical force and pain upon Faustus. The effect has been prepared for in the earlier scene with the students, where Faustus laments that the devil stops him from weeping tears of repentance, stays his tongue, and holds his hands down when he wishes to raise them in prayer. Now, the leap to God, which seems to demand an upward physical gesture, must also be followed by a stumble or fall in mid-line; bewildered, Faustus asks, "Who pulls me down?" Again, he looks skyward and sees a vision of Christ's blood streaming in the firmament. Calling on Christ, he feels a sudden inward pain, which he attributes to diabolic force. The plea, "rend not my heart for naming of my Christ," recalling those earlier scenes in which devils stormed in to stop him from repentant thoughts, is clearly directed to those same devils, as the following line, "oh, spare me, Lucifer!" confirms. The terrifying visual impact of this wrenching back and forth by unseen forces vividly expresses the cumulative reversal of master and servant roles between Faustus and the devils, as well as the theological concept of the gradual loss of self-command that inheres in habitual and repeated sin. When the tormented Faustus has his next chance to look up, the vision of redeeming blood has been replaced by one of God as wrathful judge.

Faustus, terrified, tries commanding nature once again. His next command takes the form of a Biblical image (Luke 23:30) describing fear at the time of apocalyptic judgment: "Then shall they begin to say to the mountains, 'Fall on us,' and to the hills, 'Cover us.'" His following command is addressed to the earth in which he seeks protection: "Earth, gape! O no, it will not harbour me" (5.2.88). Again, one senses an implicit pause in mid-line, as Faustus waits, ever more desperately, for his magic words to take effect. Meanwhile, the mood of hysterical hallucination is building (after all, the audience does not *see* any of these visions, mountains, and hills), and Faustus' commands become increasingly bizarre. His next, addressed to the stars, seems to ask that his body be sucked up into a thundercloud and exploded within it, so that his soul, set free from his limbs, may float up to heaven.

The clock strikes again, bringing him back to sober reality. Commands give way to a desperate prayer—for a finite rather than an eternal punishment. Faustus still tries to rewrite his world and to turn its laws his way. This time, however, he recognizes the delusion. Next, the man who once yearned for godlike status wishes he could die like a beast, leaving no soul to survive his body. Finally, as the clock strikes twelve, he reverts to commands once more, urging his body to turn into air and his soul into waterdrops. He wishes his humanity away; he wishes the extinction of self. But he is still there, screaming, as Lucifer and Mephistopheles drag him off.

In the 1616 text, the inner horrors of Faustus' last hour are compromised by the addition of scenes that frame it with spectacular supernatural machinery, on the one hand, and with gory sensationalism, on the other. The final hour is prefaced with a scene in which the devils gloat in Faustus' presence over their triumph. First, Mephistopheles happily reveals that he had control over Faustus' fateful selection of texts from the Bible at the time of his rejection of divinity (a claim that belatedly erases the ironic complexity of that decisive process). Next, the Good and Bad Angels appear from opposite directions and preside over some elaborate stage spectacle: A glorious throne "descends" to the accompaniment of music, while the Good Angel tells Faustus that this is the image of the celestial happiness he has lost; then "hell is discovered"—probably in the form of a large cloth painting, judging from the Bad Angel's detailed description:

> There are the Furies tossing damnèd souls
> On burning forks: their bodies broil in lead.
> There are live quarters broiling on the coals,
> That ne'er can die. This ever-burning chair
> Is for o'er-tortured souls to rest them in.
> These that are fed with sops of flaming fire
> Were gluttons, and loved only delicates,
> And laughed to see the poor starve at their gates. (B-text 5.2.123–30)

This lurid picture of hell as a place of grotesque physical tortures, although quite consistent with the Faust Book's imagery, is at odds with the interior, psychological torment of hell that Marlowe's earlier scenes had introduced with such telling impact. So, too, the function of the Good and Bad Angels in this scene differs from that in their earlier appearances, when they always echoed a pre-existent conflict in Faustus; they are no longer markers for the inner and spiritual problem, no longer "tuned" to Faustus' own thoughts. Even in verse style, the B-text scene shows a difference: Mephistopheles and the Angels all end their speeches in rhyming couplets. The scene's emphasis on external detail and on the external power of the devils is also at odds with the more unnerving and invisible force that Marlowe has emphasized in the student scene and in the final soliloquy. The 1616 text's closing scene, centered on the "morning after" when the students return to find Faustus' dismembered body strewn around his study, likewise derives its gory detail from the Faust Book, but, again, this seems anti-climactic and gratuitous in view of the inner disintegration revealed in Faustus' last speech. Scholars who suspect that this version of the text represents both a conception and a technique out of line with those found in the 1604 text have argued convincingly that these differences in the last scenes produce very different final responses toward Faustus. The more elaborate and spectacular context tends not only to contradict the sophisticated psychological focus built up earlier in the play but also to reduce Faustus to more of a puppet, whose intellect, will, and imagination are virtually insignificant. Ironically, such was the beginning of a history of theatrical adaptation of the play, which increasingly destroyed its tragic substructure by adding new layers of spectacle and illusory wonders, converting it eventually to farce and puppet drama.

Before those controversial "additions" of 1602 started this process, however, *The Tragical History of Doctor Faustus* had a chance to make its mark as a new kind of tragedy using some paradoxically out-of-fashion dramaturgy. In its own time, it obviously relied for much of its effect on the very serious and literal belief in witchcraft, devils, and hell; so had the very popular Faust Book. But Marlowe's adaptation of the legend, which accented its allegorical contours and deepened its psychological exploration of the self-destructive ironies of the aspiring mind, gave the Faust story a metaphorical and symbolic richness rooted in the archetype of the human being risking all to test his limits. More than the exotic adventures of a magician who dabbles in taboo sorcery, more than a negative *exemplum* of sin and punishment, Marlowe's play revisits and reshapes the ancient tragic pattern of hubris within the context of Renaissance thought and culture. Using the religious beliefs of his own time and centering his drama on the inner struggle of an extraordinary individual to redefine his own limits as well as those of the universe around him, Marlowe hit upon a formula that touched the heart of the intoxicatingly expansive spirit that we now associate with the Renaissance.

His own way of developing Faustus' inner struggle and quest, however, does not result in a schematic story of a Renaissance spirit trapped in a medieval world—a Faust too advanced for his time. Marlowe's protagonist is revealed as a doubly divided self. The inner conflict of conscience, emphasized by the Good and Evil Angels and the repeated flirtations with repentance, represents one such division within the familiar conventions (both religious and dramatic) of moral choice; the other, more original, division lies in the rift, or contrast, between imagined value and actual loss, the gap between limitless desire and all too limited achievement that Faustus plugs with self-delusion. Marlowe's most trenchant ironies—in the dialogues with Mephistopheles, in the inversions of master/servant roles, in the Helen scene—are those that expose Faustus' blindness to the full reality of what stands before him and within him, a curiously willful and arrogant blindness that is not at all like the ignorance of Oedipus or the madness of Hercules. His project of reconstructing human limits by rejecting God and joining the diabolic miracle-workers becomes a project of diminishing, rather than expanding, the human spirit. The Renaissance magician plays his biggest and most frightening trick on himself.

To appreciate this ironic split in Faustus' perception is also to understand that Marlowe's transformation of hubris places greater responsibility for destruction upon the protagonist rather than upon fate or the gods. The one who takes risks or challenges the boundary between the human and the divine is not destroyed by the higher powers to teach him or his survivors a lesson. It is more a matter of the individual forging his own destruction, not by a single critical choice, but by a pattern of repeated choices, such that he becomes his own nemesis without fully realizing it. Even the large surrounding cast of devils, focused as they are on the direction of Faustus' choice, does not diminish the crucial importance of the chooser.

Putting those devils on stage has an interesting effect with respect to what an audience judges as reality. Elizabethans may have believed in devils, but their representation on stage is hardly the image of what they are likely to have expected. Marlowe's bullying devils, with their monster costumes and firecracker special effects, are patently theatrical; they may frighten Faustus, but they are not likely to frighten us. To that extent, they lack "reality."[41] The Evil Angel's promptings, already at one allegorical remove because of their association with Faustus' own thoughts, are more credible, as is the surprising Mephistopheles when he speaks in ways that stage devils never do. Somehow we can believe in the reality of the inner pain reported by Mephistopheles, just as we can believe in the terror expressed by Faustus in his last hour and the connection of that fear to the human will that has brought it into realization. Whatever we think of hell, we can and do believe in Faustus the man who deludes and destroys himself, the man who discovers that the way up is the way down. It would be hard to explain the revival history of the play in our century if that were not the case. The inner reality of Faustus' psychological moves is what engages us: That much is more than fable.

This inward pattern, far more than the external pattern of "the fall of the over-reacher," is responsible for the core of tragic feeling in the play. Its effectiveness depends on the author's development of the inner workings of the mental processes that produce the inward fall, such as the ironically diminishing vision of what will satisfy humanity's deepest wishes. Consider, for example, the medieval stage's representation of the Fall of Lucifer in the mystery plays, where at one moment Lucifer decides to seat himself in God's throne and in the next falls through a trapdoor into a "hell" below, bemoaning his sudden transformation from angel to tormented devil. The concept of an over-reacher's self-made disaster is patent in all this, as is the theology of the sin of pride, but the theatrical effect is in fact comical, in large part because of the swift pace and external mechanics of the scene. There is clearly a fall, but it is not felt to be tragic. What Marlowe has done is to open up the mind of human ambition in its most imaginative reaches and to show, by a pattern of ironic implication and later ironic contrast to that ambition, how the chooser deludes himself and destroys his humanity—his selfhood—in the very act of attempting to enhance it. By providing for the gradual development of this process, by giving it enough time to unfold and enough context to reveal its manifold ironies, by imaging the motivation in ways that suggest understandable longings in the human spirit, and by blending one part empathy with two parts ironic detachment, Marlowe has endowed the pattern with tragic emotion.

The tragic link between choice and disastrous destiny, between aspiration and self-destruction, lies in self-delusion. Some of Marlowe's contemporaries were quick to see the poignancy of that motif. Shakespeare's *Macbeth* offers one close parallel. Another tale of crime and punishment, with much insistence on the psychological processes of the strong man tempted by ambition (with the assistance of diabolic witches and a wife who invokes the spirit world), this play's power is not felt most keenly in its ultimate scene of retribution. The fact that Macbeth is finally killed for his misdeeds is not so memorable as what Shakespeare has shown us as happening to his mind and imagination. It is the wasteland of Macbeth's inner world, expressed so unforgettably in the soliloquies "I have lived long enough" and "Tomorrow and tomorrow," that truly mirrors his damnation, and that wasteland is perceived by us to be the product of Macbeth's earlier choices and deeds. As he moved more and more savagely toward a desired consolidation of power, he cut away from his experience anything denoting a true fulfillment. It is a tribute to the play's construction that we can sense what a horrifying irony that is, even when it is overtaking a figure whose violent acts become ever more monstrous. There is sorrow and pity in the fact that a man can and does do such things to destroy himself; there is deep irony in seeing the delusions of dream-power take seductive shape, only to turn to ashes.

A similar irony and a similar process are at work in Thomas Middleton's treatment of Beatrice-Joanna in *The Changeling* (c. 1623). The title itself becomes an emblem for this character's moral transformation, a descent into a vile union with a grotesque servant whose violent agency she enlists to help fulfill her romantic aspirations. She, too, is destroyed by the one she thought would serve her, but it is her choice that initiates it all. In the end, what she realizes herself to be is more frightening than the death that overtakes her. Responding to her dying confession, her gloating servant and murderer concludes, "now we are left in hell," to which another adds, "We are all there, it circumscribes here."[42]

Although exceptional writers like Shakespeare and Middleton sensed the inner destructive dynamic in Marlowe's presentation of Faustus and appropriated it in their own ways, the more immediate legacy of Marlowe's play to the theatre generally was less profound. Its sensationalistic stage effects, its low comedy scenes (presumably already expanded by the early seventeenth-century additions), and its indulgence in hocus-pocus and horseplay were the dimensions that caught the attention of those who continued to see its revival as a commercially exploitable enterprise. After the hiatus in all theatrical activity during the Puritan interregnum (1642–60), the stage history of *Doctor Faustus* became a dizzy saga of the triumph of new stage machinery and mindless farce (Butler 1952, 52–68). Concurrently, with the rise of the anti-superstitious attitudes of the Enlightenment, even Marlowe's original play was judged a silly vestige of outmoded vulgar beliefs.

In our own time, long after the nineteenth century's revaluation of Marlowe and this play, a deep paradox continues to plague interpreters of its underlying significance. Modern readers and audiences are hardly likely to find the play's greatest appeal in the surface qualities of its spectacular or comic dimensions, yet the deeper tragic pattern within it, couched as it is in explicitly theological terms, ought to seem as foreign to our skeptical and secular age as it was to the Enlightenment. Marlowe's alleged atheism only compounds the issue: How is it possible that the most explicitly theological tragedy of its time could have been written by the scornful blasphemer described in the Baines and Kyd allegations? If we take those charges seriously, then we ought to have a play that demonstrates how Faustus sells his nonexistent soul to a nonexistent devil and eventually suffers a great deal of unnecessary anxiety over the prospect of being damned to a nonexistent hell by a nonexistent God. Yet that hardly seems to be the impression left by the play itself.

Paul Kocher has argued most strenuously that the Baines allegations are the key to Marlowe's mind, but his scholarly exploration of the play's cultural and intellectual context nevertheless has led him to conclude that *Doctor Faustus* maintains its Christian structure against the pressures of its protagonist's rebellious blasphemies and, indeed, that Marlowe included "magnificent dramatizations of Christian ideas" (Kocher 1962, 118). His way of resolving this contradiction comes from armchair psychology: Marlowe, an intellectual freethinker, was still emotionally tied to beliefs that his mind had come to scorn; in order to suppress these emotions, he resorted "the more strenuously to . . . ironical mockery" (Kocher 1962, 119). Thus, his mind articulated the statements reported by Baines, while his heart spoke in *Doctor Faustus*. The play is "an utterance of Marlowe's fears for his own destiny as a freethinking rebel from the laws of a Christian cosmos" (Kocher 1962, 306). From this perspective, the significance and appeal of the play is bound up with autobiography: The "tragedy" is in the author's own unresolved anxiety.

William Empson, who has had his notable critical quarrels even with Milton's God, does not agree that Marlowe could have been so fearful of orthodoxy. His way to explain the play's structure and emphasis is to hypothesize that Marlowe's original version did not conclude in Faustus' damnation at all; for him, the conclusion and the consequent implications of the present text result from the intervention of a more orthodox censoring hand. For Empson, the extant play is thus closer to silly superstition than to tragedy.

A third and roughly intermediate position relies on a paradigm much used in contemporary cultural criticism—the notion of "contained trans-gression." In this perspective, the radical or dissenting voice manages to express itself but can do so safely only by wrapping itself in an acceptable cover. In such readings, Marlowe did not really "mean" the orthodox parts of his play and hoped that his sympathetic audience would realize that these aspects are actually signs of institutional cultural repression.[43] Such interpretations tend also to redefine tragedy as the allegorical exposure of victimization by institutional forces (Dollimore 1984).

To attempt to locate the tragic center of *Doctor Faustus* in the presumed personal anxiety of its author, either in grappling with his own unresolved contradictions or in challenging the cultural status quo, may be to limit the play's impact too narrowly. Its thematic structure and peculiar ironies, although magnified through the allegorical and theological motifs we associate with a medieval cosmos, are at a deeper level exploring a pattern of psychological hubris, delusion, and self-diminishment that is not a "fable," even to an agnostic mind, but a recognizable experience, a pattern we sense as real. What Marlowe touched is a level of allegory that moves beyond the devil myths of Christianity, beyond the allusive myths of Icarus, Semele, and Troy, to some archetypal root, a "meta-myth" of the Autonomous Self, in which the yearning to be one's own creator and to remake the world to suit one's own unlimited desires "explodes" ironically into self-contradiction and self-destruction. That myth is not focused on the oppressive Other but on the volatile enemy within.

Chapter 8

Marlowe's Legacy to Tragedy

From the richly varied and wide-ranging experiments in playwriting that mark the Elizabethan age, one does not gather that many dramatists were engaged in a self-conscious project of "writing tragedy" in the way that a poet might attempt to write an epic. Those who came closest to that model were the Senecan imitators, such as Samuel Daniel, who produced what we now call "humanist tragedy"—a form that in England, at least, had very little success on the professional stage. In the competitive arena of the commercial theatre, we witness a kind of wild "free market" of dramaturgical styles, a mixing of classical and medieval traditions, a zestful disregard for "decorum" in genres, and a vigorous experimentation in ways to adapt historical and fictive narratives of every kind for stage presentation. In such a context, the making of tragedy or comedy or anything in between or outside those categories was a process of considerable fluidity. There was no formal mold or pattern into which new subject matter had to be shaped in order to earn a title-page label of tragedy. The "form"—if it can be called that at all—was subject to constant redefinition, as, indeed, it always has been.

Christopher Marlowe's tragedies are, in this particular context, representative rather than revolutionary. Despite the marks of a distinctive "voice" and style that we sense in all of them, they are a remarkably varied set of plays. Put any two of his plots side by side, ask whether one might expect the writer of the first to have produced the second, and you can see how difficult it is to predict where Marlowe would look for material, much less what he would do with it once he had found it. A story of doomed love from a classical epic, a heathen warlord's invincible march to empire, a pathetic English king's wretched humiliations, the atrocities of a Machiavellian French Duke, a grotesque farce of villainy in Malta, the fantastic *diablerie* and damnation of a German wizard—the subjects vary as widely as the treatments they receive. On the surface, it seems that Marlowe never, except for the second part of *Tamburlaine*, repeated himself. He was clearly not writing to formula, even when, as we have seen earlier, he appropriated certain conventions of older traditions, such as the tyrant protagonist, the *de casibus* lament, or allegorical figures, including the Vice of medieval morality drama.

Nonetheless, we can find in all this variety a radical sensibility that in its own way helped to transform the practice of dramatic tragedy, to extend its range of effects, and to suggest new themes and perspectives appropriate to it. While the broadest themes that recur in Renaissance definitions of tragedy—the mutability of Fortune, the fragility of power, the retribution for evil—overlap the boundaries of Marlowe's experiments in tragedy, they do not adequately express his particular focus or tone. The landscape (or should we call it the mindscape?) of Marlowe's tragic universe offers its own special vistas.

One way to define the character and legacy of Marlovian tragedy is to contrast it with another line of tragic development that traces back to the influential work of Marlowe's one-time roommate, Thomas Kyd. Kyd's *Spanish Tragedy*, by all the available measures of production records, frequency of printed editions, expansions, sequels, and contemporary allusions, was about as big a theatrical success as any in the sixteenth century. As is the case with so many Elizabethan plays, we cannot date it with certainty, but it seems to have been first staged at about the same time that *Tamburlaine* appeared. Its protagonist, the mad revenger Hieronimo, became as famous for his laments and mad scenes as Tamburlaine became for his astounding rant. The attendant features of Kyd's script, which includes ghosts from the underworld, doomed love affairs, sensational violence, intrigue and counter-intrigue, Machiavellian villains and their comic servants, and a climactic play–within–a–play, all served up in blank verse of a highly rhetorical form, had an enormous impact on the shape of tragedy to come. The "revenge tradition," which flourished in the seventeenth century, encompassing Shakespeare's *Hamlet* (perhaps derived from a lost Hamlet play by Kyd) and major works by John Marston, Cyril Tourneur, Thomas Middleton, John Webster, and John Ford, is clearly rooted in Kyd's bloody soil. If we measure influence by the following generation's repetition of motifs and situations, Kyd deserves major credit for defining the shape and direction of tragedy. The Jacobeans would do more than he to emphasize the *inner* violence of corruption, malice, and lust that lurks in the courts and halls of the (mainly Italianate) high and mighty, but they would continue to follow his lead in constructing highly sensational plots of complex intrigue around the central passion for revenge and in punctuating these plots with some notable *coups de théâtre*.

Marlowe obviously did not see tragedy in the same terms. His *Jew of Malta*, although the closest to the pattern of revenge tragedy, neither focuses on the frustrations of a revenger, builds a mood of terror, nor directs its poetic technique to probing and exposing the emotional depths of its protagonist. Instead, we watch the speedy and ingenious improvisations of Barabas as he invents one successful and outrageous "revenge machine" after another. He is all method and no madness, a caricature of Machiavellian deceptive cunning rather than an emotional lightning rod responding to the cruel vagaries of fate or the miasma of corruption. There is a harder ironic edge to what Marlowe was doing, both here and in his other tragedies, that cuts to the heart of his matter. He draws our eyes always to the trapdoor, whether literal or metaphorical, that awaits his protagonists. This is not merely to play upon the inevitability of the destruction that will overtake them but, more importantly, upon the links between their aspirations or projects and the fates they suffer. Marlowe spent much less energy coloring the world around his protagonists than he did in developing their inner worlds and in exposing the destructive or self-destructive germ in those inner worlds. Above all, he liked to demonstrate the ironic force of individual desire in determining one's own destruction—not just any desire, as a conventional theory of the passions might suggest, but the extraordinary desire that seeks to redefine and restructure reality so that one's obsessive needs may be fulfilled. Marlowe's tragic protagonists are all in some way myth-makers, figures who are determined to make their worlds over into more fantasy-fulfilling landscapes, whose efforts to do so inevitably collide with the harsher stuff of reality. This trajectory is not the romantic quest of the impossible dream but the ironic quest of grand delusions, a quest that leaves a trail of blood and betrayal, humiliation and pain.

For Dido, the trapdoor has been set by the gods, who push Aeneas along to fulfill his epic destiny. Her Cupid-inspired passion overwhelms her in the myth of love. Marlowe highlighted her struggle to keep that myth alive as best she can, first in desperate action, then in flights of fantasy, and, finally, in suicide.

In the case of *Tamburlaine*, Part I shadows the victories of the aspiring warlord with the savage ruthlessness that he blithely equates with honor;

Part II pits the hero's myth of himself against the more intractable forces of disease, heredity, and death. Tamburlaine's inhumanity intensifies as he lashes out, sometimes in hallucination, at unseen Death and unseen gods. His greatest humiliation is to discover that he is subject to mortality, that his myth of the invincible self is subject to correction by reality—and yet, his characteristic response is to invent a new myth of immortality for himself.

From Tamburlaine on, all of Marlowe's protagonists share a sense that they are extraordinary—as indeed they all are—but with the added confidence that such a status brings with it moral carte blanche: To the Extraordinary Man, everything is permitted. Barabas thinks himself "framed of finer mold than common men" (1.2.221) at the very moment that he sees the need to revenge himself on others. The Duke of Guise scorns "peasants" and philosophers, religion and kings. Edward II's idea of kingship is founded on a consummate self-indulgence so absolute as to crowd out any sense of responsibility to the realm; Marlowe was also intent to show that Mortimer, too, can grow into such a myth of self. Faustus adopts diabolic magic as his means of remaking the world to suit his more immortal longings—which he is already equating with "all voluptuousness" as he drafts his contract.

All of them are allowed to "touch" fulfillment, to enjoy some measure of the dream they have projected for themselves. Dido and Edward are rapt in love, Tamburlaine glories in his barbaric triumphs, and Barabas and the Guise gloat over their deceptively manipulated power. Faustus is delighted with the comic pageantry of the Seven Deadly Sins, ecstatic with his preternatural Helen. But, for one and all, Marlowe wove the web of ironic context that allows us to see the germ of destruction in these myths of self-fulfillment.

To focus tragedy in this way is to give new importance to the mental and imaginative process that motivates and enacts the quest, to the depiction of mindscape. Plot becomes a function of character, subplot often a parodic comment upon character, and poetic imagery and rhetoric the means to define the innermost core of character. Character itself, its extraordinary and often outrageous desires amplified by hyperbole, its obsessions hovering on the border of caricature, takes on a special intensity. Intensity does not always mean complexity, for few of Marlowe's chief figures are "divided selves" (Faustus is the great exception); in fact, many are close to monomania. The complexity comes from the ironic framework of context or allusion that coaxes us to see the character's motives and deeds in terms quite other than those that are paramount to himself. Tragic irony for Marlowe is most often revealed in what a character *prefers* not to see, rather than in what a character is not permitted to see. Marlovian tragedy is more psychological than metaphysical.

Playwrights with an eye for more than the surfaces of rhetoric and spectacle would clearly be able to adopt this insight into tragic character as the age went on. Shakespeare, Jonson, Chapman, Middleton, and Webster were all in Marlowe's debt, although none was content merely to imitate him.[44] Marlowe's work also encouraged them to extend the range of tone in tragedy, from pathos at one end of the spectrum to satire at the other. His application of mythological allusion as a means of both establishing character and ironically critiquing it provided an important lesson on how to move beyond Seneca's more mechanical style of amplifying emotions by piling up mythological references. His "mighty line" proved to them how flexible and effective blank verse could be, and his sense of a correspondingly "mighty scene" or visually emblematic staged moment was also instrumental in suggesting how tragic effects could be engineered in the theatre. Above all, he taught them how word and action, rhetoric and spectacle, could be so counterpoised in ironic opposition to one another that the combined effect could mirror thematic contrarieties.

Tamburlaine's bravura mode of self-expression would be mocked by Jonson, Shakespeare, and others; Faustus would be transformed into a figure of farce in a later theatrical generation; all of Marlowe's plays would suffer centuries of neglect as fashions in theatre moved on to other modes. Nevertheless, the deeper dimensions of Marlowe's dramaturgy would, in fact, live on in more subtle and creative ways, not only helping to transform the practices and directions of tragedy as it developed in the reigns of Elizabeth and James, but also encouraging a new poetics of the theatre—a way of combining word and sight to provoke the experience of infinite and infinitely disturbing riches.

Appendix A

Thomas Kyd's Accusations of Marlowe

After his release from prison in 1593 and after Marlowe's death, Kyd
wrote two letters to Sir John Puckering, Lord Keeper of the Privy Seal,
pleading for his assistance in restoring him to the good graces of an
unnamed former patron (possibly Lord Strange, for whose company
Kyd had recently been writing plays) and in clearing his name of the
charges of atheism and seditious libel. The full texts from which these
extracts have been taken are provided in Wraight 1965, 314–16. I have
modernized both spelling and punctuation.

When I was first suspected for that libel that concerned the state, amongst
those waste and idle papers (which I cared not for) and which unasked I
did deliver up, were found some fragments of a disputation touching that
opinion, affirmed by Marlowe to be his, and shuffled with some of mine
(unknown to me) by some occasion of our writing in one chamber two
years since.

My first acquaintance with this Marlowe rose upon his bearing name to
serve my Lord, although his Lordship never knew his service but in writing
for his players. . . .

That I should love or be familiar friend with one so irreligious were very
rare, when Tully sayeth *Digni sunt amicitia quibus in ipsis inest causa cur
diligantur* ["Those are worthy of friendship in whom there is cause for
esteem."] which neither was in him, for person, qualities, or honesty;
besides, he was intemperate and of a cruel heart, the very contraries to
which my greatest enemies will say by me.

It is not to be numbered amongst the best conditions of men, to tax or
to upbraid the dead *Quia mortui non mordent* ["Because the dead do not
bite"], but thus much have I . . . dared in the greatest cause, which is to
clear myself of being thought an atheist, which some will swear he was.

For more assurance that I was not of that vile opinion, let it but please
your Lordship to enquire of such as he conversed withal, that is (as I am
given to understand) with Harriot, Warner, Royden, and some stationers
in Paul's churchyard, whom I in no sort can accuse nor will excuse by
reason of his company.

Pleaseth it your honorable Lordship, touching Marlowe's monstrous
opinions, as I cannot but with an aggrieved conscience think on him or
them, so can I but particularize few in the respect of them that kept him
greater company. . . . First, it was his custom when I knew him first (and
as I hear say he continued it) in table talk or otherwise to jest at the divine
scriptures, gibe at prayers, and strive in argument to frustrate and confute
what hath been spoke or writ by prophets and such holy men.

He would report St. John to be our savior Christ's Alexis (I cover it with
reverence and trembling): that is, that Christ did love him with an extraordinary love.

That for me to write a poem of St. Paul's conversion, as I was determined, he said would be as if I should go write a book of fast and loose,
esteeming Paul a juggler.

That the prodigal child's portion was but four nobles, he held his purse
so near the bottom in all pictures, and that it either was a jest or else four
nobles then was thought a great patrimony, not thinking it a parable.

That things esteemed to be done by divine power might have as well
been done by observation of men. All which he would so suddenly take
slight occasion to slip out, as I and many others (in regard of his other
rashness in attempting sudden privy injuries to men) did overslip, though
often reprehend him for it; and for which, God is my witness, as well by
my Lord's commandment, as in hatred of his life and thoughts I left and
did refrain his company.

He would persuade with men of quality to go unto the King of Scots,
whither I hear Royden is gone, and where, if he had lived (he told me when
I saw him last) he meant to be.

Appendix B

Richard Baines' Note

Wraight (1965, 308–9) supplies a photographic reproduction of the original manuscript signed by Baines as well as an old-spelling transcription. My modern-spelling adaptation of the full text follows.

A note containing the opinion of one Christopher Marly concerning his damnable judgment of religion, and scorn of God's word.

That the Indians and many authors of antiquity have assuredly written about 16 thousand years agone, whereas Adam is proved to have lived within 6 thousand years.

He affirmeth that Moses was but a juggler, and that one Heriots [Harriot] being Sir W. Raleigh's man can do more than he.

That Moses made the Jews to travel forty years in the wilderness (which journey might have been done in less than one year) ere they came to the promised land, to the intent that those who were privy to most of his subtleties might perish and so an everlasting superstition remain in the hearts of the people.

That the first beginning of religion was only to keep men in awe.

That it was an easy matter for Moses, being brought up in all the arts of the Egyptians, to abuse the Jews, being a rude and gross people.

That Christ was a bastard and his mother dishonest.

That he was the son of a carpenter, and that if the Jews among whom he was born did crucify him, they best knew him and whence he came.

That Christ deserved better to die than Barabbas and that the Jews made a good choice, though Barabbas were both a thief and murderer.

That if there be any God or any good religion, then it is in the Papists because the service of God is performed with more ceremonies, as elevation of the Mass, organs, singing men, shaven crowns, etc. That all Protestants are hypocritical asses.

That if he were put to write a new religion, he would undertake both a more excellent and admirable method, and that all the New Testament is filthily written.

That the woman of Samaria and her sister were whores and that Christ knew them dishonestly.

That St. John the Evangelist was bedfellow to Christ and leaned always in his bosom, that he used him as the sinners of Sodom.

That all they that love not tobacco and boys were fools.

That all the apostles were fishermen and base fellows, neither of wit nor worth; that Paul only had wit, but he was a timorous fellow in bidding men to be subject to magistrates against his conscience.

That he had as good right to coin as the Queen of England, and that he was acquainted with one Poole, a prisoner in Newgate, who hath great skill in mixture of metals, and having learned some things of him he meant, through help of a cunning stamp maker, to coin French crowns, pistolets, and English shillings.

That if Christ would have instituted the Sacrament with more ceremonial reverence it would have been had in more admiration; that it would have been much better being administered in a tobacco pipe.

That the Angel Gabriel was bawd to the Holy Ghost, because he brought the salutation to Mary.

That one Ric Cholmley hath confessed that he was persuaded by Marloe's reasons to become an Atheist.

These things, with many other, shall by good and honest witness be approved to be his opinions and common speeches, and that this Marlow doth not only hold them himself, but almost into every company he cometh he persuades men to Atheism, willing them not to be afraid of bugbears and hobgoblins, and utterly scorning both God and His ministers, as I Richard Baines will justify and approve both by mine oath and the testimony of many honest men, and almost all men with whom he hath conversed any time will testify the same, and as I think all men in Christianity ought to endeavor that the mouth of so dangerous a member may be stopped. He saith likewise that he hath quoted a number of contrarieties out of the Scripture which he hath given to some great men who in convenient time shall be named. When these things shall be called in question the witness shall be produced.

Richard Baines

Notes

1. Calvin Hoffman, an American journalist, proposed this in *The Murder of the Man Who Was Shakespeare* (New York: J. Messner, 1955).

2. Frederick S. Boas has noted that on the evidence of the buttery books, Marlowe's only lengthy periods of absence were in the third or fourth terms of 1584–85 and the third of 1585–86, adding that a more probable time for performing his government "service" would have been "after he had 'gone down' in or after the Lent term 1587" (Boas 1940, 14).

3. The last name is spelled in various ways in contemporary documents: Marley and Morley, with or without the "e," are common; Morle and Marle are also found in older family records; Marlin and Marlyn appear in university accounts.

4. John Bakeless' two-volume biography (1942) is still the most comprehensive collection of facts and documents, although important new facts have since been published by Boas (a discovery in 1949 about the background of Richard Baines), Arthur Freeman (background on the Dutch Church libel, which spurred the arrest of Kyd and Marlowe), R. B. Wernham (Marlowe's arrest in Flushing), and William Urry (Marlowe's 1592 case of assault in Canterbury).

I have rendered all quotations in modern spelling (except for proper names) and with abbreviations silently expanded.

5. Data on the production history of Elizabethan acting companies are notoriously scant. The major source of information is a collection of business papers and journals belonging to Philip Henslowe, a leading theatre manager and entrepreneur who was associated both through business and family ties to Edward Alleyn, the celebrated actor, who married Henslowe's step-daughter. Henslowe's journal of play calendars and receipts began only in 1592 and was not continued in detail after 1597. More than half of the 113 plays whose performances he recorded are known only through his list. His Diary has been edited by Foakes and Rickert. Its play calendars have been incorporated into a very useful chronological list of documented play performances and publications

in Barroll, Legatt, Hosley, and Kernan (eds.), *The Revels History of Drama in English, Vol. 3: 1576–1613* (London: Methuen, 1975, 55–94).

6. For details about the libel, see Freeman 1973.

7. A slightly altered second copy of the Baines note that was prepared for the Queen contains the confusing notation: "A note delivered on Whitsun Eve last of the most horrible blasphemies and damnable opinions uttered by Christopher Marly who within three days after came to a sudden and fearful end of his life." Bakeless has commented that, since Whitsun Eve fell on June 2 in 1593, the note erroneously implies that Marlowe died on June 5 (Bakeless [1942] 1970, 1:112).

8. More puzzling is the implication of the phrasing in Kyd's first letter concerning the "fragments of a disputation touching that opinion, affirmed by Marlowe to be his, and shuffled with some of mine." If Marlowe's affirmation refers to "fragments of a disputation" rather than to "opinion"—which the syntactic parallel with "affirmed/shuffled" suggests—then Kyd seems to be saying that Marlowe corroborated the claim that the heretical document belonged to him. Could this have been the case, and also the reason for Kyd's eventual release? Unfortunately, we do not know when Kyd was set free.

9. This remark, together with instances of homosexual subject matter in *Dido, Edward II,* and *Hero and Leander,* has led to considerable modern speculation about Marlowe's sexual orientation. The nineteenth-century sexologist, Havelock Ellis, who edited the first Mermaid anthology of Marlowe's plays in 1887, including in its initial run the full text of the Baines note, was also the first to suggest, in *Sexual Inversion* (1897), that Marlowe probably "possessed the psychosexual hermaphrodite's temperament." See Dabbs (1991, 122–35) for a fuller treatment of the context for Ellis' verdict. Constance Kuriyama's *Hammer or Anvil: Psychological Patterns in Christopher Marlowe's Plays* (New Brunswick, NJ: Rutgers University Press, 1980) has argued on the basis of a somewhat outdated Freudian theory of homosexuality that this is the key to understanding the playwright and his plays. It is common to find modern playbills and notices of Marlowe play productions asserting confidently and absolutely that Marlowe was homosexual. There is no clear and reliable historical evidence to substantiate that claim, however, whatever the suggestions that invite conjectures of this sort.

10. That Baines was an underworld informer is further witnessed by a letter by one other such informer, Thomas Drury, written in August 1593 to Anthony Bacon, seeking his aid in requesting a reward from the Lord Treasurer for a number of his recent achievements (Sprott 1974). One achievement was to track down Baines for a "secret" about a libel for which the city had proclaimed a bounty (the description fits the proclamation and search for the authors of the Dutch Church libel that had led to Kyd's arrest). Another (which might possibly refer to Kyd's arrest) refers to his men having taken "a vile book" and "a notable villain or two," now imprisoned. Still another concerns his procuring and delivering to the authorities "the notablest and vilest articles of atheism that I suppose the likes were never known or read of in any age"—which might have something to do with the Baines note.

11. Thomas Fineux's atheism was noted in a common-place book kept by Henry Oxinden of Kent during 1640–1670. He attributed the information, along with other notes about Marlowe, to one Mr. Aldrich, presumably Simon Aldrich of Canterbury, who had also attended Cambridge in the late 1590s. In 1641, Oxinden noted that Aldrich said:

that Mr. Fineoux of Dover was an atheist and that he would go out at midnight into a wood, and fall down upon his knees and pray heartily that the Devil would come, that he might see him (for he did not believe that there was a Devil). . . . He learned all Marlo by heart and divers other books: Marlo made him an atheist. This Fineaux [*sic*] was fain to make a speech upon "The fool hath said in his heart there is no God," so got his degree.

At another point, Aldrich noted that Marlowe "wrote a book against the Scripture, how that it was all of one man's making, and would have printed it but would not be suffered" (Bakeless 1970, 1:119–23). The latter statement might be derived from the Beard anecdote, which seems to have been the source of still another Aldrich citation: "he was stabbed in the head with a dagger and died swearing."

12. In May 1591, another arrest warrant had been issued for him and for Thomas Drury at Drury's residence. Drury, as noted above, claimed in 1593 to have found Baines for the authorities.

13. Cited by Dabbs (1991, 119), whose *Reforming Marlowe* traces in telling detail the transformation of Marlowe's reputation effected by a succession of scholars, critics, and poets who have "read" Marlowe through very selective lenses. Maclure's collection (1979) of critical excerpts on Marlowe from the sixteenth through the nineteenth centuries is an excellent resource for tracing shifts in judgment and appreciation.

14. Gerald Eades Bentley has summarized the usual grounds for the censor's objections as (1) critical comments on the policies or conduct of the government; (2) unfavorable presentations of friendly foreign powers or their sovereigns, great nobles, or subjects; (3) comment on religious controversy; (4) personal satire of influential people; and, after a special edict in 1606, profanity (Bentley 1971, 167).

15. If, as some scholars have conjectured, it is the play that Shakespeare's Hamlet describes when he asks for a sample speech from the traveling players, that description (*Hamlet* 2.2.454–70) may be its most notable memorial. But the player's speech is definitely not an excerpt from the text of *Dido*, nor is its style an accurate reflection of the play's verse technique.

16. Michael Shapiro has provided a full study of the boy companies and their repertories. For essays on the relationship of *Dido* to the conditions of production by these companies, see Cope (1974), Gibbons (1968), and Smith (1976, 1977). There are contemporary references to a play about Dido and Aeneas performed by the Admiral's Men in 1598, but we have no way of telling whether this was Marlowe's play (Oliver 1968, xxxi).

17. Turner (1926) and Bono (1984) have provided extended studies of the Italian and French plays; Bono also includes Marlowe's play. Allen (1963) and Smith (1976, 1977) have treated Marlowe's play with reference to the European analogues. Boas has discussed a Latin *Dido* produced at Oxford in 1583, which blended Virgil and Seneca while adding some notable spectacle (1914, 183–91).

18. Martin Mueller's (1980) first chapter provides a succinct look at the European attempt to imitate classical tragedy. T. S. Eliot's (1950) essay on "Seneca in Elizabethan Translation," which treats actual translations as well as plays imitating Senecan features, remains one of the best analyses of the phenomenon.

19. There is a marked tendency in Marlowe's other plays to "score" his female parts according to the limits and specialties of the boy members of adult companies: Zenocrate

and Olympia in *Tamburlaine*, the Queen in *Edward II*, and Abigail in *The Jew of Malta* all tend to express themselves in fairly formal, declamatory complaints.

20. Ellis-Fermor's edition (1951) includes a helpful review of the sources (17–48) as well as excerpts from them (286–307).

21. The combination of delirious commands and hallucinations in the midst of greatest stress is a technique that Marlowe used to portray the suffering of Dido and Faustus in their last extremities and of Edward II in his deposition scene.

22. There is no record of a second part. For a detailed analysis of this and other plays inspired by *Tamburlaine*, see Berek (1982), who finds them generally sharing an implied negative judgment of the kind of "hero" Tamburlaine represented.

23. For a detailed analysis of the English reception, see Bawcutt (1970), who has put earlier treatments by Ribner (1949, 1954) and Raab (1964) in perspective. Gentillet's role in the polemics that followed the Bartholomew's Day massacre has been analyzed by Anglo (1989).

24. Oliver's edition (1968) includes extracts from one of the major sources published in 1574 (167–80).

25. In early 1592, Henslowe's repertory at the Rose included *The Jew of Malta* and a lost play entitled "Machiavelli."

26. For extended discussions of the development of the Vice figure in English drama, see Spivack (1958) and Potter (1975).

27. Entered in the Stationers' Register in July 1593, the earliest edition of the play appeared in 1594, with Marlowe's name on the title page. Later editions between 1598 and 1612 mention its having been acted by the Earl of Pembroke's company, who were apparently first active in 1592. The 1622 edition mentions that it was acted by "the late Queen's Majesty's Servants" (Queen Anne's Men) at the Red Bull theatre, a public theatre built around 1604.

28. Farnham (1936) has provided a full discussion of the tradition.

29. Because it is so difficult to fix dates for the composition and first productions of Shakespeare's *Henry VI* plays and of Marlowe's *Edward II*, and because there are mutual echoes of each author's works in certain lines of the other's, scholars have disagreed about who was influencing whom. The more recent majority opinion posits a chronology that puts the *Henry VI* trilogy first (giving Shakespeare the precedent for the "weak king" play) and *Edward II* second: see Wilson (1953) and Manheim (1969). Henslowe's list of plays produced at the Rose in the 1590s includes several titles indicative of sources in the chronicles of English history; few of those still extant reflect a pattern of tragic downfall.

30. See Cunliffe's collected edition (1912) for texts of *Gorboduc* and of another early attempt to merge Senecan form with English history, *The Misfortunes of Arthur*.

31. Queen Elizabeth's sensitivity to certain analogies between her situation and that of Richard II seems to lie behind the absence of the deposition scene in the 1597 edition of Shakespeare's play. There was no such censorship, however, of the deposition scene in Marlowe's play.

32. It is tempting to think that Michael Drayton's description of Edward's behavior in his *Mortimeriados* (1596) owed something to his having seen Marlowe's play:

> He takes the crown, and closely hugs it to him,
> And smiling in his grief he leans upon it;
> Then doth he frown because it would forgo him,

Then softly stealing, lays his vesture on it;
Then snatching at it, loath to have forgone it,
He put it from him, yet he will not so,
And yet retains what fain he would forgo. (Drayton [1597] 1931, 1688–94)

Drayton's king, however, does not "rage."

33. The statistic is derived from the list by Cronin (1987) of productions since 1880 of Tudor and early Stuart plays.

34. See my essay, "The Impact of Goethe's *Faust* on Nineteenth and Twentieth Century Criticism of Marlowe's *Doctor Faustus*," in Boerner and Johnson (1989, 185–96).

35. Helpful summaries of the textual controversy are provided by Ormerod and Wortham (1985, xxi–xxix), and by Bevington and Rasmussen (1993) in their edition of both texts.

36. The full text of the English Faust Book is included in Palmer (1965, 134–236).

37. For this and many other references to contemporary theological texts, both popular and learned, see my chapter on *Doctor Faustus* in Cole, *Suffering and Evil* (1972) and the introduction and notes to the Ormerod and Wortham edition (1985).

38. For more detailed analyses of the morality play tradition, see Bevington (1962) and Potter (1975).

39. Modern productions of the play have nearly always managed to make this scene especially memorable in one spectacular way or another. Presuming this was also the case in Elizabethan times, one wonders whether Marlowe, bargaining on that effectiveness, was not also thinking about trapping his audience into feeling that the Seven Deadly Sins were indeed delightful entertainment. This choice would be similar to his strategy in setting up unsettling audience complicity with Barabas in *The Jew of Malta*.

40. For a detailed discussion of the relation of Doctor Faustus to the morality tradition, see Cole, *Suffering and Evil* (1962, 231–42). Far more important than the use of specific devices associated with morality drama (Good and Evil Angels, Seven Deadly Sins, comic depictions of vice) is the allegorical habit of mind that posits the protagonist's career, for all its exceptional details, as fundamentally representative of a broader human pattern of behavior.

41. A 1620 pamphlet, J. Melton's *Astrologaster, or, the Figure-Caster*, deriding the frauds of astrologers and weather prophets, cites the artificial stage effects in the production of *Doctor Faustus* at the Fortune theatre as the more likely place to witness predicted foul weather: "There indeed a man may behold shaggy-haired devils run roaring over the stage with squibs in their mouths, while drummers make thunder in the tiring-house, and the twelve-penny hirelings make artificial lightning in their heavens" (31).

42. Gardner (1948) has traced the thematic debt to Marlowe in Shakespeare, Middleton, and Milton.

43. A more sophisticated variant of this argument suggests that Marlowe, rather than consciously shielding himself from censorious authority by reverting to *apparently* orthodox frameworks or resolutions, was illustrating the predicament of a rebellion that defines itself by merely reversing the value-terms of the opposed authority, thus unwittingly accepting the structural grounds of its power. See Greenblatt (1980, 209, 212).

44. James Shapiro (1991) has provided an extensive study of Marlowe's impact on Jonson and Shakespeare.

Works Cited

Quotations from Marlowe's plays are from the following editions:

Dido Queen of Carthage and The Massacre at Paris. Ed. H. J. Oliver. The Revels Plays. London: Methuen, 1968.

Doctor Faustus: A- and B-texts (1604, 1616). Ed. David Bevington and Eric Rasmussen. The Revels Plays. Manchester: Manchester University Press, 1993.

Edward II. Ed. W. Moelwyn Merchant. New Mermaids. London: Ernest Benn, 1967.

The Jew of Malta. Ed. T. W. Craik. New Mermaids. London: Ernest Benn, 1966.

Tamburlaine. Ed. J. W. Harper. New Mermaids. London: Ernest Benn, 1971.

Allen, Don Cameron. "Marlowe's *Dido* and the Tradition." In *Essays on Shakespeare and Elizabethan Drama in Honor of Hardin Craig*, ed. R. Hosley, 55–58. Columbia, MO: University of Missouri Press, 1962.

Anglo, Sydney. "Henri III: Some Determinants of Vituperation." In *From Valois to Bourbon: Dynasty, State and Society in Early Modern France*, ed. Keith Cameron, 5–20. Exeter: Short Run Press, 1989.

Anonymous. *Art of English Poesy, The*. (1589). In *Elizabethan Critical Essays*, vol. 2, ed. G. Gregory Smith. Oxford: Oxford University Press, 1904.

Bakeless, John. *The Tragicall History of Christopher Marlowe*. 2 vols. Cambridge, MA: Harvard University Press, 1942; Westport, CT: Greenwood Publishing Group, 1970.

Bawcutt, N. W. "Machiavelli and Marlowe's *The Jew of Malta*." *Renaissance Drama* n.s. 3 (1970): 3–49.

Bentley, Gerald Eades. *The Profession of Dramatist in Shakespeare's Time, 1590–1642*. Princeton: Princeton University Press, 1971.

Berek, Peter. "*Tamburlaine*'s Weak Sons: Imitation as Interpretation Before 1593." *Renaissance Drama* n.s. 13 (1982): 55–82.

Bevington, David. *From* Mankind *to* Marlowe: *Growth of Structure in the Popular Drama of Tudor England.* Cambridge, MA: Harvard University Press, 1962.

Boas, Frederick S. *Christopher Marlowe: A Biographical and Critical Study.* Oxford: Clarendon Press, 1940.

———. *University Drama in the Tudor Age.* Oxford, 1914.

———. "Informer Against Marlowe." *Times Literary Supplement*, Sept. 16, 1949.

Boerner, Peter, and Sidney Johnson, eds. *Faust through Four Centuries: Retrospect and Analysis.* Tübingen: Max Niemeyer Verlag, 1989.

Bono, Barbara J. "Renaissance Dramatic Transvaluations." In her *Literary Transvaluation: From Vergilian Epic to Shakespearean Tragicomedy*, 83–139. Berkeley: University of California Press, 1984.

Briggs, Julia. "Marlowe's *Massacre at Paris*: A Reconsideration." *Review of English Studies* n.s. 34 (1983): 257–78.

Brooke, Tucker. "The Reputation of Christopher Marlowe." *Transactions of the Connecticut Academy of Arts and Sciences* 25 (1922): 347–408.

Butler, E. M. *The Fortunes of Faust.* Cambridge: Cambridge University Press, 1952.

Cassirer, Ernst, ed. *The Renaissance Philosophy of Man.* Chicago: University of Chicago Press, 1948.

Chapman, George. *The Conspiracy and Tragedy of Charles Duke of Byron.* Ed. John Margeson. Manchester: Manchester University Press, 1988.

Cole, Douglas. *Suffering and Evil in the Plays of Christopher Marlowe.* Princeton: Princeton University Press, 1962; New York: Gordian Press, 1972.

———. "The Impact of Goethe's *Faust* on Nineteenth and Twentieth Century Criticism of Marlowe's *Doctor Faustus*." In *Faust through Four Centuries: Retrospect and Analysis*, ed. Peter Boerner and Sidney Johnson, 185–96. Tübingen: Max Niemeyer Verlag, 1989.

Cope, Jackson I. "Marlowe's *Dido* and the Titillating Children." *English Literary Renaissance* 4 (1974): 315–25.

Cronin, Lisa. *Professional Productions in the British Isles since 1880 of Plays by Tudor and Early Stuart Dramatists (excluding Shakespeare).* Renaissance Drama Newsletter, Supplement Seven. University of Warwick, 1987.

Cunliffe, J. W., ed. *Early English Classical Tragedies.* Oxford: Clarendon Press, 1912.

Dabbs, Thomas. *Reforming Marlowe: The Nineteenth-Century Canonization of a Renaissance Dramatist.* London and Toronto: Associated University Press, 1991.

Daniel, Samuel. *The Tragedy of Cleopatra* (1599). In Geoffrey Bullough, *Narrative and Dramatic Sources of Shakespeare*, vol. 5. New York: Columbia University Press, 1966.

Dollimore, Jonathan. *Radical Tragedy.* Chicago: University of Chicago Press, 1984.

Donne, John. *Sermons.* Ed. George R. Potter and Evelyn M. Simpson. 9 vols. Berkeley: University of California Press, 1953–59.

Drayton, Michael. *Mortimeriados* (1596). In *The Works of Michael Drayton*, ed. J. William Hebel. Vol. 1. Oxford: Shakespeare Head Press, 1931.

Eccles, Mark. *Christopher Marlowe in London.* Cambridge, MA: Harvard University Press, 1934; New York: Octagon Books, 1967.

Eliot, T. S. *Selected Essays.* New York: Harcourt, Brace, 1950.

Ellis-Fermor, Una, ed. *Tamburlaine the Great: In Two Parts*. 2nd ed. London: Methuen, 1951.

Empson, William. *Faustus and the Censor: The English Faust-book and Marlowe's Doctor Faustus*. Oxford: Basil Blackwell, 1987.

Farnham, Willard. *The Medieval Heritage of Elizabethan Tragedy*. Berkeley: University of California Press, 1936.

Foakes, R. A., and R. T. Rickert, eds. *Henslowe's Diary*. Cambridge: Cambridge University Press, 1961.

Fortescue, Thomas. *The Forest* (1571). In *Tamburlaine the Great: In Two Parts*, ed. Una Ellis-Fermor. London: Methuen, 1951.

Freeman, Arthur. "Marlowe, Kyd, and the Dutch Church Libel." *English Literary Renaissance* 3 (1973): 44–52.

Gardner, Helen. "Milton's Satan and the Theme of Damnation in Elizabethan Tragedy." *English Studies* (English Association) n.s. 1 (1948): 46–66.

Gibbons, Brian. "'Unstable Proteus': Marlowe's *The Tragedy of Dido Queen of Carthage*." In *Christopher Marlowe*, ed. B. Morris, 27–46. London: Ernest Benn, 1968.

Greenblatt, Stephen. *Renaissance Self-Fashioning*. Chicago: University of Chicago Press, 1980.

Greene, Robert. *The Life and Complete Works in Prose and Verse of Robert Greene*. Ed. Alexander B. Grosart. 15 vols. London, 1881–86.

Greg, W. W., ed. *Marlowe's Doctor Faustus 1604–1616: Parallel Texts*. Oxford: Clarendon Press, 1950.

Gurr, Andrew. "Who Strutted and Bellowed?" *Shakespeare Survey* 16 (1968): 95–102.

———. *The Shakespearean Stage 1574–1642*. 3rd ed. Cambridge: Cambridge University Press, 1992.

Hazlitt, William. *The Complete Works of William Hazlitt*. Ed. P. P. Howe. Vol. 6. London: J. M. Dent, 1931.

Higgins, John. *The First Part of the Mirror for Magistrates* (1574). In *Parts Added to The Mirror for Magistrates by John Higgins & Thomas Blenerhasset*, ed. Lily B. Campbell. Cambridge: Cambridge University Press, 1946.

Hoffman, Calvin. *The Murder of the Man Who Was Shakespeare*. New York: J. Messner, 1955.

Holinshed, Raphael. *Chronicles of England, Scotland, and Ireland* (1577, 1587). Vol. 2. London: J. Johnson et al., 1807.

Horne, David H. *The Life and Minor Works of George Peele*. New Haven: Yale University Press, 1952.

Hotson, J. Leslie. *The Death of Christopher Marlowe*. London: Nonesuch Press, 1925.

Jonson, Ben. *Discoveries*. In *Works*, ed. C. H. Herford and Percy Simpson, vol. 8. Oxford: Clarendon Press, 1947.

Kocher, Paul. "Contemporary Pamphlet Backgrounds for Marlowe's *The Massacre at Paris*." *Modern Language Quarterly* 8 (1947): 151–73, 309–18.

———. *Christopher Marlowe: A Study of his Thought, Learning, and Character*. Chapel Hill: University of North Carolina Press, 1946; New York: Russell & Russell, 1962.

Kuriyama, Constance. *Hammer or Anvil: Psychological Patterns in Christopher Marlowe's Plays*. New Brunswick, NJ: Rutgers University Press, 1980.

Leech, Clifford. "Marlowe's *Edward II*: Power and Suffering." *The Critical Quarterly* 1 (1959): 181–96.

Machiavelli, Niccolò. *The Prince*. New York: Modern Library, 1940.

Maclure, Miller, ed. *Marlowe: The Critical Heritage, 1588–1896*. London: Routledge & Kegan Paul, 1979.

Manheim, Michael. "The Weak King History Play of the Early 1590s." *Renaissance Drama* n.s. 2 (1969): 71–80.

Mirror for Magistrates, The. Ed. Lily B. Campbell. Cambridge: Cambridge University Press, 1938.

Mueller, Martin. *Children of Oedipus and other essays on the imitation of Greek tragedy*. Toronto: University of Toronto Press, 1980.

Nicholl, Charles. *The Reckoning*. London: Jonathan Cape, 1992.

Oliver, H. J., ed. *Dido Queen of Carthage and The Massacre at Paris*. London: Methuen, 1968.

Ormerod, David, and Christopher Wortham, eds. *Dr. Faustus: the A-text*. Nedlands: University of Western Australia Press, 1985.

Palmer, Philip Mason, and Robert Pattison More, *The Sources of the Faust Tradition from Simon Magus to Lessing*. New York: Oxford University Press, 1936; New York: Haskell House, 1965.

Potter, Robert. *The English Morality Play*. London and Boston: Routledge & Kegan Paul, 1975.

Raab, Felix. *The English Face of Machiavelli*. London: Routledge & Kegan Paul, 1964.

Ribner, Irving. "The Significance of Gentillet's *Contre-Machiavel*." *Modern Language Quarterly* 10 (1949): 153–57.

———. "Marlowe and Machiavelli." *Comparative Literature* 6 (1954): 348–56.

Selimus, The Tragical Reign of (1594). Malone Society Reprints. London: Chiswick Press, 1908.

Shapiro, James. *Rival Playwrights: Marlowe, Jonson, Shakespeare*. New York: Columbia University Press, 1991.

Shapiro, Michael. *Children of the Revels: The Boy Companies of Shakespeare's Time and Their Plays*. New York: Columbia University Press, 1977.

Sidney, Philip. *An Apology for Poetry* (1595). In *Elizabethan Critical Essays*, ed. G. Gregory Smith. vol. 1. Oxford: Oxford University Press, 1904.

Smith, Mary E. "Marlowe and Italian Dido Drama." *Italica* 53 (1976): 223–35.

———. "Staging Marlowe's *Dido Queen of Carthage*." *Studies in English Literature* 17 (1977): 177–90.

Spivack, Bernard. *Shakespeare and the Allegory of Evil: The History of a Metaphor in Relation to His Major Villains*. New York: Columbia University Press, 1958.

Sprott, S. E. "Drury and Marlowe." *Times Literary Supplement*, August 2, 1974, p. 840.

Stow, John. *The Chronicles of England*. London, 1580.

Strathmann, Ernest A. *Sir Walter Raleigh: A Study in Elizabethan Skepticism*. New York: Columbia University Press, 1951.

Strauss, Gerald. "How to Read a *Volksbuch*: The *Faust Book* of 1587." In *Faust through Four Centuries: Retrospect and Analysis*, ed. Peter Boerner and Sidney Johnson, 27–39. Tübingen: Max Niemeyer Verlag, 1989.

Sugden, Edward H. *A Topographical Dictionary to the Works of Shakespeare and His Fellow Dramatists*. Manchester, U.K.: Manchester University Press, 1925.

Swinburne, A. C. *George Chapman: A Critical Essay*. London: Chatto & Windus, 1875.
Tannenbaum, S. A. *The Assassination of Christopher Marlowe*. 1928. Hamden, CT: Shoestring Press, 1962.
Turner, Robert E. *Didon dans la Tragédie de la Renaissance Italienne et Française*. Paris: Fouillot, 1926.
Urry, William. *Christopher Marlowe and Canterbury*. Ed. Andrew Butcher. London: Faber and Faber, 1988.
Wernham, R. B. "Christopher Marlowe at Flushing in 1592." *English Historical Review* 91 (1976): 344–45.
Wilson, F. P. *Marlowe and the Early Shakespeare*. Oxford: Clarendon Press, 1953.
Wraight, A. D. *In Search of Christopher Marlowe: A Pictorial Biography*. Photography by Virginia F. Stern. London: Macdonald, 1965. Re-issued in paperbound edition, 1993, London, Adam Hart.

BIBLIOGRAPHICAL NOTE

In addition to works cited above, the following items may prove helpful for further consultation.

General History of the Elizabethan Theatre

Barroll, J. Leeds, Alexander Leggatt, Richard Hosley, and Alvin Kernan. *The Revels History of Drama in English, Vol. 3: 1576–1613*. London: Methuen, 1975.
Bentley, G. E. *The Profession of Player in Shakespeare's Time, 1590–1642*. Princeton: Princeton University Press, 1984.
Chambers, E. K. *The Elizabethan Stage*. 4 vols. Oxford: Clarendon Press, 1945.
Clemen, Wolfgang. *English Tragedy Before Shakespeare: The Development of Dramatic Speech*. Trans. T. S. Dorsch. London: Methuen, 1961.
Wilson, F. P. *The English Drama 1485–1585*. Ed. G. K. Hunter. Oxford History of English Literature. Oxford: Clarendon Press, 1969.

Bibliographical Surveys of Marlowe Studies

Friedenreich, Kenneth. *Christopher Marlowe: An Annotated Bibliography of Criticism since 1950*. Metuchen, NJ: Scarecrow Press, 1979.
Kimbrough, Robert. "Recent Studies in Marlowe." In *The Predecessors of Shakespeare: A Survey and Bibliography of Recent Studies in English Renaissance Drama*. Vol. 1, pp. 3–55. Ed. Terence P. Logan and Denzell A. Smith. Lincoln: University of Nebraska Press, 1973.
Levao, Ronald. "Recent Studies in Marlowe (1977–1986)." *English Literary Renaissance* 18 (1988): 329–42.
Post, Jonathan F. S. "Recent Studies in Marlowe (1968–1976)," *English Literary Renaissance* 7 (1977): 382–99.
Tydeman, William, and Vivien Thomas. *Christopher Marlowe: A Guide through the Critical Maze*. State of the Art Series. Bristol, U.K.: Bristol Press, 1989.

Texts of Marlowe's Plays

Standard Old-Spelling Editions

The Complete Works of Christopher Marlowe. Ed. Fredson Bowers. 2 vols. Second ed. New York: Cambridge University Press, 1981.

The Works of Christopher Marlowe. Ed. C. F. Tucker Brooke. Oxford: Clarendon Press, 1910.

Modern Spelling Editions

New Mermaid Series. London: Ernest Benn.

Doctor Faustus. Ed. Roma Gill. 1990.

Edward II. Ed. W. Moelwyn Merchant. 1967.

The Jew of Malta. Ed. T. W. Craik. 1966.

Tamburlaine. Ed. J. W. Harper. 1971.

The Revels Plays.

Dido Queen of Carthage and The Massacre at Paris. Ed. H. J. Oliver. London: Methuen, 1968.

Doctor Faustus: A- and B-texts (1604, 1616). Ed. David Bevington and Eric Rasmussen. Manchester: Manchester University Press, 1993.

The Jew of Malta. Ed. N. W. Bawcutt. Manchester: Manchester University Press, 1978.

Tamburlaine. Ed. J. S. Cunningham. Manchester: Manchester University Press, 1981.

Index

acting companies (adult), 32–34;
    aristocratic patronage, 23–24;
    repertory system, 34, 36–38. *See
    also* children's (acting) companies
Admiral's Men, Lord, 5, 8, 32–34, 104;
    lost Dido play in repertory, 161 n.16;
    Marlowe's plays in repertory, 5, 27,
    33, 36
Aeneid (Virgil), 43–44, 46–47, 49, 51,
    54–55
Aldrich, Simon, 160 n.11
allegorical representation: in *Dr.
    Faustus*, 132–35, 143, 163 n.40; in
    Edward II, 101, 118; in morality
    drama, 30, 132; in Tudor drama, 31,
    73, 103
Alleyn, Edward, 5, 32, 34–35, 159 n.4;
    celebrated roles, 38
Alphonsus, King of Aragon (Greene), 6,
    75
Amores (Ovid), 17, 51, 140
Amyntae Gaudia (Watson), 6
Apology for Poetry (Sidney), 31, 63
Ariosto, 73
Art of English Poesy, 63–64
Astrologaster, or, the Figure-Caster
    (Melton), 163 n.41

Athenae Oxonienses (Wood), 12

Baines, Richard: accusations of
    Marlowe's atheism, 11, 14, 16, 160
    nn.7, 9; accusations of Marlowe's
    Dutch counterfeiting, 8–9; arrest at
    Rheims, 9, 159 n.4; and Drury, 160
    n.10, 161 n.12
Bakeless, John, 159 n.4, 160 n.7
Bartholomew's Day massacre, 81, 83
Beard, Thomas, 11–12, 14
Bentley, Gerald Eades, 161 n.14
Berek, Peter, 162 n.22
Birde, William, 122
Blackfriars playhouse, 24; second
    Blackfriars playhouse, 27
Blind Beggar of Alexandria, The
    (Chapman), 77
Blount, Edward, 7, 15
Boas, Frederick S., 159 nn.2, 4
Boccaccio, Giovanni, 101
boy actors, 24, 27, 37; in *Dido*, 43,
    47–48, 56–57; in Marlowe's other
    plays, 161 n.19. *See also* children's
    (acting) companies
Bradley, William, 6
Bull, Eleanor, 2, 12–13

Bussy D'Ambois (Chapman), 77

Cambridge University, 2–3, 11, 14, 30,
    160 n.11
Canterbury, 3, 10, 159 n.4, 160 n.11
Castle of Perseverance, The, 132
censorship of plays, 37, 161 n.14, 162
    n.31
Cerne Abbas, 17
Chamberlain's Men, 32
Changeling, The (Middleton), 145
Chapman, George, 7, 13, 15, 32, 34,
    77–78, 153
Chaucer, Geoffrey, 101
children's (acting) companies, 4–5, 24,
    32–33, 161 n.16; Children of Her
    Majesty's Chapel, 43. *See also* boy
    actors
Cholmeley, Richard, 14, 16–17
Cinthio, Giraldi, 44
classical drama, in sixteenth-century
    schools, 30. *See also* Seneca
classical mythology, 31, 44, 113, 153;
    in *Dido*, 46–49; in *Dr. Faustus*, 125,
    138-39; in the Faust Book, 125; in
    Tamburlaine, 65
Cleopatra, The Tragedy of (Daniel),
    45–46, 58
*Conspiracy and Tragedy of Charles
    Duke of Byron* (Chapman), 77–78
Contre-Machiavelli (Gentillet), 81
Corkine, William, 10
Corpus Christi College (Cambridge), 3,
    14, 18
court performances, 5, 23–24, 27, 32, 34
Curtain playhouse, The, 6, 24

Dabbs, Thomas, 19–20, 161 n.13
Daniel, Samuel, 45–46, 58, 149
De Casibus Virorum Illustrium
    (Boccaccio), 101
Dekker, Thomas, 69
Deptford, 2–3, 11, 12
Diary (Henslowe), 34, 36–37, 123, 159
    n.4
Dido, Renaissance plays about, 30,
    44–45, 49; 161 nn.16, 17

*Dido Queen of Carthage, The Tragedy
    of*, 17, 33, 43–58; boy actors, 43,
    47–48, 56–57; comic scenes, 46–50;
    fantasy, 52–54, 58, 162 n.21;
    Ovidian influence, 46, 51, 53, 55.
    See also classical mythology
*Doctor Faustus, The Tragical History
    of*, 121–47; allegorical devices,
    132–37, 141–43, 147, 163 nn.40,
    41; associations with Renaissance
    aspiration and exploration, 129, 131,
    143; audience complicity, 163 n.39;
    B-text version of final hour, 142–43;
    classical mythology, 125, 138–39,
    147; comic elements, 124, 132;
    farcical adaptations, 121–22, 146; in
    Henslowe's repertory, 17, 33, 36;
    influence on Middleton and
    Shakespeare, 145; morality play
    elements, 124, 132–37, 141–43;
    relationship to Marlowe's alleged
    atheism, 146–47; relationship to the
    Faust Book, 124–25, 130–32,
    135–37, 139–40, 143; revival by
    Poel, 19; Seven Deadly Sins,
    132–34; textual history, 122;
    unconventionality of the devil,
    Mephistopheles, 135–37
Dolce, Lodovico, 44, 49
Donne, John, 35, 127
Dowden, Edward, 19–20
Drayton, Michael, 69, 162 n.32
Drury, Thomas, 160 n.10, 161 n.12
Dunciad, The (Pope), 122
Dutch Church libel, 159 n.4. *See also*
    Kyd, Thomas

Eccles, Mark, 6-7, 9
*Edward II, The Troublesome Reign and
    Lamentable Death of*, 17, 33, 47,
    99–119; audience complicity, 119;
    deposition scene, 112–15; early
    editions, 162 n.27; emblematic
    scenes, 101–3, 113–14, 117–19;
    historical alterations, 107–9, 115;
    and Shakespeare's *Henry VI* plays,
    103–4, 162 n.29; and Shakespeare's

Richard II, 103–4, 114, 116, 162 n.31

Eliot, T. S.: on farce and caricature in *The Jew of Malta*, 92–93; on translations and imitations of Senecan drama, 161 n.18

Elizabeth I, Queen, 2, 13, 16, 17, 23, 30, 84, 160 n.7, 162 n.31

Ellis, Havelock, 160 n.9

emblematic scenes, 55–56, 153; in *Dr. Faustus*, 132–33, 138–39; in *Edward II*, 101–3, 113–14, 117–19; in *Tamburlaine*, 61, 68, 73–74

Empson, William, 147

Essex, Earl of, 2, 13

Everyman, 30

Fall of the Late Arian, The (Proctor), 7–8

Farrant, Richard, 24

Faust (Goethe), 121–22

Faust Book, 122–25, 130–33, 135, 137; depiction of hell's torments, 136, 140; Faustus' last sentiments, 139–40; Faustus' motivations, 137; parallels between Faustus and Lucifer, 124–25; Seven Deadly Sins, 133

Fineux, Thomas, 14, 160 n.11

Flushing (Netherlands), 8–9, 14, 159 n.4

Ford, John, 150 Freeman, Arthur, 159 n.4

Frizer, Ingram, 2, 12–13

Gager, William, 30

Garnier, Robert, 31, 45

Gentillet, Innocent, 81

Gilbert, Gifford, 8

Gismond of Salerne, 31

Globe playhouse, 27

Goethe, Johann Wolfgang von, 19, 121–22

Gorboduc, 31, 64, 103

Greene, Robert, 4, 10, 32; allusions to Marlowe, 5–6, 10, 14

Harlequin Doctor Faustus (Thurmond), 121–22

Harlequin Necromancer (Rich), 121

Harriot, Thomas, 8, 17

Harvey, Gabriel, 14–15

Hazlitt, William, 20

Henslowe, Philip, 17, 34–39, 159 n.4, 162 n.25; additions to *Dr. Faustus*, 122. *See also* Rose playhouse

Hero and Leander, 7, 15, 17, 20

Heroides (Ovid), 46, 53, 55

Hogarth, William, 122

Holinshed, Raphael: *Chronicles of England, Scotland, and Ireland*, 103, 108, 112, 114–15, 117; judgments of Edward II and Gaveston, 104–6, 109

Hotson, J. Leslie, 11–12

Hues, Robert, 8

Inns of Court, 30-31

Jew of Malta, The, 9, 88–97; audience complicity, 89, 94, 96; elements of farce and caricature, 92–96; in Henslowe's repertory, 17, 33, 36, 96; Machiavellian attributes in Barabas, 80, 93; Machiavelli's prologue, 88–89; and revenge tragedy, 97, 151; seventeenth- and nineteenth-century revivals, 19, 96; Vice attributes in Barabas, 90–92

Jocasta, 31, 73

Jodelle, Estienne, 44

Jones, Richard, 63

Jonson, Ben, 17, 32, 34, 92, 96, 153

Kean, Edmund, 19

King's Men, 27

King's School (Canterbury), 3

Kocher, Paul, 146

Kuriyama, Constance, 160 n.9

Kyd, Thomas, 7; accusations of Marlowe, 7–8, 13–14, 160 n.8; arrest, 10, 160 n.10; influence of his *Spanish Tragedy*, 150-51

Lamb, Charles, 19–20

Lectures on the Age of Elizabeth (Hazlitt), 20
Legge, Thomas, 30
Life and Death of Doctor Faustus, Made into a Farce, The (Mountfort), 122
Locrine, The Lamentable Tragedy of, 65
Lodge, Thomas, 32
Lucan, 17
Lydgate, John, 101
Lyly, John, 4, 32

Machiavelli, Niccolò, 81, 93
Machiavelli (lost play), 162 n.25
Marlowe, Christopher: alleged atheism, 2, 8, 11–12, 14–16, 160 n.11; alleged homosexuality, 160 n.9; arrest for counterfeiting, 2, 8–9; arrest for London street duel, 2, 6; assassination theories, 2, 13; and Baines, 8–9, 11; birth and education, 3; charged for Canterbury street brawl, 10; contemporary allusions to, 3–6, 10, 11–12, 14–15; death, 2, 11–12; and Kyd, 7, 10; literary reputation in decline and revival, 19–20; posthumous publications, 17; Privy Council intervention for his M.A. degree, 3–4; Privy Council warrant for his arrest, 10; and Raleigh, 15–17; Renaissance qualities expressed in his plays, 1; service for the Queen, 2–4; spellings of last name, 159 n.3; supposed portrait, 18; and Thomas Walsingham, 7, 10; and Watson, 6–7, 10
Marston, John, 150
Massacre at Paris, The, 79–88; Guise/Tamburlaine parallel, 87; in Henslowe's repertory, 17, 33, 36, 82; historical alterations, 85, 88; Machiavellian attributes in Guise, 80, 85, 87; pirated script, 34, 82; propaganda aspects, 83–84, 86; "tyrant-tragedy" aspect, 83–85

Meliboeus (Watson), 7
Melton, J., 163 n.41
Metamorphoses (Ovid), 125
Middleton, Thomas, 145, 150, 153, 163 n.42
Milton, John, 133, 136, 163 n.42
Mirror for Magistrates, The, 101, 103, 106–7
Misfortunes of Arthur, The, 64
morality drama, 30, 89–90, 132; elements in *Dr. Faustus*, 124, 132–37, 141–42; elements in *The Jew of Malta*, 90–92; role of angels and devils, 135; role of the Vice, 90, 118, 132. *See also* Vice
Mortimeriados (Drayton), 103, 162 n.32
Mountfort, William, 122
Mueller, Martin, 161 n.18
mystery plays, 27, 30; representation of Lucifer's fall, 144

Nashe, Thomas, 4, 13, 15, 32, 43
Niccols, Richard, 103
Nicholl, Charles, 2
Northumberland, Earl of, 8, 17

Oliver, H. J., 56
Oration on the Dignity of Man (Pico della Mirandola), 131
Orlando Furioso (Ariosto), 73
Ovid, 17, 46, 51, 53, 55, 102, 125, 140
Oxford University, 30–31, 161 n.17
Oxinden, Henry, 160 n.11

Parsons, Robert, 17
Peele, George, 4, 15
Peirs Gaveston (Drayton), 103
Pembroke's Men, Earl of, 33, 162 n.27
Perimedes the Blacksmith (Greene), 5
Petowe, Henry, 15
Pharsalia (Lucan), 17
Pico della Mirandola, Giovanni, 131
Plautus, 30, 38
playhouses (in sixteenth-century London): physical characteristics,

24, 28; "private" and "public" distinction, 24, 27
Poel, William, 19
Poley, Robert, 12–13
Poole, John, 9
Pope, Alexander, 122
Privy Council, 7, 16, 32; intervention for Marlowe's M.A. degree, 3–4; warrant for Marlowe's arrest, 10
props, emblematic, 39, 96; in *Dido*, 47, 53; in *Edward II*, 101, 114. *See also* emblematic scenes
Puritan opposition to stage, 2, 11–12

Queen Anne's Men, 162 n.27
Queen's Men, 27

Rabelais, François, 92, 96
Raleigh, Sir Walter, 2, 15–17
Ralph Roister Doister (Udall), 30
Red Bull playhouse, 162 n.27
Renaissance: aspiration and exploration in *Dr. Faustus*, 129, 131, 143; image of human potentiality in Pico della Mirandola, 131; qualities expressed in Marlowe's drama, 1
Revenger's Tragedy, The, 97
Rheims, 3–4, 9, 84
Rich, John, 121
Rose playhouse, 7, 9, 27, 29, 34, 82, 162 n.25; production of *Machiavelli*, 162 n.25; repertory in 1590s, 36, 38, 162 n.29. *See also* Henslowe, Philip
Rowley, Samuel, 122
Royden, Matthew, 13
Rudierd, Edmund, 12

"School of Night," 17
Selimus, The Tragical Reign of, 75–77
Seneca, 31, 38, 43–44, 96, 101, 153, 161 nn.17, 18. *See also* tragedy
Shakespeare, William, 1, 6, 17, 24, 27, 31, 34, 153; *Hamlet*, 37, 126, 150, 161 n.15; *Henry V* and *Tamburlaine*, 67; *2 Henry VI* and *Tamburlaine*, 59–60; *Henry VI* plays and *Edward*

II, 103–4, 162 n.29; *Macbeth* and *Dr. Faustus*, 145; *Merchant of Venice* and *The Jew of Malta*, 96; *Richard II* and *Edward II*, 103–4, 114, 116
Shapiro, James, 163 n.44
Shapiro, Michael, 56
Sidney, Mary Herbert, Countess of Pembroke, 6, 31, 45
Sidney, Sir Philip, 31, 63, 103
Sidney, Sir Robert, 8
Skeres, Nicholas, 12–13
Spanish Tragedy, The (Kyd), 7, 38; influence on later tragedy, 59, 150–51
Specimens of English Dramatic Poets (Lamb), 19–20
Spies, Johann, 123
Stow, John, 107, 117
Strange, Lord, 8
Strange's Men, Lord, 32, 82, 96
Strathmann, E. A., 17
Swan playhouse, 27–29
Swinburne, Algernon Charles, 19–20

Taine, Hippolyte, 19
Tamar Cam, 38, 59
Tamburlaine the Great, 59–78; allusions to, 4, 14–15, 59–60, 69, 75; comic elements, 63, 71; debt to chivalric romance, 68–69, 72–73; Elizabethan imitators, 75–77; emblematic scenes, 61, 68, 73–74; in Henslowe's repertory, 17, 36; historical alterations, 66–68, 72–73; influence on Chapman, 77–78; relationship to tyrant tragedy, 65–66; title page, 33, 62
Tannenbaum, S. A., 2
Terence, 30, 38
Theatre of God's Judgments, The (Beard), 11–12
Theatre playhouse, 6, 24, 32
Thunderbolt of God's Wrath (Rudierd), 12
Thurmond, John, 121
Thyestes (Seneca), 101

Timur Khan (Tamburlaine), 60, 68
Tournour, Cyril, 150
tragedy: comic elements in Elizabethan
  popular tragedy, 47, 65; *de casibus*
  tragedy, 101–3, 106–7, 114;
  humanist (or neo-Senecan) tragedy,
  31, 44–46, 58, 149, 161 n.18;
  Marlowe's reformulations, 39–41,
  57, 69, 75, 97, 104, 116, 143–44,
  149–53; Renaissance conceptions,
  41, 62–64, 107, 150; revenge
  tragedy, 150–51; Senecan tragedy,
  46, 49, 97, 161 n.18; tyrant-tragedy,
  63–65, 81–82

"University Wits," 4, 31–32
Urry, William, 159 n.4

Vice: in morality drama, 90, 132; traits
  in Barabas, 90–92; traits in
  Lightborn, 118
Virgil, 43–44, 161 n.17. *See also Aeneid*
Volpone (Jonson), 92, 97

Walcheren, Isle of (Netherlands), 8
Walsingham, Sir Francis, 7, 9
Walsingham, Thomas, 2, 7, 10, 12–13,
  15, 78
Warner, Walter, 8
Watson, Thomas, 6–8, 10
Webster, John, 88, 97, 150, 153
Wernham, R. B., 8, 159 n.4
White Devil, The (Webster), 97
Wood, Anthony à, 12
Worcester's Men, 32, 37

About the Author

DOUGLAS COLE is Professor of English at Northwestern University. He is author of *Suffering and Evil in the Plays of Christopher Marlowe* and editor of two volumes—*Twentieth-Century Interpretations of Romeo and Juliet* and *Renaissance Drama XI: Tragedy*.

ISBN 0-313-27516-5

90000>

EAN

9 780313 275166

HARDCOVER BAR CODE